MY BOY

THE FULL STORY OF PHILIP LYNOTT
& THE FAMILY HE NEVER KNEW

Fully Updated with Remarkable New Revelations

PHILOMENA LYNOTT
with Jackie Hayden

The original version first published in 1995 by Hot Press Books, 13 Trinity Street, Dublin 2.

This new, fully updated version published in 2011.

Copyright © Philomena Lynott and Jackie Hayden 1995.

The right of Philomena Lynott and Jackie Hayden to be identified as the authors of this work has

been asserted by them in accordance with the Copyright, Design and Patents Act 1988.

British Library Cataloguing in Publication Data is available for this book.

ISBN No: 978-0-9553419-5-3

Design: David Keane

Production Manager: Mairin Sheehy

Studio Manager: Graham Keogh

Cover photograph by Andre Csillag

Printed by Clays Ltd, Bungay, Suffolk

Photographs are from Philomena Lynott's personal collection. Every effort has been made to trace
the copyright holders of the additional photographs in this book but one or two were unreachable.
We would be grateful if photographers concerned would contact us.

INTRODUCTION

Since the first edition of *My Boy* was published in 1995, a series of often bewildering and momentous events have occurred in my life. Some of these have been private, others public. In a manner that I could never have anticipated, the publication of *My Boy* triggered events that set me off on a rollercoaster voyage of personal discovery during which I've had to confront aspects of my past that I had thought would remain hidden forever. As a direct result, the meaning of family was renewed afresh for me in a truly magical way.

At its most dramatic, the first edition of *My Boy*, which primarily dealt with the close and often wonderful relationship I enjoyed with my rock star son Philip, changed my life forever. It became the catalyst to my reunion with my second son Leslie, the brother Philip never knew. While her existence was kept secret in the original *My Boy*, I was enjoying an inspiring personal relationship with my only daughter, also called Philomena. The reasons I had kept the existence of both of these children secret, even from Philip and my own mother, are explored in depth for the very first time in this new and fully updated edition of the story of my life.

This, of course, is not just my story. Both Philomena and Leslie graciously agreed to their first ever interviews about growing up as adopted children and how they, completely separately, and a number of years apart, came to the stunning realisation that I was their birth mother. You could say that this is first and foremost a book about the brother they never met, one of the greatest talents Ireland has ever produced, my first son Philip. After all, I knew Philip better than almost any other man on the planet. But it is also much more than that. It is the story of how a family was sundered all of those years ago, in a way that would never happen now, or almost never, in this part of the world at least. And of how they came back together through a series of accidents, adventures and clandestine meetings that at times must have seemed like something out of the Soviet era, with all the intrigue and subterfuge we had to engineer. It is a shame that my first son Philip could not be around to be a part of it all. He'd have loved every minute of it…

For an ever-increasing number of music fans spread right across the globe, the name Philip Lynott conjures images of a hugely successful rock star, the Black Irishman vocalist with the unmistakable voice, a musician whose work captured the imagination of millions, and whose songs live on in the hearts of fans everywhere.

Although those images are tinged with the sadness of his personal life and the tragedy of his death, for me, Philip Lynott was more than just a talented creative artist. He was, above all, a generous and loving son, with an indomitable spirit and a warm personality who, although he spurned the more ostentatious trappings of wealth, thoroughly enjoyed his glamorous lifestyle, the opportunities it brought him and the characters that peopled it.

Enjoyed it too much at times: I think we all know that by now. The events of his life as a world-famous celebrity were played out between traumatic events, at one end the hardship of his birth and upbringing and, at the other, his wasting away though a drug habit that turned out to be the only serious challenge in his entire life with which he failed to cope.

My Boy first enabled me to set the record straight – to the best of my ability at the time – regarding the many spurious rumours and often cheap speculation about the circumstances of Philip's birth, life and death. This is something we still have to put up with. And so I am really gratified that this dramatically expanded narration of my life story gives me the opportunity to celebrate the re-emergence into my life of my other son and my only daughter.

So this book is neither the story of Philip Lynott – Rock Star, nor the sordid tabloid tale of a drug addict. This is my personal story of our deeply affectionate mother-son relationship, as well as a welcome opportunity for me to finally lift from my 80-year-old shoulders the burden of concealment in relation to the rest of my family.

It covers the trials and tribulations of a black child born out of wedlock and growing up in a Catholic working-class suburb in the Ireland of the harsh 1950s, his ascent to the dizzy heights of international rock celebrity and the heart-break of his failed marriage and tragic death. It also graphically describes the pressures and heartaches a single mother had to endure, through not one but three pregnancies, in a rough and often condemnatory world. Some of the names of the people who figure prominently in the early part of my story have been changed in order to protect their privacy. But that is just a measure of how tough it was for us, and how hard we all had to battle.

Above all else however, this is a love story. But one with a bigger cast than readers will have imagined when *My Boy* was originally published back in 1995. And it is now yours, to keep and to treasure…

PHILOMENA LYNOTT, January 2011.

MY BOY

THE FULL STORY OF PHILIP LYNOTT

CONTENTS

1. THE EMIGRANT TRAIL

"How can I leave the town
that brings me down
that has no jobs
is blessed by God
and makes me cry, Dublin"
– from 'Dublin' by Philip Lynott

Growing up in working-class Dublin in the 1940s and 1950s had many similarities with the experiences and prospects of young Irish people in later decades. In particular, the related threats of joblessness and emigration hung over many of us, just as they did again in the 1970s, the 1980s and as they do in 2011. In contrast, the influence of the Catholic Church on the society in which I was reared was much deeper than it is today or ever will be again. In general, authority figures, whether that of Church, School, State or parents, expected and received far greater respect than is evident these days. People have learned the hard way that they are scarcely to be trusted.

I had been born in a part of the inner city of Dublin known as The Liberties on the 22nd of October 1930, but when I was about four years of age the family moved to Crumlin, then a growing working-class suburb further out on the south side of the city. During the often anxious and uncertain years of my childhood, the Irish economy was in a deep depression. Unemployment was high, and the evidence of poverty and squalor on the streets of Dublin was striking. A report published in the *Irish Journal of Medical Science* in 1932 revealed that one in eight children in the inner-city slums suffered from malnutrition. Diseases such as tuberculosis were rife, claiming hundreds of lives annually.

It is estimated that about 15% of the Irish population of that time took the emigrant boat to England in search of employment. The number doesn't surprise me: I remember it as a daily fact of life, with friends and neighbours waving goodbye to husbands, off to England in search of work, or to children who took the same way out as soon as they'd left school. The Irish newspapers regularly ran advertisements from companies offering not only to pay travel fares from Ireland to England, but also to arrange jobs and accommodation for those who set off on the emigrant's trail. I answered one of those advertisements, and not long afterwards a letter arrived confirming that my application had been successful. So I left the childish cosiness of our family home at 85 Leighlin Road, Crumlin halfway through 1947, heading for Birmingham, to stay in a hostel and to train as a nurse.

We had never had any money, but I had been happy in Dublin. For a naïve seventeen year old, the shock of arriving in what seemed like a whole new world was enormous. I remember thinking, at first, that everything looked different here, even the sky, the clouds, and the air so crisp and clean you felt you could almost drink it. Still, I settled down quickly in the strange land to which I had moved and made friends with numerous other Irish girls from similar backgrounds to my own. We were, you might say, all in it together.

In its own funny way, Birmingham was an exciting place in the late 1940s. Vast areas of the largely Victorian city centre had been decimated by Hitler's World War II bombs, but a campaign of rebuilding was already underway. There was an energy and excitement about it. Everywhere you looked, shattered old houses, shops and offices were being salvaged and reconstructed, and foundations for brand new roads and buildings were being laid. Strolling, as I often did, though Brum's many parks and green spaces, I reflected on how lucky I was to be part of this burgeoning sense of a 'fresh start'.

The events that were subsequently to have such a profound bearing on the rest of my life can be traced back to one night in 1949 when one of my friends, Annie Brennan, suggested that we go to a dance at a Displaced Persons' Hostel on Wolverhampton New Road in Birmingham. Oh the glamour! But for us it really was all new. There were similar hostel sites in various parts of England, intended for Poles, Lithuanians and people of other nationalities, mostly displaced from their homelands by the Second World War. They were like army camps, and they often contained a large community centre, canteen, cinema, church and virtually every other essential amenity.

Loving the freedom of being away from our parents for the first time, Annie and I began to attend dances regularly in one such hostel. The ballroom was like the old-time dance halls which would be familiar to anyone who remembers the Ireland of the fifties or who saw the film *The Ballroom of Romance*, where all the ladies stood on one side of the room and gentlemen on the other, and the music would be provided by a big band.

Such places of entertainment probably attracted Irish girls like Annie and me because they reminded us of home as well as, perhaps, holding out the prospect of meeting a future husband. But, as often happens in these matters, fate had a slightly different plan, for me at least.

Annie and I had been going out to dances at the hostel for about a month. It wasn't something that I'd have remarked on at the time, but the different nationalities used to keep apart from each other in a casual way, not unlike the tradition in Irish dancehalls. But when the music struck up, such differences were usually put aside and we danced the night away, mixing perfectly naturally with each other and with what I remember was a great sense of fun.

Two Polish boys took a shine to Annie and me and they often danced with us. My Polish friend was called Janek. Apart from enjoying lots of dancing with them, they also took us one night to see the film *Forever Amber*. Whenever I see that film on television it brings back memories of those far-off days during which Janek and I dated for about two months in spite of the fact that he, like many of his fellow countrymen in England at that time, had very little English. In fact, he grew rather fond of me to the extent that I think he regarded me as his girlfriend and wanted to have every dance with me.

One night when we were all in the dancehall, a tall black gentleman walked across the dance-floor and invited me to dance. His name, as I later found out, was Cecil Parris. He was from Guyana in South America, and little did I know it then, but he was to become the father of my son, Philip. When we finished our first dance, which had three encores, I walked back to where I had been standing. I remember vividly that the other ladies moved away from me, and I heard somebody angrily mutter "nigger-lover" within my earshot. That was my first encounter with any kind of racial intolerance, and for obvious reasons it shocked and upset me.

I had grown up totally unaware of such racial prejudice. Black people were a rarity in Dublin, apart from those one would see in the movies, or the occasional black student I might have observed around Trinity College, when I travelled into the centre of Dublin with my school friends or on an errand for my mother. So I could not understand what was supposed to be so dreadfully wrong, dancing with a black man, or why anyone would call me horrible names just because I had done so. Indeed, how could I have refused a man who had walked the length of the dance floor to invite me to dance? In my eyes, to have done so would have been an act of extreme rudeness. Besides, I thought, that's what ladies went to dances for, to be invited to dance! I could never, and would never, refuse to dance with any man who politely asked me. There might have been times when I did not like the appearance of a guy who approached me, but I would not hurt any individual by rejecting him so openly in a public place.

Out of a fairly packed attendance at that dance there were probably only about a dozen black men, but I could not help noticing how they too tended to gather together in part of the hall, much like the other ethnic groups and nationalities. Of course when I agreed to dance with this man, I didn't even know his name or anything about him. I was simply hoping for a pleasant dance, nothing more, nothing less. And so it turned out, that night.

Unfortunately, my Polish friend Janek did not see things quite so simply. As Annie and I made our way out of the hall, we were confronted by Janek and his Polish buddy, both of whom were showing the effects of having had too much to drink. They both started to rough me up because I had been dancing with Cecil. Their aggression frightened me, but when I tried to run away they grabbed me and forced me up against a wall. By this point I was really terrified and did not know what might happen to me until, from the darkness, I heard a stern voice telling them to let me go. It was Cecil, who had seen what was going on. As soon as Janek and his cowardly friend saw that Cecil meant business, they threw me on the ground and ran off into the night. I cannot describe how relieved I was to have been rescued from what was a thoroughly frightening experience.

Determined not to let such boorish behaviour stop us enjoying ourselves, Annie and I attended that same dancehall several more times, and on nearly every occasion, I danced with the same friendly black man. He was handsome as well as tall and I was gradually getting to like him more. Then, one night, he asked me for a date. I didn't hesitate about saying yes and on this occasion he took me to a different dancehall. For about three months, we did what in the 1940s and 1950s was called 'courting', and spent a lot of time in each other's company in and around Birmingham. But whenever we were seen together in a public place, people would stare at us; the sight of a black man and a white woman together was unusual in those days.

Over a period of time, our relationship blossomed as we discovered we really liked one another and a close, reasonably serious relationship developed. Then, one sunny day, we made love. For me, it was the very first time, and it happened on a local golf course. It might not seem like the most romantic place but we were able to find a quiet spot where we would not be disturbed and he was very gentle and loving. Young love is such a strange thing. We were kids, really, finding our way and enjoying the pleasures of being together fully for the first time. Our sexual relationship continued intermittently for a while. However, within a matter of weeks, Cecil informed me that he was being transferred down to London because of his work in the services. I didn't think it was the end of the world. I loved him but I also had a sense that if he was the right man for me then we would work things out in the long run. And if he wasn't then I would form other relationships. I had lots of time – or so it seemed! He promised to keep in touch. Shortly afterwards, I was horrified to discover that I was pregnant. It was as sudden and simple and life-defining as that.

By what seemed like a remarkable coincidence – although it wasn't that surprising if you thought about it for more than a few minutes – my Irish girlfriend Annie told me that she had missed her period and she thought she too must be pregnant. And of course she was. I suppose we were equally alarmed by our plight, both of us alone in a strange country, expecting babies out of wedlock, against all the teachings of our Irish Catholic upbringing. We didn't know what to do, and didn't feel we had anyone to turn to.

It was a popular belief at the time – a superstition I suppose – that if a pregnant woman drank boiled gin with some pennies in it, her periods would return and the pregnancy would miraculously disappear. The only thing was that you had to act during the first month of your pregnancy! So Annie and I furtively gathered together a miniature bottle of gin, a bundle of wood, a discarded bean-can and some newspapers and took them to a field. We dug a shallow hole in the ground in which to burn the wood to heat the gin in a billycan we had borrowed from the hostel canteen.

As I neither smoked nor drank at the time, I had no previous experience of alcohol. Annie swallowed hers without difficulty, but when I raised mine to my mouth, the smell of it made me retch. Thus ended my first amateurish attempt at aborting my pregnancy! God help me but I really was innocent!

Then someone told us that quinine tablets, which were often used to alleviate malaria, would bring back our periods. We tried that method too, but all I got was a severe headache. Gradually, I realised that I would have to accept the fact that none of these tricks would work. I suppose

I had also begun to understand what was really happening to me – and to accept it too. Apart from that naïve, failed attempt, I did not for a moment consider any other means of aborting my pregnancy. It's not that I'm against abortion. I have always believed in the woman's right to choose, but for me to have my baby was definitely the right decision – I was never in any doubt about that, despite the terrible treatment I would subsequently be subjected to along the way.

After four months, my pregnancy really began to become obvious, and a source of intense whispering in the hostel where I was staying. When my secret was exposed, I was ruthlessly expelled and my career as a nurse abruptly ended before it had even begun. So much for the ethics of the caring profession in that era.

Fortunately, Birmingham, the second largest city in England, was in those days a thriving industrial capital in which work was, comparatively speaking, widely available. Scores of famous British business names had their roots in Brum, from Cadbury chocolates, HP sauce and Typhoo tea to breweries such as Davenport's, Ansell's, and Mitchell's and Butler's. The biggest employers of all, though, were Dunlop tyres, and the vast Austin Motor Company.

Established by Herbert Austin in 1906 in Birmingham's Longbridge area, Austin Motors was one of the world's first mass-production car factories. In the post-war years it was to become one of the most successful companies in Britain. And it was in the Austin Motors foundry that I managed to find a job, at piece-work rates. Conditions at the foundry were primitive, and the foremen were all ferocious taskmasters, their minds set on nothing but meeting the crushing weekly quota figures. It was strenuous and often dirty work for a lonely young girl, unmarried and four months into an unplanned pregnancy. Every evening, as I clocked out, exhausted, grimy and weak from the day's efforts, I would stare at the beautiful pastoral countryside of the Lickey Hills that rose up behind the foundry, and wonder despondently what was to become of me and my unborn child. But I continued working at Austin Motors right up to the week before my baby was born, struggling to disguise my swollen shape by holding my tummy in and wearing a tight corset.

Meanwhile, I desperately needed to find a place to stay. It wasn't easy, but eventually a childless married woman called Mrs Beardsley, who was crippled with a very bad leg, gave me a bedroom to share with another Irish girl.

At the time, I was rather fond of knitting, and I produced many items of clothing for my baby over those months, as well as a jumper and some white socks for Mr Beardsley because he was a keen cricket fan. When I think about it now, it all seems so innocent. The couple seemed to have taken a liking to me and were very kind, although they knew that I hadn't had the courage to inform my parents in Dublin about the secret I was still trying to conceal from the world – the first of many it's fair to say.

The Beardsleys promised that, when my baby was born, we could both return to live with them and they kindly offered to take care of my baby if I later chose to return to work. Even today, so many decades later, I carry a precise picture of their house, and its pleasant surroundings, in my mind. It is worth emphasising that such kindness and generosity can have a hugely positive impact on a lonely and vulnerable girl in a time of crisis. But, unfortunately, it was not to last.

. . . .

As nature took its course, there came a day when I began to feel a little strange and was taken by ambulance to Hallam Hospital, in the West Bromwich part of Birmingham, where I was eventually to endure a full 36 hours in labour. The nurses knew that my baby was illegitimate, and I was convinced that this knowledge gave some of them delusions of superiority over me. I walked around a lot trying to ease my labour pains until one of them forced me to drink a cup of thick, unpleasant, castor oil. She said it would make the baby come quicker, but I suspected that she was just being cruel. It was horrible.

I heard some mothers screaming, "Oh, I'll never forgive you, oh, I'll never forgive you! Never again," and so on during their deliveries, but I never once called out. I bore my son proudly despite experiencing the most intense labour pains. I remember grabbing the iron bars on the bed with white-knuckled ferocity and holding on for dear life. I was aware of the nurses gathered around me, perhaps waiting for a glimpse at the comparative novelty of an unmarried Irish woman bringing a black child into the world, but I didn't care. They wouldn't intimidate or upset me. Such was their curiosity that some of them even took pictures of us!

My boy was born on 20th August, 1949. He weighed nine and a half pounds and was twenty-one and a half inches long at birth. A big fella! Only another mother will fully comprehend the overwhelming feeling of elation and the sense of wonder I felt at first seeing and holding my beautiful new baby, the difficult circumstances of his birth and our uncertain future temporarily banished from my mind. I was put in a ward with six beds, and can recall that room to this day, with the babies' cots standing at the foot of the beds during visiting hours, while at all other times they were kept in a separate nursery.

I named him Philip Parris Lynott. I chose the name Philip because during my mother Sarah's pregnancy with me, my father Frank became very ill. My mother prayed to St. Philomena, promising that if Frank regained his strength she would call her baby Philomena, or the male equivalent, Philip, in the case of a boy. Shortly before I was born, my father began to enjoy his full health again and that's how I became Philomena, or Phyllis for short.

When it came to my turn to be a mother, I remembered that story. Throughout my life, I had often prayed to St. Philomena, and it had seemed to me that she regularly eased my troubles. So it really disappointed me when in 1961 it was officially announced by the church authorities in Rome that there had been no such person as St. Philomena, and that the feast of St. Philomena, on August 11th, was to be discontinued. I mean, where had all those prayers gone? Out into the wild blue yonder, I suppose!

For Philip's second name, I chose Parris after his father, Cecil Parris. The horrible thing was that throughout my trauma, Philip's father was still unaware of my situation. He had written from London to me at the hostel, but because I had been evicted, none of his letters was forwarded. When visitors came to see the other women with their babies, I used to bury my head and cry, wondering what would become of my beautiful, innocent, little baby and me. I had no visitors. The Beardsleys never came to see me, and I envied the other mothers who all received regular visits from husbands, family and friends.

But difficult though my plight was, it was as nothing compared to the experience of one lady there, who had unfortunately lost her baby at birth. A couple of days after Philip was born, her relations called to take her home. Understandably, she could not bear to remain in the same ward as us, with our healthy babies. As she was waving good-bye to me, her own mother handed me about four boxes containing all the clothes that had been bought for the dead baby. That was the first act of genuine kindness shown to me since becoming a mother, and it came from a total stranger.

About four days later, the matron casually dropped a real bombshell. "Philomena," she said, "you have nowhere to go when you leave here. Your landlady has sent us all your bits and pieces in a suitcase, so we have to make arrangements to place you in a home." This news hurt me desperately. My landlady and her husband had promised to visit the hospital, and I had been deeply disappointed that they had not done so.

But I discovered that, unknown to me, they had actually arrived at the hospital, had been shown Philip in the nursery and had walked straight out again on seeing that he was black. They had returned to their house immediately, packed up all my belongings and delivered them to the matron who was now, without any forewarning or any hint of Christian sympathy, giving me the dreadful news that I was bound for a home for unmarried mothers.

I had never heard of the Selly Oak Home for Unmarried Mothers before this. It was located amid the lush daffodils and tulip beds of the Selly Oak suburb in Birmingham, and I was taken there with my baby in my arms. It was a beautiful old mansion-type building set among vast grounds, with a small chapel visible at the end of the gardens. There was also a very old Victorian outhouse – the purpose of which I discovered later.

I was allotted a bed in a dormitory with several other young mothers, while Philip was put in a nursery full of babies in cots, arranged in neat rows. The Mother Superior sternly informed me that, as long as I was staying there, I would have to work to earn my keep. The jobs for the girls included keeping the dormitories clean, looking after the nurseries, polishing the dining room and assisting the cook. Having spent so long working in a car foundry, to me these seemed like potentially pleasant tasks by comparison.

But the Victorian outhouse turned out to be the laundry and, unfortunately, I was put to work there. To reach it, you had to leave the big warm house, and walk across the yard to this old, unfriendly building with its cold, stone floor. It was fitted with large sinks, or troughs as they were called, and in the corner stood an enormous drum full of water and a gas heater to boil it. The drum had a big stick in it for pounding the clothes up and down, and one of the sinks was used only for dirty nappies. This was long before the days of the disposable nappy, so I had to stand in that laundry for hours on end and let the water wash the smelly dirt from each nappy into a sluice, before putting it into a second sink to be rinsed, and then into the big boiler.

They had clearly given me the toughest job going and I believe this was a deliberate form of punishment, not only for having an illegitimate child, but perhaps more especially because he was black. Maybe that's being paranoid, but I certainly could sense that they looked down on me from the moment I arrived, and most of them clearly did not even want to talk to me, including some of the nuns.

Every weekend, the mothers were ordered to make their babies look pretty and all the cots would be set out on the lawn. Visitors, strangers to us all, would parade around peering closely at our babies in their cots. This activity puzzled me. I did not understand who these people were or what they were doing, and I became particularly intrigued whenever I saw them standing over Philip's cot, staring intently at my baby, who always looked gorgeous in the blue clothes I had knitted. One day, I asked one of the other mothers, a tough young girl named Mary, to explain what this was all about. "Don't you know?" she said, "they've come to adopt the babies. The day your baby is adopted that's the day you get out of this prison."

I was astonished at this. Indignantly, I said: "I'm not giving my baby up for adoption," but she repeated the same refrain. "I'm telling you, that's the only way you'll get out of here," she insisted. I was distraught at the very idea of losing my beautiful baby boy. If there was anything I could do to prevent it, I determined that I would.

Next day, I met Mary again. She asked me, "How old are you?" I told her I would be eighteen before too long. "Oh, you'll be alright then," she said casually. "They can't take your baby from you when you're eighteen." But I thought it extraordinary, and extremely cruel, that nobody had even bothered to tell me what was going on here. I also realised that, in sharp contrast to my own feelings of protectiveness towards my baby, Mary actually wanted hers adopted so that she could quit the home and continue her life as before.

She was not alone in that, something which I would come to understand – though for very different reasons. A Polish girl called Maria had a baby called Johnny. I'll never forget him. He was as blonde as the driven snow, with lovely blue eyes, but an unusually enlarged head. Mary pointed at Maria one day, "See her?" she said. "She can't wait to have her baby adopted so she can get back to her boyfriend!" Maria had managed to maintain contact with the father of her baby because we were allowed out one afternoon each week, to walk to the nearby village of Selly Oak. But I could not understand how she could be so casual about something as important as her baby, although Mary reckoned that Maria was going to be in the home a long time, because, as she callously believed, nobody would want to adopt a baby with an abnormal head.

Then while having my bath one night in the ground floor bathroom close to the laundry, I left the window open to let the steam out, and I was shocked to hear Maria loudly arguing, "No, no, I'm not doing that job," she said. "Let the mother of the nigger do it." Her words – cruel and ignorant as they were – echo in my mind still because it was the first time I had heard my baby referred to as a nigger.

I leapt angrily out of the bath, probably not even stopping to dry off. I charged across to the laundry where I found Maria with one of the nuns, of whom she seemed to be a particular favourite, and I furiously launched myself at her. "Don't you dare call my baby a nigger!" I roared. She abused me in turn and left no doubt about how much she despised any mother who would give birth to a black baby. It was a terrible scene, but I was so upset that I couldn't help myself. I continued swinging at her while the nun struggled to restrain me, but I broke free, grabbed the pounding stick from the drum and swung it at the pair of them in such a wild temper that others heard the commotion, rushed in and forced me down.

I was then instructed to go to the chapel to ask God to forgive me. Marched to the chapel, I stood before the altar screaming at them: "What am I asking forgiveness for? Why are they calling my baby a nigger?" I was in complete emotional turmoil and was totally distraught at the injustice of the situation. I couldn't understand why they were treating me like this. I calmed down eventually but, in the days that followed, I wondered if life for Philip and me was always going to be fraught with such pain.

One day soon afterwards, the Matron ordered me to report to the Committee Room, which was furnished with a table so beautifully polished that, whenever the nuns in their habits were seated around it, you could see their faces clearly reflected in the furiously waxed surface. When I entered the room, the Mother Superior was already seated, with two nuns and a priest from Selly Oak village church and a sheaf of official looking documents spread out before them.

After ordering me to sit down, one of them said: "Philomena, we are making arrangements to send you back to Ireland to start a new life and we have some good news for you. We have found a married couple who are willing to adopt your Philip." This was put to me with a great sense of authority, and it was emphasised that they knew how good this move would be for me. If they had had their way, I would have been given absolutely no say in the deliberations. But a primal instinct took hold. I wasn't going to let them take my child away from me.

"Just a minute," I said. "This is my baby and I'm not parting with him." With that, I fled from the room, ran upstairs, grabbed Philip and locked us both inside the nursery. It may sound melodramatic now, but at the time I was in desperation. Apart from anything else, I think they were concerned that I might be going to harm myself or Philip, which was not my intention at all. There was much pounding on the door, and, eventually, and after much negotiation, I agreed to come out. Realising the extent of my determination not to allow anyone to separate us, they then threatened to inform my parents in Dublin. I had been terrified that my mother and father would hear of my predicament. My family was a conventionally respectable Catholic Irish family, and my father had proudly walked my older sisters down the aisle on their wedding days. I was, as it were, the 'wild one', and now I had a baby outside marriage to prove it.

So I was presented with a simple but cruel choice, bordering on blackmail. Unless I was prepared to surrender Philip for adoption, the home no longer wanted me, and they would have to pass me – and Philip – over to whoever would then be legally responsible for us. Because I still received none of his letters and didn't know where to write to him, Cecil remained unaware of Philip's existence – although whenever I bumped into anyone who had news of him, they would tell me that he had been enquiring about me. Without him, I was in a real quandary.

A photographer called regularly to the home to take pictures of the babies, and any mother who so desired could be photographed with her baby. It makes my skin crawl when I think about it: though I didn't know it at the time, those photos were intended to be shown to potential adoptive parents. This was why my photo had been taken with Philip, but it would now be used for a different purpose. I was now forced to write a letter, informing my mother in Crumlin that I had a baby, and that I did not know where the father was. From what I can remember, the letter simply went, "Dear Mummy, I am enclosing a photograph of me with a little baby, and the little baby is my son and he's three months old."

I later found out that when my mother opened the envelope she looked at the picture and initially thought, "What a lovely black baby with our Phyllis." But when she read the letter through, and discovered the reality of my position, she collapsed in a heap on the floor.

I suppose most Irish mothers at the time, faced with a revelation of this kind, would have reacted similarly. It may be difficult now for people to understand the social pressures prevalent in the Dublin of the early 1950s, compared to the liberalism of today, but to my mother this news was a tremendous shock that went against all her religious beliefs and her expectations for her daughters.

But she was generous at heart and so when she recovered and talked things over with my father, she dispatched my brother John to England to meet me. As he was obviously from a respectable background, his arrival at least proved to the nuns in the Home that I came from a caring family. I was again summoned to the Committee Room, so that arrangements could be made for my brother to take me back to the family home in Crumlin. For me, that wasn't part of the plan. Not at all. I was convinced that the family, including my brother John, had already decided to bring me back merely in order to persuade me to let Philip go for adoption, and I adamantly refused to co-operate with this new plan. I had been through such emotional upheaval that I didn't know whom I could trust. I was full of fear and paranoia, as well as an inevitable sense of loneliness by being separated from the father of my little baby.

At yet another meeting in the Committee Room, John, who was himself about to get married, again attempted to persuade me, but I insisted, "no, no, no." That was it. I wasn't going to go back in disgrace. I can still remember the look in his eyes as he said goodbye to me before returning to Crumlin, obviously feeling so sorry for me, both because of my situation and because I was stubbornly making life even more difficult for myself.

Shortly afterwards, the Home authorities delivered me an ultimatum. If I found a place for Philip and me to live, we would be permitted to leave, but since I would not have my baby adopted I could not stay indefinitely in what, they kept reminding me, was a "respectable" Catholic home. Irrespective of any threats or schemes, I was more determined than ever to keep my baby, no matter what difficulties or obstacles might lie in waiting for us. But I still felt terribly isolated and alone.

2. MY GUARDIAN ANGEL

One day, totally out of the blue, a knock came to the door of my dormitory at the Home and the Mother Superior informed me that a man had arrived claiming to be the father of my baby. It was Cecil and, as we held each other for the first time in many months, we both broke down in tears. "Why didn't you find some way to tell me about all this?", he asked me through his sobs, and I explained that, in my lonely, confused state, I had no way of contacting him. I was so relieved to finally have at least one sympathetic person to talk to. I told him about everything that had happened to me and to Philip since I had last met him. When he had absorbed the story fully, he promised to find a place, or digs as they were called, for us to stay.

To his eternal credit, despite the fact that winter was coming on and the weather was awful, he went out searching for lodgings. Unfortunately, the evils of racial prejudice were rooted far deeper in English society than I could possibly have imagined and, try as he might, nobody wanted us. Much later, John Lydon, the singer with the Sex Pistols, wrote a book about his life called *No Irish, No Blacks, No Dogs*. I know only too well what he was talking about. Those offensive words frequently appeared on signs placed in the windows of houses that had vacancies. Equally, even when prejudice wasn't so obviously articulated, there prevailed an unwritten, unspoken but deeply ingrained attitude based on ignorance and fear.

Eventually, after much heartache and many point-blank refusals, Cecil found a Mrs. Cavendish with a house in the working-class suburb of Blackheath in Birmingham, who said she would take me into her house on condition I agreed to share a double-bed with her teenage daughter, Dorothy. Cecil would not be staying with us because of his work in London, but he would be allowed to visit frequently and I would be permitted to keep Philip's cot with me in the bedroom. Of course, when the Social Welfare people came to inspect our living quarters, Mrs. Cavendish said nothing about the bed-sharing arrangement. The inspectors found a nice clean house, approved the situation, and gave us the all-clear to move in.

But, as it turned out, there were further indignities to come. After my first night under a new roof, I awoke to find that Dorothy, who was about the same age as myself, had wet our bed and urinated all over me. It was a ghastly feeling, waking up in someone else's wet sheets but there was no point in being unpleasant. I realised then that she must have a slight mental problem and acted accordingly. Besides, this was the only half-decent place Cecil could find for us after trudging all over Birmingham for weeks, and so I was thankful that we were at least free of all the unpleasantness of the dreadful Home.

And there were compensations. Edith, the second daughter in the house, became a really close friend to me. She was a bonny looking girl with a nice smile and I liked her from the first time we met. It was uncanny: I was only about two months in the house when she confided that she was pregnant. The first question I asked her was, "Does your Mother know?" She said, "No." And then she told me what was really bothering her. "The baby's going to be black," she whispered, "and I can't stay here much longer. I'm going to have to run away."

It emerged that Cecil had been able to arrange these digs because he was acquainted with the black man who was the father of Edith's baby. Ironically, if not for that coincidental connection, there might have been no escape for me and Philip from the Selly Oak Home. Who knows what fate might otherwise have overtaken us? Or where I'd have ended up?

I had already decided that I would have to try to earn some money, even though Cecil was sending me as much as he could towards Philip's upkeep. After several attempts, I secured yet another job amid the noise, grime and back-breaking quotas of my old friend, the Austin Motor Company. In order to be on time for work in Longbridge on the other side of Birmingham, I left the house at six-thirty every morning to travel in a type of motor-bus called a charabanc. I would arrive home after a heavy day's work as late as seven-thirty in the evening.

Mrs. Cavendish had agreed to mind Philip while I was at work in return for payment, but the arrangement never really worked satisfactorily. The long trek to and from work, and the arduous working day, drained all my energies. As you can imagine, it used to anger me greatly to arrive home most evenings to find Philip still wearing the same nappy I had put on him before leaving early that morning. It was obvious that Mrs. Cavendish hadn't even bothered to attend to such a basic chore, even though she was charging me a lot of money for minding him *and* for my digs, in which I didn't even have a bed of my own. So every evening, after a hard day's work, I would have to spend hours washing Philip and his clothes. Needless to say, I was disgusted at the way we were being treated.

Yet again when I recalled with far greater horror the indignities I had endured at the Home, not to mention the extreme difficulties Cecil had experienced in getting us even this meagre accommodation, I realised that there was no alternative but to persevere. I could at least draw some consolation from having Philip with me, and with my wages and the occasional contribution from Cecil, we were able to get by despite the headaches.

Unfortunately, this comparative security was not to last for long. While standing in a queue one day at a local fish and chip shop, another neighbour asked me, "Don't you live around the corner with Mrs. Cavendish?" I said yes, I did. Then she said, "Haven't I seen you wearing a lovely maroon-coloured coat?" She was referring to a beautiful coat Cecil had given me as a Christmas present around the time that I left the Home. I said "Yes, you probably have." Then she continued, "Well, I often see that landlady of yours wearing it when she goes out to the pub."

Bloody hell! It finally dawned on me the extent to which my precious baby was being cruelly neglected by the very woman who was actually being paid to mind him. I knew I could not tolerate this situation much longer, so I asked Edith when she was planning to move away. "As soon as possible," she told me. And so we agreed to run away together to Manchester.

On reading about my experiences, some people may, understandably I suppose, suspect that I just had a little too much to drink one night, met a man, had sex and became pregnant. Others may even presume that I was promiscuous and that I was just one of those who got caught. But the truth is somewhat different and far less dramatic. In reality I had simply been enjoying a genuine, very loving relationship with a man for the first time in my life. We cared about each other very dearly and our relationship was such that I even corresponded with Cecil's mother and sisters for a time afterwards. And the reason our relationship eventually ended is not particularly earth-shattering.

Cecil's reputation for wearing good clothes had earned him the nickname 'The Duke'. While I had been in the digs in Blackheath with Mrs.Cavendish, he used to travel up from London sometimes to take me to a dance, while Edith looked after Philip. During one dance, I visited the powder room and overheard two girls discussing a man. One of them said something like, "Did you see The Duke with a new girl tonight? He took me home the other evening." I was devastated to hear this. I realised that, in spite of all I had been through, he was carrying on with other girls behind my back. I suppose I was naïve to assume that I was the only one he was seeing – but that was what I had believed. The prolonged separations, which circumstances had imposed on us, obviously hadn't helped, but I couldn't stand the thought that he had been two-timing me. Our relationship had lasted for about two years – but after much heart-searching, just before Edith and I resolved to abscond to Manchester, I decided there was no long-term future in a relationship with a man I could no longer trust. I'm sure there are lots of women reading this who will sympathise.

Since I had first discovered I was pregnant, there had been many times when I was almost completely overwhelmed with anxiety. The fact that most of my family were far away in Dublin meant that I was often prey to deep insecurity. I had two older sisters living in Leeds but only one of them, Monica, had kept in regular contact with me. She knew about Philip – I had told her – and she felt sympathy for me, particularly after I had written to Mammy with news that, predictably, had resulted in more than a few people wanting to forget all about me.

Everywhere I turned, I was reminded of the extent to which an unmarried Irish girl with a black baby was a social outcast. Monica was married and while she was expecting her own baby I asked if I could visit her and take Philip with me. She agreed, but after she met us off the train at Leeds station we had to walk around until darkness fell, to make sure that her landlady didn't see her bringing a black baby into the house. It was that kind of awful, mean-spirited world back then, where anything unconventional was frowned upon and people were made to feel guilty, even about the most natural and innocent things.

Monica arranged for me to sleep on the settee in her small flat that night. It sounds crazy looking back from this modern vantage point, but every time Philip cried we were terrified in case the landlady would become aware of his illicit presence in the house. Unfortunately, the landlady did eventually hear him and promptly came to investigate. When she saw Philip, she was determined to throw both of us into the street in the middle of the night, but after much pleading she relented and allowed us stay until morning. I cried again, because of the unfair way that my baby and I were being treated. It was heartbreaking – but at least I knew that in my sister Monica I had found someone who was not too far away and who genuinely cared about us. At a time when I most needed some kindness and charity, they had become very rare commodities indeed.

. . . .

After fleeing from Blackheath, Edith and I arrived in Manchester by train. An energetic industrial city, then encircled by an enormous ring of active collieries, Manchester was, as I was ultimately to learn, a place of many faces, from the conspicuously ritzy to the dreadfully impoverished. To the outsider, however, it can be a cold, unwelcoming landscape, its air of rush and bustle serving only to alienate anyone who does not already have a secure foothold within the life of the city.

All of a sudden, I now found myself in what I took to be a strange and ugly world with ramshackle houses and foul back-alleys, with not a tree or a flower to be seen. I was genuinely frightened by the bleak and forbidding atmosphere we encountered, but there was little time to dwell on my fears. Our first priority was to find somewhere to stay. From previous bitter experience, I knew that our only chance would be in the poorer districts, where a woman with a black baby would be more easily accepted.

Finally, after much searching, we found a place with an African landlord who gave us a room and, in the beginning at least, was generally very kind to us. At this point, we had cut ourselves adrift from virtually everybody. None of our friends or family knew where we were, with the exception of the father of Edith's baby because she had written to him. In a sense, we were two girls alone against the world – with one baby to take care of and another one on the way.

To help us get by, Edith and I came to an arrangement whereby I would go out to work to earn enough money to keep all three of us, leaving her free to concentrate on taking care of Philip and looking after herself as her own pregnancy developed. Out of necessity, we had postponed fretting about the long-term future until after her baby was born. That said, we were not so naïve as to imagine that there was anything other than stormy waters ahead. We were to encounter them sooner than anticipated.

As I said, it seemed that our landlord was a decent sort, even giving us bundles of wood for the fire. His place wasn't exactly the lap of luxury, but everything seemed to be going fine. Or so I thought. Our lodgings contained a cellar which had been converted into a kitchen. The pregnant Edith found it increasingly difficult to make it down the steps, so it fell to me to do all the trips to the cellar to cook and to put pennies in the meter. My weight had dropped to about seven stone by this time, and I was as skinny as a rake. But there's something in the human spirit that makes it hard to crush, and in spite of all the difficulties and anxieties we were managing to get by quite merrily. Then, an unexpected problem raised its ugly head. Many women have had this experience, so I know that I'm not at all unique, but that doesn't make the memory any more palatable.

One night, I was in the cellar cooking dinner when the landlord, who as far as I knew, up until then, had behaved very well towards us all, started fondling me. I told him, "No, no, no, go away," and after much struggling I shook him off. I was disgusted by his behaviour. But when I told Edith, she said it had actually been happening quite a lot to her and while she too had been able to fend him off, the pattern was beginning to unnerve her. Still, having tried it on with me and been rebuffed, we hoped he had got the message and that there would be no further repeats of this kind of unacceptable sexual bullying. Then, another night soon afterwards, without any warning he came in drunk and said he wanted to sleep with the two of us. We were genuinely afraid, with him beating on our door demanding to be allowed into the room we shared. We were so terrified that I ran straight to the nearby police station and screamed at them that our landlord was getting heavy with us. They immediately dispatched a couple of policemen to accompany me back to our lodgings, but when they saw Philip in his cot they assumed the black landlord was Philip's father and that we were two white women living in some kind of weird arrangement with a black man. They looked at us as if we were two tramps and adopted an extremely unsympathetic attitude towards us. I remember exactly the words that one of them used. "What do you expect?" he said with a tone of contempt. And they walked out and left us with this awful man. They didn't give a damn what happened to us.

When I think about it now, the behaviour of the police was absolutely disgraceful – there's no knowing what our presumptuous landlord friend might have done to us, now that I had gone to the police. But as luck would have it, an Irish lady living across the road from our lodgings had heard the commotion, with Edith and me screaming at the tops of our voices and had observed the policemen entering the house. After the police had gone back to the station we stood outside the house, wondering if we could afford to brave it inside. The Irish woman came over to us and asked if we were alright. We explained how our landlord was trying to take advantage of us. I remember I used the word 'disgusting' to describe him because that was how I felt. In fact Edith felt even more strongly: she explained that she was so unhappy with the situation that she had been in touch with her mother and had decided to go back to Birmingham.

This was news to me, but I can't say I was very surprised. Being in the house all day, she was more vulnerable than I was and I knew now that she hadn't been making up stories about the landlord trying to molest her. Seeing how upset we were, and perhaps realising that the police were totally indifferent, the neighbour invited us, there and then, in the middle of the night, to move into her house temporarily. As it happened I was in luck – if you could properly call it that! When this neighbour realised I'd be on my own with no way of earning any money because there was nobody else to look after Philip, she told me that she might be able get me a job minding children – which would allow me to earn money and be with Philip at the same time. It seemed like a good idea at the time. Things moved quickly. My neighbour made a phone call and the following day, I moved into an attic room in a very large house owned by a woman called Jo Freeman and her African husband, in the black area of Manchester.

Mrs. Freeman owned a nightclub in Manchester and needed what was then referred to as a skivvy – someone to do household chores for her. She would provide Philip and me with board and lodgings in an attic, in return for me having to take care of her three children – thus leaving her free to run the nightclub. It seemed like a decent, straightforward arrangement. My main responsibilities were to keep the house clean, take her children to and from school, feed them, dress them, and so on. So once again we found ourselves living under a different roof, but it was better than having to fend off the advances of Edith's tormentor, that's for sure. In retrospect, I suppose this was my first real contact with the entertainment business, which was to play such a huge part in my future life. Jo's nightclub had a bit of glamour about it. It attracted lots of the top names in show business like Shirley Bassey, who sang there when she was only 14. It didn't close until 2am, so as often as not my new employers would come in drunk, at 3am or 4am, leaving me to raise their kids more or less on my tod. I had to work morning, noon and night, scrubbing and cleaning the front doorsteps, taking care of the shopping, bringing the kids to the pictures, giving Mrs. Freeman and her husband their breakfast in bed and doing any other chore Jo could think of. But the fact that the two of us had children by black men at least gave us something in common, and there was no fear of anyone in the house being prejudiced against Philip because of the colour of his skin. And besides, a lot of people had to work extremely hard to get by in the 1950s. They were hard times all round.

As you can imagine, I was far too busy simply surviving even to think of starting a relationship, platonic or otherwise, with any man. In fact, friendships of that kind could not have been further from my thoughts – not because I had developed a dislike of men, or bore a grudge against them, but simply because I was physically and mentally exhausted working from dawn till dusk. I know that I could begin to sound like a perpetual moaner going on like this, but I do think that I was taken advantage of, for although I had comfortable lodgings, my new boss virtually enslaved me. At the end of each gruelling day, all I was fit for was sleeping and cuddling Philip. Every ounce of energy was drained from me by a woman whom I gradually perceived to be tyrannical and heartless.

I remember one Sunday when three men arrived at the house. They were tall, dark – I should really say black – and handsome. And one of them said to me, "I'm going to marry you." I laughed him off. He might have been thinking that if he married me he'd get a visa and be able to stay in Britain. I don't know. But there always seemed to be a man with a proposition of some kind waiting around the proverbial corner.

Having grown up in Ireland in the bosom of a close family, and as what people would probably describe as a 'good Catholic girl', I was totally bewildered by the turmoil that had overtaken me and the absence of any signs of friendship in the alien and difficult existence I was forced to lead in order to keep my son. There was not a soul I could turn to, yet not for a second did I entertain the thought of giving in. I was fiercely determined to overcome all these trials, particularly after all the hurt and abuse we had suffered to date, and to allow nothing – or nobody – to get the better of us. I'd look at little Philip and shudder as I asked myself, "What if I never saw him again?" I was young and inexperienced, and didn't have any idea what was involved in bringing up a child, but he was all that mattered to me. Without him, I would be nothing, and life would not be worth living. I know I was horribly confused, but in my heart of hearts that was how I felt.

Although some people have since asked me where I drew my strength from, I have never really seen myself in any kind of heroic light. When my own mother had babies, and she had five more after I was born, I had helped nurse them from their earliest days. Mammy would say, "You walk him up and down, Phyllis, and make him tired while I do the washing." I had a lot of responsibility thrust upon me from a very early age, so when I had my own baby, I instinctively felt I could love him and care for him as much as any mother.

Of course, some people will say that the father should have been there to share that responsibility, and ideally he would have been, but in fairness to Cecil, it was I who had broken off the relationship and was as determined as ever to make a life for Philip and myself away from him. Of course, I was not so stupid as to imagine that we would have an easy passage through life. Mrs. Freeman, my latest "employer", did not even pay me wages. She found it cheaper to turn a blind eye to me drawing the dole and receiving child allowance. I was useful to her as a skivvy, and she would pretend to the social security people that I rented my room. I was too young and too insecure to break free.

Despite the fact that I felt badly exploited, there was no point in complaining since I had no real alternative. And, deep down, I have to admit that, in some ways, I was reasonably happy with the situation, all things considered. Philip had other children to play with, and sometimes I would take them all to the cinema, where seats, I still remember, cost four old pence each. That was our only weekend treat, but we were well fed, we had a comfortable room and I often had to remind myself that there were many other people enduring far more austere conditions than ours.

One night, a taxi called to the house after the children had gone to bed, and the driver told me "Jo wants you to leave the children asleep and come over to the night-club straightaway." I didn't like leaving the kids unattended, but I didn't feel I had the authority to tell the taxi man to go away either. On arriving at the club, she put me behind the bar where they seemed to be short-staffed, and where, without any prior warning or discussion, washing glasses became yet another of my regular duties. I suppose that was another way in which people's respect for authority worked. I did what I was told. Again, I didn't feel that I had any other option.

While working at the bar one night soon afterwards, I felt someone staring intently at me. When I looked up, I saw a black GI who was drinking on his own. American soldiers were not an uncommon sight in Britain in those days, as the U.S. Army still had numerous bases located throughout the country. But this particular one made a big impression, and it was obvious that he couldn't take his eyes off me either. This scene was repeated over several nights, the same dark eyes fixed on me as I worked behind the busy bar.

When the taxi delivered me back to the house one particular night I hadn't noticed that a big green American Buick had followed the cab, and just as I was putting my key in the door, a voice behind me said, "Excuse me." When I turned around, it was the same GI. "Can I have a word with you?" he asked, and then told me he'd taken a shine to me and that he'd like to take me out some time. I should have said something funny like 'You caught me at a bad time, why don't you come back in a few years?'

But he was quite polite and persistent, and I was terribly apprehensive.

"What's the deal with you?" he said. "Every night they bring you to the club to wash glasses and then you're brought straight back to this house. It doesn't make sense." Or words to that effect.

My initial response was to feel that he was putting my work and my security at risk. "I can't talk to you, and if they catch you here you'll get me thrown out and I'll lose my job," I explained to him. "I've got a little baby and he's black, and I can't afford to risk losing my lodgings by being seen talking to you."

"I'll go now, but I'll be back," he said, and he got into his Buick and drove off. But, typically, it wasn't long before he came back sniffing around. Are all men like that, prairie dogs that persist in their badness till a woman finally gives in? I don't know – maybe it was just the type I attracted!

Anyway, he kept at me at the club, inviting me for a date again and again and again until he slipped a note to me asking me to telephone him. When I rang him the next day, he asked me how I'd got into this situation. "Tell me everything," he insisted. I had no idea what he really wanted, but I suppose it was nice to be able to pour out my troubles to somebody, so I told him my story from start to finish. He listened intently, which made me feel good.

When I finished, he said: "Why don't you let me take care of you?" It was the last thing I expected to hear. I remember feeling that nobody at all wanted to know me, so why should this fellow? Besides, what did he mean when he said he'd take care of me? I had no reason to trust anybody at that point. At the same time, I was finding all the work and the heavy responsibilities hard going. I didn't know how long I could survive combining the duties of a mother, a baby-minder, a house cleaner and an over-stretched dogsbody in a bar in a late-night club. It wasn't the kind of life that anyone would choose to live – not anyone in their right mind, anyway.

"Don't worry, I'll find you somewhere to live," he told me. "I'll pay your rent. I'll look after you and your baby." I promised to think it over, though I honestly hadn't a clue what to make of a proposal that was as frightening as it was surprising. Looking back, I don't know whether

I thought he'd fallen in love with me or was just being kind. Either way, I was probably less inhibited than most Irish girls at the time, and there was something in me that was attracted to the possibility of an adventure. I kept turning his conversation over and over in my mind and wondering what did I have to lose? Not a lot, I reckoned, given the situation I was in.

The following week, I wasn't taken to the nightclub as normal. Apparently, somebody had told my boss that I had been seen in conversation with a strange man outside the house. It may seem bizarre from the perspective of the 1990s, but I was still very young – and she felt that this gave her the right to dictate what I could, and more importantly what I couldn't, do. It didn't matter that I'd already had a baby. So she threatened to write to my parents and create all kinds of trouble for me.

When I look back, it seems strange that this threat would have assumed such an exaggerated sense of importance to me – after all, my mother already knew about my situation – but it did. The irony is that I was the only real mother this woman's own kids had known. I'd been her baby-sitter, housekeeper, bottle-washer, nanny, cook, cleaner, the whole caboodle, and all for no wages and even less appreciation. Now, under threat of being further exposed to my own mother, I gathered Philip and our few belongings and left this part of our lives behind. I knew that I was taking a risk – but I was driven by a desperate need to keep my independence intact and to experience the respect and warmth of another human being who cared for me. Besides, I was worn out slaving day and night for Jo and her husband, and so I felt a great sense of relief when I made the decision to take my new friend up on his offer.

My new American GI buddy was called Jimmy Angel and he came from South Carolina. He fulfilled his promise and found us digs, which were nice, if nothing special – but I now had the time and space to begin to get myself organised and in a lot of ways I felt like a new woman. And I had the space to – maybe, just maybe – begin to enjoy life again! After I moved in, I made friends with another girl who was also going out with an American. It was the beginning of a good phase in my life that

I still remember fondly all these years later. Jimmy began taking Philip and me to the American base in which he was stationed, at Warrington in Cheshire, although there was nothing he loved more than going out on the town. We couldn't do it often but we were beginning to fall in love, and so I embarked on a full blown affair. We enjoyed ourselves laughing and dancing and having a good time – always under the cloud of knowing that I was still an unmarried mother. Yes, he was good to me, was Jimmy Angel, and a decent man.

For the first time in my life, I was able to indulge in big, juicy t-bone steaks, nylon stockings, Hershey bars and all sorts of treats like barbecues, that I'd never experienced before, and, in those still-rationed years, was otherwise unlikely to experience for quite some while. In time, I began putting Philip's father, who I believed was now living in Birmingham, well behind me.

I had remained in contact with my sister Monica in Leeds, and kept her informed about my developing friendship with Jimmy. One day, she invited us down to visit, and we all travelled in Jimmy's big car, with its green-tinted windows. Her house was situated on a hill, and sometime after we arrived, Philip, who was now almost three years old, went out to play with the other kids. I don't know how he did it, but he managed to get back into the car. He must have released the handbrake, because the car took off down the hill with Philip in it. You can imagine the fright I got when one of the neighbours raised the alarm. Luckily, neither the car nor Philip came to any harm, but he could have been seriously hurt. To say that he demanded constant watching is to put it mildly!

Meanwhile, I was extremely happy in my relationship with Jimmy. He was a tall and very handsome man who took great pride in his appearance. From the time I had discovered him staring at me in the bar, I have to admit I was genuinely and thoroughly hooked on him.

I have never made any apology, and never will, for any of my relationships with black men. Black, white, yellow, brown – to me none of it makes a blind bit of difference. It was infuriating that so many white men, as soon as they discovered I had a black baby, would have nothing to do with me anyway. It was awful to suffer rejection in this way – and so it was doubly uplifting to have a true friendship, where the colour of my skin and my child's skin were irrelevant.

At that time, I had very little confidence in my attractiveness to the opposite sex. Perhaps now, when I look back at photographs of myself in my early twenties, with my jet-black hair, I can see that I looked rather well, but I was not conscious of it at the time. On the contrary, when I used to look in the mirror before going out to a dance, despite being all dolled-up, I never thought much of my appearance. I used to think my green eyes were like cat's eyes, and I hated them.

Part of the reason I was so lacking in self-confidence was that I had very little time to develop any awareness of my sexuality. I had become pregnant after having sex a couple of times with the first man with whom I had a sexual liaison. I became a mother before I had the chance to enjoy anything like a full teenage life, and I'd had to proceed through life wary of getting pregnant a second time. But I never felt any resentment against men, neither then nor later. Jimmy had taken a shine to me, we had fallen in love – he had actually wanted to marry me at one point – and I was delighted to be rescued from the awful drudgery of the life I had been leading. In modern parlance, it was all good…

Of course, I had to deal with considerable inner trauma throughout that part of my life. The traditional teachings of the Catholic Church had been deeply ingrained in me since my earliest schooldays in Ireland and I had to accept that I was basically a sinner in the eyes of the church. An unmarried mother, with a black child, now living with a man I was not married to, and who was not the father of my son: dear, oh dear, I was the kind of person that we'd all been taught to shun. Some inner part of me was probably deeply ashamed or riddled with guilt about the whole thing. It would take me a long time to rid myself of that horrible legacy, but I eventually did.

I have always believed that sex is beautiful, and once you have enjoyed it as a teenager you want it again. That is a perfectly natural response. Anyone who tries to suggest otherwise is plain daft. And there's nothing wrong with it either. Nothing. That doesn't mean it's always going to be easy. While I endeavoured to cope with the practical pressures of my situation, I also had to deal with the various deep emotions I was experiencing and without anyone else to turn to or to share feelings with.

Whether other people approve or not, I cannot alter the experiences I went through, and I'm certainly not going to pretend I'm sorry now, just for the sake of propriety. Survival was the over-riding priority for me, and my son, but I needed love and tenderness too, and I got it, living very happily with Jimmy Angel as my boyfriend, for what certainly felt like a couple of years. We were reasonably well off by the standards of the time, with me drawing the dole while Jimmy covered the cost of our lodgings and most other expenses. With his companionship, I was rediscovering that life could have some wonderful moments, and I reckon I was enjoying a reasonable share of them. No more than I deserved though, I can assure you!

Because I was drawing the dole, one day the welfare people demanded that I name Philip's natural father, and I had no alternative but to comply with their command. They in turn informed me that they were taking him to court to insist that he pay me my due maintenance. Cecil, who was still sending me some money irregularly, then came to visit me in Manchester and told me he wanted Philip and me to live with him and that he wanted us to be married. I don't know whether he knew what he wanted at all – or understood the level of responsibility involved in bringing up a child. Either way, that prospect no longer had any appeal for me, assuming it ever might have had, because I was now extremely content with Jimmy and we were in love with each other. But when I refused Cecil's proposal, he was so incensed he threatened to take Philip away from me.

When the maintenance case came to court, I was terrified. The cold, grey courthouse, and the snooty, stern-faced barristers who swaggered and strutted through the long corridors with their wigs and gowns, did little to reassure me. In the event, Cecil did not appear in person, but instead wrote a letter to the magistrate in effect saying, "I am Cecil Parris. I do not deny the parentage of the said child and whatever you decide that I should pay towards his maintenance I will willingly do so."

Cecil's generous and frank admission not only surprised me after his threat to take Philip, but his attitude was in sharp contrast to the other cases I observed while in the court, where the usual approach was for the man to deny fatherhood so that blood-tests were often required. When Cecil's letter was read out, I was absolutely thrilled, because it put the whole issue of Philip's parentage completely beyond a shadow of doubt. Here was an honest man, accepting without any prevarication, that he was the natural father of my son. A spiteful man could have denied his responsibility and thereby caused me endless grief, but that was not Cecil's nature, and it made me eternally grateful to him, in this regard at least, for his decency.

Obviously, the kind of situation I found myself in reflected much of the bias against women that was then – and still is – too common in our society. Back then, a man could have sex with a woman, and if she became pregnant she was literally left holding the baby if the man decided to deny all knowledge and evade all responsibility. It isn't as easy to get away with that kind of stuff nowadays but back then it was what men did. But Cecil behaved very honourably, despite the fact that it might not have been easy for him, and particularly since I had refused his offer of marriage. I know I loved him at one point, but after discovering that he was two-timing me, I knew that I didn't want to spend the rest of my life with him.

Meanwhile, my sister Monica made it abundantly clear to me how she felt about him. She was bitterly opposed to him after she realised how he had been behaving with other women – especially since he knew all too well that I had borne his child. She told me quite bluntly: "If you marry him, I'll swing for you." And she meant it.

Although I was tremendously relieved at the outcome of the court case, there were even further difficulties ahead. My life with Jimmy Angel, full of joy and contentment despite the hardships of the time, was not destined to last for very much longer. While America is much troubled by racism today, the situation at that time was far worse. Blacks in certain States were forced to sit in segregated sections of restaurants, cinemas and buses, and this bigoted, separatist outlook was reflected in the attitudes of large sections of the ordinary American public. It hardly seems credible at this point, but many of Jimmy's fellow Americans at the base in Warrington objected to his close association with a white woman. As time passed, the antagonism towards him increased, and he was eventually transferred to another base overseas, apparently for his own safety. I really don't know how he felt about this deep down, but soon he was gone almost completely from my life except for the letters we exchanged. He said all the right things in these but the truth is that there was no way for us to get back together.

Naturally, and inevitably, we gradually lost touch. It took a while but, after I became reconciled to the permanence of his departure, I hoped that he might find his way back to his old routine in South Carolina where maybe he might marry his childhood sweetheart. I never did find out what became of him.

Philip took his absence very badly. At around the same time, he was beginning to be the direct recipient of the same kind of disgusting racial taunts that had previously been hurled at me. One instance occurred in the Chorlton area of Manchester, when we were living with a family called Nimro. There was a friendly, neighbourly woman who often shared with us some of the tasty bread she used to bake in her house.

One day, I sent Philip to collect some from her and, when some considerable time had elapsed with no sign of him returning, I anxiously set off in search of him. Not far along the road, I came upon two kids playing on the path, with another up a tree throwing chestnuts down to them. Before I could ask them if they had seen my Philip, I realised that they boy up the tree was Philip. When I chastised the boys for encouraging such a small boy to climb a tree, they told me that he was well able to climb trees because he was a monkey! I know the children meant no harm, but that example shows what dreadful prejudices were planted in the minds of innocent white kids concerning members of other races.

Sadly, there are still too many similar instances where that same blind ignorance forms an integral part of the world in which innocent children grow up. One wonders if such bigotry will always be with us. But with Jimmy Angel only recently having departed from his life, Philip was being forced to begin learning how to face such ignorance – and he had not yet even started attending school.

3. A TALE OF TWO CITIES

We stayed on in Manchester after Jimmy's departure and it was not long before my parents came over to visit my sister Monica in Leeds. Monica then suggested they should travel down to Manchester to meet Philip for the first time. He was three years old.

It was bound to be a difficult occasion for everyone involved, and for some time beforehand I had been preparing Philip by repeatedly telling him, "You're going to meet your grandma and grandad." For days the poor kid had been repeating the words 'grandma' and 'grandad' over and over.

Inevitably, by the time we got to Victoria railway station, Philip was very excited by all the fuss. And it got worse. There was, as yet, no sign of my parents, but as we waited I noticed a commotion centred around a group of about ten men passing through the station. The object of everyone's attention was a well-known Red Indian wrestler called Billy Two Rivers, who actually lived very close to my flat and later became a national celebrity on British television because of his spectacular Red Indian wrestling attire.

Just then, I spotted my mother approaching us with tears in her eyes. But before she got to us, Billy rushed over, lifted me up and swung me around, right there in front of her. She, of course, did not know that, being neighbours, we knew each other rather well, and was astonished at what was going on in public, between her daughter and this huge, burly man with a very weird Mohican hair-style (of exactly the kind which, oddly enough, was to become very popular with so many young people when punk rock arrived about two decades later – I guess Billy was before his time!). My father was so taken aback that he could only burst out, "Sacred Heart of Jaysus!" – a familiar Dublin exclamation that could be heard all over the station. As we found out later, he thought Billy Two Rivers was Philip's dad! I will never forget the expression on my father's face as long as I live, with the whole station, including little Philip, looking on in amazement at this extraordinary spectacle. What a way for my parents to meet my son for the first time!

After an initial tentativeness, Mam and Dad discovered that they really liked Philip, who was an extremely lovable kid anyway, and, from that point on, they enjoyed a very close relationship with him for as long as they both lived. To help cement the new relationship, I invited them for a little holiday to where we were now living, in Didsbury, and made as much of a fuss of them as I could because I knew only too well how tough all this was for them. We had a lovely time together, but of course it couldn't last, and they returned to Dublin. At least now, however, I felt reassured of the love of my parents – not just for me, but for Philip also. That was very important, because in truth I was gradually finding it harder and harder to cope on my own.

At this distance, it seems virtually impossible to convey the difficulty faced by a young unmarried mother in the early 1950s, trying to hold on to her child in the kind of circumstances I found myself in, striving to dress, feed and clothe a child while holding down demanding jobs – and, in my case anyway, at the same time having to do whatever I could to protect myself in a very vulnerable and lonely predicament. Even a trip to the local shop could become a taxing ordeal in such situations.

There were times when I had no job and even having enough to eat was a major problem. Through one bad patch, I remember cooking a pan of porridge over an open coal fire for myself and Philip, and putting some of it aside for the next morning's breakfast. That was all the food we had. Another time, my resources had sunk to the point where I was reduced to asking the butcher for some bones, which I pretended were for a dog. Later, I added a carrot, one onion and a couple of small potatoes to those bones to make us a stew.

To add to the obvious problems of racism, loneliness and poverty, I also had to endure occasional public indignities that I can only put down to the fact that Philip was black. It came to a head one day when I was queuing for a bus, hungry and bitterly cold, with Philip in his buggy. When the bus pulled up at the stop, I expected the conductor to offer the customary courtesy of helping me on with the buggy. But to my great distress, he didn't lift a finger. Instead of helping me, he maliciously rang the bell for the bus to move on without us. This was the last straw for me, and I collapsed on the street. A woman went for assistance to a nearby chemist and they kindly brought me a glass of ice-cold water with some peppermint, although it was hardly much help, given the state I was in.

I think that was the straw that broke the camel's back. I had been under pressure for a long time but had kept going, unaware of how close I had come to a complete and total physical breakdown. I think that incident finally brought it home to me that it was no longer feasible for me to care for Philip adequately on my own. What if it happened to us in a more isolated or threatening place? And what if I was so depleted that I couldn't get up or recover? It became obvious to me that I was in serious danger of permanently damaging my own health, and possibly even Philip's. I know it doesn't sound very brave, but I had reached the point where I simply could not bear any more hardship.

I sometimes wonder might I have done things differently – and how would our lives have turned out if I had? In the face of the overwhelming difficulties, I had struggled to avoid becoming too depressed and I certainly never sank so low, in spite of pressures, as to contemplate anything as drastic as suicide. Nor did I pray very often, probably because I had become so utterly disillusioned by this so-called Christian society and the hateful way it had treated both me and my innocent baby. But I was desperately in need of help and there didn't seem to be a great deal of it about in Manchester at the time.

Things might have been different too if all this had happened in the 1960s, because of the development of the Welfare State and, in particular, the level of support available for unmarried mothers. But in the 1950s that support simply didn't exist. Against that background, the avenues of escape from the predicament we faced were few and far between. Cecil and I were by now living totally separate lives. He was not sending me the maintenance money, which the court had ordered him to, but I had no stomach for the prospect of having to pursue him for it. And, besides, I had neither the inclination nor the resources to embark on a legal battle – at least partly because I realised that if you looked at it only from *his* perspective, I had selfishly taken his child away from him.

Equally, there was no point in me harbouring plans to move back to Dublin with Philip because this was still the dour, depressed 50s, and the chronic jobs situation in Ireland had not improved. People were emigrating in their droves, so how could I possibly expect to get a job if I went back?

Marriage was not an option either, given my circumstances at that time. In those narrow-minded days, it was tough even for women who had given birth to illegitimate *white* babies to form new relationships. As a result, back-door abortions were common, and many unfortunate women, who found themselves in a similar position to mine had no alternative but to go down that road. I have met several of them since, and they are amazed that I stubbornly insisted on continuing my pregnancy, notwithstanding that I had made that crude attempt at abortion myself.

I have never fully understood where my stubbornness came from, since my sisters were all rather quiet, inoffensive and easy-going. Perhaps it developed in me as a direct response to the pressures assailing me on all fronts. Or maybe it's just the way that I was born, because even today I will not tolerate anybody talking down to me.

There are some people who meet me, and who probably leave with the impression that I am a hard woman. Others might think more kindly of me. But I do know that I was faced with difficult decisions along the way and that I had to make them on my own. So, after much heart-searching and agonised deliberation, I decided that the only sensible course of action was for me to ask Mam to take Philip into her house in Dublin, while I would stay in England. It was hard to ask, I don't mind admitting, because I had to swallow my pride to do so. It was made even harder because the prospect of being separated from Philip appalled me. But

I knew that I would be relieved of a burden of responsibility that I was finding really difficult to bear. Looking back, it could, I know, seem like a very selfish option to have chosen, but I can say this much for certain – it didn't feel like that at the time.

About a year after the emotional reunion with my parents and their first meeting with Philip in Manchester, I wrote to Mum and asked her to consider taking Philip to live with her in Dublin.

In my head, I genuinely knew that sending Philip to Dublin was the right thing to do. But, in my heart, I was torn apart with sorrow at the very idea. But when Mum kindly agreed, I decided to go through with it, for my own sake as much as for Philip's. She fully understood that I badly needed the space that the arrangement would give me, and that otherwise I would never be free to build a real life for myself.

I promised to send her as much money as I could spare, and I intended to look out for clothes for Philip since I would probably pick up better bargains in Manchester than my mother could afford back in Dublin. That kind of thinking might seem crazy now, but it's the way your mind works in a situation like that. You focus on the inconsequential details a lot of the time, in an effort to shut out the harsh realities. That's certainly what I did.

I will never forget the morning I had to leave four-year-old Philip behind in Dublin. I was due to go back to Manchester alone, taking the boat to Liverpool and making the short journey from there. As I packed my bag for the trip, my fingers were literally trembling with anguish and distress. I couldn't speak properly. The muscles around my throat had tightened, and I could barely look at Philip without wanting to cry. After everything we had been through together I could only hope that the little trouper, my loyal friend, wouldn't experience it as a betrayal, and that he would settle down and be happy in my absence. With all the strength I could muster, I fixed a smile on my face and cuddled Philip for all my life was worth, whispering to him that it wouldn't be long before we would be together again. At the same time I knew that I was lucky that I had a loving mother and father to turn to. So many young women in circumstances similar to my own don't have that luxury.

I returned to Manchester, and soon afterwards, I picked up not one but three part-time jobs, including one on a stall in an open market and another as a barmaid. Although my standard of living and my health had improved somewhat now that I did not have a small, demanding child to look after, life was still difficult. My child, for whom I had sacrificed so much to hold on to, was now in another country. Living on my own again since Jimmy Angel had been posted overseas, there was very little in the way of joy in my life. It was an austere time generally. All my clothes were purchased from second-hand stores or from market stalls. I was constantly on the look-out for bargains, and did a lot of my shopping at Woolworth's, where you could purchase popular items like Evening In Paris perfume for two shillings and sixpence. In fact, I still have one of those distinctive blue bottles, which I kept as a memento. It also serves as a constant reminder of a memorable occasion on a train journey with Philip, when he was only about three years old. Out of the blue, he said to me, "Ma, you smell lovely," and when I explained to him about perfume he said, "When I grow up I'm going to buy you lots and lots of perfume and a big, big house." In the long run, he did buy me a house and, right from the time he first started travelling, he never came home without a bottle of perfume for me. But I am getting ahead of myself!

It goes without saying that there was real consolation for me in the knowledge that Philip was now living in a secure, loving household with a standard of life which, though relatively poor by modern standards, was a lot better than anything I could have provided for him at the time. He now had regular food, proper nourishing meals and a clean, warm bed among people who cared for him and loved him. Yet my heart still ached to have him with me. But I derived some pleasure from writing regular letters to my mother, and I'd enclose as much money as I could afford.

Not that the situation was without its difficulties for my family in Dublin. When Philip first moved in with them, the social pressures were so intense that they conspired to pretend to their neighbours that Philip was the son of a friend of mine – or alternatively, probably depending on whom they were talking to, that his mother had died. Indeed, they'd have spun any yarn they thought people would swallow to avoid telling the truth. And you couldn't blame them. The level of shame and embarrassment that surrounded the idea of a child being born to an unmarried mother in Ireland at the time was frightening. And so numerous estates all over Dublin had their mystery children – kids who appeared out of nowhere at the age of three or four or five, and no-one quite knew for sure if they were adopted, or were family – or if they were just staying for a while…

In retrospect, it has to be acknowledged that it was extremely courageous of my Mam to take Philip in. There was no way his presence in the house wasn't going to become a source of unpleasant gossip, given the social and religious climate of the time, and especially given that he was a little black boy. To say that he'd stand out in Dublin in 1954 is to put it mildly! I know I had never seen a black child in Dublin when I was growing up – which is why Philip became commonly known as the first black man in Ireland. Besides, my mother already had her hands sufficiently full with my father Frank, my ten-year-old sister Irene and my younger brothers Tim, who was seven, and Peter, only a year older than Philip.

For her courage and limitless generosity, especially to me, I have always been deeply grateful to Mam. When she herself was coming to the end of her life, I was able to return the favour, albeit in a very small way, by ensuring that she would not have to enter a home – and I greatly treasure the memory of holding her in my arms when she died.

Living on my own, I no longer had to endure the unpleasant innuendo or the outright offensive remarks that I had often been subjected to while Philip was with me, except on those occasions when I visited Dublin, which I did about five times each year. Back home, I found myself defiantly fighting my ingrained Irish tendency to be ashamed of my circumstances. There was a constant process of awakening taking place within me, as I questioned, again and again, the conventional attitudes my upbringing had instilled in me, and indeed in virtually every other young woman of my generation.

Illegitimate offspring – an offensive term in itself, as if the birth of any human being could actually be deemed illegitimate – are often referred to as 'love children', but in my time they were considered 'sin children'. You were expected to hang your head in shame if you gave birth out of wedlock. It was not until I reached my thirties that I believe I finally shook off the last residues of that shame. I have always resented the fact that it has traditionally been the pregnant woman who has been despised. How many others in my time were enjoying sexual relationships and were lucky enough to avoid becoming pregnant? And why was no shame attached to the men in these situations? And what is wrong, anyway, with love freely given and freely shared? And if a child results, is it not the most important thing that he or she, in turn, is loved?

It was that sense of shame, unjustly imposed by an intolerant society, which forced my family to keep up one pretence or another about Philip for several years, but I believe that most of the neighbours saw through it anyway and knew that he was my child. For my mother's sake, and her sake alone, I played along with her stories, but before those who dared to look me in the eye and defy me to tell the truth, I would openly behave as if, yes, he was indeed my son. The more often I visited Crumlin, the more rebellious I became in the face of the offensive taunts I would be subjected to by some of the more vicious and xenophobic neighbours.

Like many other working class areas of Dublin, Crumlin was a tough place to grow up in. Located on the south west of the city, there was nothing intrinsically attractive or pretty about it. Row upon row of faceless, terraced houses to some degree obscured the depths of poverty, which often existed side by side with the relative prosperity of others. It was easy to lose yourself in the anonymity of the estates, which ran like rabbit warrens throughout the area. But while violence and crime were not uncommon, it was, for the most part in those days, a seemingly friendly place with a real sense of community spirit. Behind closed doors, however, all manner of prejudices were nurtured, and gossip, of both the malicious and harmless varieties, was as much a part of the daily diet as potatoes, cabbage and – for those who could afford them – pork chops.

One particular Crumlin neighbour would regularly, and very pointedly, remark to me, while looking at Philip, "Isn't he just like you when you were a child?" I suppose I should have taken it as a compliment, but I don't think it was intended that way. When he was about seven, the local shopkeeper very skittishly passed a similar remark and I couldn't restrain myself from shouting back at him, "I know, sure isn't he mine?"

Small incidents linger on in the mind, which suggest what must have been a horrible level of stress in maintaining the pretence. On another occasion when we were out shopping, Philip had smeared chocolate all over his face. I must have been reaching breaking point with the way we were being treated, because when a woman went to wipe his face, I said, "Oh look, the colour comes off." I said it with real venom and bitterness, and I can still remember the anger I felt welling up inside me.

It'd be easy to conclude that I was being paranoid, but there was a dreadful, parochial small-mindedness about. While travelling on the ferry between Holyhead and Ireland, I once overheard a group of people gossiping about "a girl over on Kildare Road in Crumlin who had given birth to a black baby." They agreed how shocking it all was. As it happened, I was acquainted with the girl under discussion. Cathleen was her name and, when I arrived in Dublin again, I called to her house to show her that she was not the only one in that particular predicament, and to offer her some advice based on my own experience.

Of course, not all Irish people were so petty and so prim – there were many good-natured individuals who would compliment me on my beautiful child, and some who would stare admiringly at his lovely hair and ask me for a curl.

Meantime, while I was away in Manchester, my mother coped admirably. She had given birth to my younger brother, Peter, at the grand old age of 51. As he was only a year older than Philip, she raised the two of them together as if they were brothers. Indeed she had nine children in total, so Philip, growing up with his uncles Peter and Tim for company, was not the enormous extra burden for her that some people might imagine.

That was one of the good things about the large families prevalent in Ireland at the time – to an extent, the kids took care of one another, and even though it was hard, especially for mothers, adding another one to the flock wasn't the major decision it sometimes seems like nowadays.

The passage of time had helped my mother recover from the shock of Philip's birth – and his unexpected colour. My father Frank, meanwhile, like many Dublin working-class men of that era, dutifully went to and from work each day and popped out for his pint in the local at night. They were happy together, and I suppose the pretence about Philip's origin probably helped him more than anybody else in that respect. Much as he loved Philip, I don't think he'd have been comfortable if he'd had to properly explain the circumstances to his friends. Sadly, he died of a heart-attack in May 1964 and Philip, who was only fourteen at the time, was heartbroken. Because of his sudden death, his grandfather missed out on all of Philip's later successes, which he would have thoroughly enjoyed, as he was the first to spot the showman in the young Philip.

On my trips home, I would treat Philip, his uncle Peter and my nephew, Ronnie, to whatever was appropriate at the time: it might be a pantomime, a visit to Santa or to the cinema. Alternatively, I might simply take them shopping in the centre of Dublin, which was then considered a real treat for children, although few of today's worldly-wise kids would be so easily impressed! We would have great fun together, but it was soul destroying having to leave Philip behind each time I returned to Manchester.

Visits home also offered me the opportunity to contact some of my Dublin friends and to go dancing. Mostly these were good times – Philip, I knew, was safe and I didn't have to worry about the prospect of having to get up for work the next day – but there were incidents which underlined the fact that my experiences marked me down as an outsider. I remember cycling to the house of Geraldine, a pal of mine who was now married, and while I was there her husband Harry arrived in. It did not take me long to spot that he was very much the worse for drink. When the time came for me to leave, Harry was persuaded to show me a short-cut back to Mam's house.

We were both on bikes, but after we had cycled only part of the way he cut across me and tried to push me up against a wall and drunkenly attempted to have sexual intercourse with me. Horrified by his behaviour, I pushed him away, but that made him even more furious, and he shouted at me, "You let niggers have you, but one of your own kind is not good enough for you." Thankfully he didn't become violent as I feared he might have, but I was so frightened that I could never bring myself to meet Geraldine again. In a way, I regret that I could not pluck up the courage to tell her the reason why – I probably should have, since it was not her who had tried to rape me, but who knows how she would have responded or what the effect on their relationship might have been?

Unfortunately, that sort of reaction from men was not uncommon. On the rare occasions when I had time to go out for a date, I could see the adverse response as soon as I admitted that I had had an illegitimate child. For some of them, inevitably, my child's colour was the central problem. Also, the fact that I told them about Philip upfront often seemed to be taken as an indication that I must be a sex-starved nymphomaniac only too keen to jump into bed with any man who offered himself. It was a constant dilemma that seemed to rear its head almost as soon as I thought any man might be taking a genuine fancy to me. I had the awful choice of telling the truth early on, or allowing the relationship to develop and then probably having it ruined anyway, as soon as the truth was revealed.

Sadly, that kind of overt racism is still to be encountered to this day, although I like to think it is not quite as prevalent as it was in my time. Back then, I could not help worrying how Philip, growing up in a tough, no-holds-barred area of Dublin, was going to cope with this problem. I knew it inevitably would catch up with him, and that my family's protection could not or would not shield him forever.

4. REMEMBERING PART 1

And that, more or less, is the story of that part of my life as I told it for the first edition of this book in 1995. But not all of that account is true. Or rather it is selective, in that it deliberately omits certain crucial facts. What no readers or fans could possibly have known back then was that I was hiding two enormous secrets that I dared not reveal. It wasn't a new experience for me. Concealing the truth about my personal life had racked me with guilt throughout virtually all of my adult life but, even then, well into my sixties, when I was engaged in looking back over my whole life and trying to make sense of all the things that had happened to me, there was still no way that I could have gone further than I did.

Well, comes a time. I can tell the full story now. I know I'm not meant to say this, but it certainly is a curse, age. Perhaps because I never really was one, I like to think of myself still as a carefree 18 year old – but, as I write this, there's no denying that I am all of 80 years old. I don't feel it. And my friends tell me that I don't look it. But much as I might like to pretend otherwise, in my heart of hearts I know that there is no turning the clock back.

There are some compensations that mitigate the knowledge that our best years are probably behind us (see how I cling to the hope of better things to come!). The wheels of fate have ground on in the intervening years and I am freer now than ever before of the need to put a different face on, in the morning, to greet the day. We are all too fond of dissembling anyway, myself included. We're addicted to subterfuge, to mirrors, to make-up and to masks. Well, there's too little time left to continue with all of that. And besides the people that might have been hurt, had I told all then, are now in a different place. And so I can finally be true to myself and to the hand I was dealt.

And so to repeat what I have already said at the start of this book, Philip was not my only child. I am aware that it might shock some people that this revelation is directly contrary to what I said back then. Certainly, the truth of my situation would have shocked anyone who knew me in Dublin, when all of this was unfolding – in fact it might even have killed my own mother if she'd found out. For, truth be told, in the few years after Philip was born I gave birth to two other children, a sister and a brother that Philip never knew. The naked reality of what transpired is that I had to give both of them up for adoption because of the awful circumstances I was living in at the time.

Why did I keep this stark fact a secret for so long? Well, there isn't really any great mystery. I went to extraordinary lengths to hide the truth because of the effect these new revelations might have had on my mother. In time I revealed the essential details to a small number of trusted friends, including my long time partner Dennis Keeley and my sisters.

But living as she did in a working-class, conservative Catholic suburbs of Dublin in the 1950s, I felt my mother already had enough pressure to cope with. Remember, at the age of seventeen I had given birth, out of wedlock – a major crime in the unforgiving eyes of the Catholic Church in those oppressive days. But what complicated matters irretrievably, of course, was the fact that my first baby was black.

It wasn't that my mother held any racial views. She might have had the apprehension that a lot of Irish people felt about black people because of their unfamiliarity, but in the long run she demonstrated that she never had an ounce of prejudice in her, something I hope I inherited. But she admitted to me later that she'd had to bear the brunt of offensive racist taunts. The rest of the kids said that she handled these with a fierce stoicism but it was tough for her and she didn't like it at all, being made to feel like an outsider in her own hometown. But if I had revealed the truth, the whole truth and nothing but the truth – that I'd had two more babies that had also been born out of wedlock, and to different fathers, and both put up for adoption – well, you can imagine the likely reaction.

The shame would have been bad enough for me, but for her I think it would have been impossible to bear. Anyway that was the judgement I made at that time: In the long run I would owe her so much for taking on the responsibility for feeding, clothing, housing and rearing Philip, and I simply couldn't bear to add to her burden. Such was the debt I owed this generous, and in many ways heroic woman, having given my children up for adoption, I preferred to shoulder the burden of secrecy, deceit and guilt myself rather than burdening her with any further turmoil.

Was I stupid? I don't know. Sometimes there is an element of self-delusion in the decisions we make. Maybe I was thinking less about her than I was about myself. Who really knows what lies in the heart of man? Or woman? I never regretted keeping my mother in the dark – although I paid a heavy cost in terms of having to bottle up my secrets for so many decades, permanently on alert in case I blurted something out by mistake.

Later on, I had to deal with the dilemma that almost every mother who gives a child up for adoption eventually faces. Having let the child go off into the world, hopefully to find a different family, have you a right to start rummaging around when it suits you, in what might be a very settled situation – until you intervene, that is, potentially stirring up old ghosts that would be better left in peace? It is very hard to know the right thing to do. But of course that works both ways and in the end what you can say for sure is that children have a right to know where they came from. Certainly if they initiate contact, it seems better, to me, that we should embrace it wholeheartedly.

In any event, the way things unfolded, I also felt I had to protect the privacy of my two other children, and their adoptive parents, who could have so easily become tabloid targets as the siblings of the rock star Philip Lynott. Over the years, I am not afraid to say that I have had to accept that, having dug a deep hole of untruths, I found it increasingly difficult to confront the unreconstructed reality, even after my mother died. But now, for the first time ever, I want to reveal the complete details of the circumstances surrounding the births of my two other children. That, I think, is the least I owe to the world.

. . . .

Philip Parris Lynott was born in August, 1949. My lovely daughter Philomena followed in March 1951, and then came a second son, the wonderful Leslie in June 1952. Those are not the names I gave the younger two on their birth certificates, but rather the names they use now. So there it is. By the age of 21, I was three times a mother. But to reveal the full details of how, where and when, I need to rewind a little bit. The funniest thing, looking back, is just how little I knew about sex even then. Like most parents at the time, my mother had given us no sex education at all. But of course she'd had none herself and so I'm sure it never even remotely occurred to her that she might have a responsibility in this regard.

When I had my first period at the age of about eleven, she must have noticed something, because she enlisted my eldest sister to act as my 'governess'! "Take Philomena into the bathroom and talk to her," she instructed. My sister did what she was told and explained to me that whenever this happens to you, you must not go near boys. "But you're not to be worried," she said. "You're not sick."

While that came as a bit of relief, the rest of what she said was misleading, to put it mildly! But that was the end of it. In fact, my sexual education before I met Cecil was so lacking that, at one point, I was convinced that if a boy kissed me I'd get pregnant. So in reality, when I left home, on my own, to go to England at 17 years of age, I was as pure as a lily. Well, nearly…

This was not very long after the war had ended in 1945 and I gradually became aware that there were lots of men in uniform about the place. They might have provided a distraction on occasion, but in general life was dull. There was no clear air, what with smoke coming out from fires in houses, the heavy fog, shortages of goods and so on. My life had been pretty drab after Philip was born, and it got worse after his father Cecil, moved to London. So with Cecil off the scene, I began another affair – with a white American serviceman. He was stationed at the US base in Burtonwood, a few miles outside Liverpool, where lots of GIs were garrisoned. Local girls would meet the US army men in the dancehalls in the area, and get up to all sorts of mischief.

As for me, I know it doesn't sound very romantic, but I actually met my suitor at a phone-box. Although it was obvious to me at least that Cecil and I were unlikely to spend our lives together, we kept in touch while he was up in London and he'd visit on occasion. We had an arrangement that he would ring a particular phone-box at an agreed time, which might seem a bit mad now, with mobile phones and how easy communications have become, but it was the way long distance relationships had to be conducted at the time, unless you were well off enough to have a phone installed, which I certainly wasn't.

One day, after I'd picked up the receiver, I noticed there was a man outside the phone-box, waiting to make a call. As I chatted away to Cecil, this chap kept knocking on the window to get me to finish off, so he could use the phone. Bloody impatient he was! Or that was what struck me at the time. Underneath I was thinking that maybe there was some crisis in his world and that he really did need to use the phone quickly. It was raining too, I remember, and Philip was in the pram outside the phone-box with the hood up.

But, in between his banging, this man started to play with Philip, keeping him amused. I saw him giving Philip a tiny bit of a Hershey bar, which got me to bring the conversation with Cecil to an end pretty sharpish. Philip was less than nine months old at the time and, in all honesty, I was afraid that he might choke. I mean you don't give sticky toffee to a baby. So I finished talking to Cecil, came out, and said hello to this stranger. I was still shy, and so I thanked him for the chocolate, grabbed the pram and headed off towards the house I was staying in.

It turned out he was the persistent type. As I pushed the pram ahead of me, instead of him making his precious phone call, he traipsed after me, right around to where I was living. If it happened nowadays, you'd feel nervous, and maybe think of reporting the man to the police as a potential stalker. But back then it just seemed normal. It was what boys did, sniffing after us like stray dogs. And, of course, in a way I was flattered. In fact, I thought about him quite a lot that evening – but in truth I assumed that it was a one-night wonder and that I was unlikely ever to see him again.

The next day, however, one of the other tenants came knocking on the door of my room and told me that there was an American GI in uniform asking at the door for the lady with the little black baby. My heart was palpitating as I went down the stairs to see who it was, though I had my suspicions. It was him alright, the guy who had followed me home. He handed me a package of nylon stockings, which I can assure you were a very sought-after luxury at that austere time, and a box of chocolates. As if that wasn't enough for me to deal with, in a way that was quite touching, he asked if I'd like to go to the pictures. I had to explain that since I had a baby to look after there was no way I could go on a date just like that.

I went back upstairs and, a little bit later on, took the nylons out and tried them on. I thought I looked wonderful in them, which added to the spark. There was something about his face that I had liked. In fact the more I thought about him, the more I agonized about the fact that I'd had to turn him down. How could I be so rash?

His name, as I later found out, was Louis Caldwell. Louis was white, but he didn't seem to have any problem with me having a black baby – which seriously mattered to me given the extent of racial prejudice at the time. Far from being put off, Louis kept pleading with me for a date until – eventually – I did what I had secretly wanted to do all along. I got a babysitter for Philip, and we went out together, beginning what I suppose was really an affair. After all, I was still in a relationship of sorts with Cecil, who came back to visit us as often as he could get away from his London duties and at one stage had even tried to persuade me to move to London with him.

Despite the hardships, I felt I was better where I was; I was also beginning to make friends in the area around where I lived and I didn't want to walk away from that unnecessarily. And so I admit I was being a bit sneaky when I hooked up with Louis – and the truth is that I felt bad about it at least some of the time. But he was a really nice guy and he was persuasive – and so we started to have sex, which needless to say I hadn't planned.

Was I silly and naïve? Of course I was. Was I an innocent taken advantage of by a more experienced man? A lot of women might like to present it like that, but it's just not true: even looking back on it with the benefit of hindsight, there is no way I can escape the reality that I was equally responsible. I'd already had one child. I should have made sure I knew how to avoid becoming pregnant again, but I didn't and so – almost inevitably – I was soon to be hit by another bombshell.

When I discovered that I was pregnant again, I was launched into a repeat spiral of panic and helplessness. What the hell was I supposed to do now? I was distraught. I didn't know where to turn. Should I tell Louis? Should I confess to Cecil that I'd been sleeping with someone else behind his back? No, I didn't have the courage to do that. But Cecil inadvertently made the whole situation easier for me. For obvious reasons, he assumed he was the father of the baby, and so we proceeded on that basis, me knowing in my heart that this wasn't really the case. Would I ever have to come clean? Would I have to confess? I didn't know, and in a way I didn't care. On the one hand I was in blind panic. On the other, I felt I was becoming more bloated with each passing week.

I still had Philip to mind and so I went into a kind of denial. Every day I got up in the morning and eventually went to bed at night. And in between, there was just the process of getting through each day the best way I could. I'm optimistic by nature, but I really didn't know what I was going to do or where to turn. I probably figured deep down that I'd be in a position to let everyone know the truth in the future, hopefully in a way that no one would get hurt. But for the moment I just kept my mouth tightly shut and struggled on.

. . . .

Philip was still not much more than eighteen months old when his sister arrived in Sefton General Hospital in Liverpool, in March 1951. The fact that she was white at least meant that neither of us would have to suffer the racist comments I'd endured with Philip. But that does not mean it was all plain sailing. The fact that I was not wearing a wedding ring seemed to give the nurses a license to look down on me as a single mother, a shameless sinner in many eyes. I even thought of getting an old brass ring or one out of a Hallowe'en barmbrack to put on my finger to keep up appearances, but I was defiant enough not to give in to them.

But she was my beautiful daughter and I wanted everything to be right for her. Not that I felt confident. On the contrary, just after she was born, looking at her pale white skin, I had a terrible sense of foreboding: when Cecil saw that she was white, might the game be up? How was I going to explain it to him? I had no idea. Might he immediately guess that he wasn't the little girl's father? He might. And if he did, would he be angry?

I remember breaking out in a cold sweat and imagining the worst – Cecil shouting and roaring and maybe taking a swing at me. I could hardly swallow thinking about it, tossing over in my mind all of the terrible things he might do. Talk about wasted energy! Even though the new arrival was white, in his innocence Cecil immediately accepted her as his own; it helped that he had a sister Ernestine who was light-skinned, and he assumed that the new baby shared in that particular strand of the family DNA. We called her Jeanette after his mother. Remember, for a lot of black people back then, the lighter your skin was the better.

Now I want to make it clear that I never actually told Cecil he was the father. I don't mind telling white lies, in fact I'm pretty good at it – but that would have been a whopper, and so I stopped short of deliberately misleading him. But I allowed the charade to go on and I consciously didn't correct it; it suited me, in my fear and loneliness, to allow him to think that he was the father of this lovely girl. Looking back now I know that this was dishonest and wrong, but what can I say?

We sometimes do things that we know we shouldn't – and convince ourselves that it is just for now and that we'll fix it all up later. Objectively, I was under a lot of pressure and I didn't really have anyone I could confide in or seek help from. The irony is that, if the second baby had been black, then it's quite possible that I would have ended up marrying Cecil. Instead, everything I had been through, and especially the isolation and turmoil I felt inside, convinced me that I didn't love him enough to make a life together – and so I let him slip gradually away.

I had no real regrets about that then, and I still don't. I was about to go through a desperately tough few years – but unlike a lot of other Irish women of that era, the gut feeling I had against the idea of marrying for convenience sake or to appease my parents or the neighbours or the Church, or anyone else for that matter, was too strong. I couldn't do it. He wasn't for me. I would never marry him. What would be the point in prolonging a relationship that could never satisfy me, and that might involve living a lie – until such time as one or other of us inevitably decided to walk away? Better to do that now…

Of course none of us can ever know what might have been. Cecil stayed in London and met a woman there, whom he later married. Once he had moved permanently to London, he forgot his son – and indeed the daughter he thought was his too. In fact we didn't even receive a card from him for birthdays or at Christmas, which is something I was bitter about for a long time afterwards. Small kindnesses make a big difference. I know it happened a lot in those days that men disappeared if and when it suited them. They hadn't been taught to be responsible and the laws didn't exist which might have brought fathers who were in denial to account. But I couldn't pretend to be on any high moral ground. In truth he was the father of only one of my children. And so I was destined to struggle alone through whatever adversities were about to be unleashed against me.

And I was literally on my own. After an affair that lasted no more than six weeks, Louis had had to go back to America, back to whatever life he had been living there before he'd begun his tour of duty in Europe. There was no way he could have taken me, a white woman with a black child, to the USA with him. But the truth is that we never even discussed the possibility. Looking back on it all now, the worst thing – the thing I really do feel sad about – is that he never knew anything about his daughter, because he was already gone by the time I found out I was pregnant. He left no forwarding address, so I had no way of letting him know. Of course I could have gone to the US army and asked them to track him down for me – but the cultural differences between then and now are immense. The thought simply never occurred to me. There was a fatalistic aspect to the way I looked at things. I was aching inside: my heart was broken at the realisation that he'd had to leave me. But I accepted it. He was gone.

So now I had two babies to mind, one black and one white. I had no one to blame except myself, but I was still genuinely distressed imagining what people might think of me – and, worse still, I was sick with worry that my family might find out the horrendous predicament I'd gotten myself into. Somehow I managed to find a more suitable place to stay and was at least comforted by the fact that we'd have a roof over our heads. It wasn't much, but as the old saying goes, beggars can't be choosers. The house was near an area with a black community, which meant I would get less hassle over Philip around the streets and in the shops. But, being an unmarried mother for a second time, I was inevitably drawn back into the grip of the people who had made my life such a misery when I was pregnant with Philip. Nuns and welfare people were on my case. Throughout Jeanette's first year, and beyond, they used to visit us to check out how we were living. This was fine, except that I constantly felt that they were disapproving of me – and of the children. One of the welfare women seemed to like me, though, and so when I had the opportunity, I said to her, "My mammy wants me to go home to Dublin for Christmas".

Like a good Dublin girl, I still called my mother 'mammy'! And she said to me, "That sounds like a great idea. I'll mind the children for you."

What she really meant was that the welfare people in Manchester had a place they could take babies into for the Christmas, but I felt liberated all the same. Most young mothers will know what I mean: you've got two kids to worry about 24/7 and then somebody swoops in to take them off your hands for a few days! It is sheer bliss, to be freed from the responsibility if only for a while. I had also been missing my family in Dublin, and so I was delighted to get the chance to see them. Over the few days I was back in Crumlin, I thought about the possibility of telling them the full story but I decided to play it by ear. Too often, that can prove to be a mistake. You really need to have built up the resolve to do a horribly tough thing like telling your parents that you're a fallen woman not once but twice over! If you let it drift, looking for the right moment, in my experience anyway, the likelihood is that you'll never pluck up the courage to say anything to anyone. And so it transpired.

I went to Dublin and had a lovely time, but I never got around to telling my parents what had been going on in my life. What would have happened if I had revealed to them the whole unvarnished truth? Now and then those questions come back to taunt me, but there is no point in dwelling on them too heavily. You have to play the hand that's dealt you. And so I returned to Manchester with no better understanding as to how I was going to make sense of my life in the long run.

I'll never forget what greeted me when I got back from Dublin. My lovely daughter was dressed in clothes like I'd never seen before and she was playing with toys she'd been given for Christmas. I felt both jealous and protective at the same time. But it also made me feel less adequate, that someone else had made my daughter special in a way that I couldn't afford to. The social worker explained to me that while I was at home in Dublin, a married couple from Blackpool, both school-teachers, had asked if they could take Jeanette to their house to see their Christmas tree as they had no children of their own to share Christmas with. If the same thing were happening to me now I'd spot the emotional blackmail a mile off. And I'd be far more assertive of my own rights. But back then I didn't see that this was how the Catholic authorities worked. They needed children to give up for adoption and, therefore, for them, my daughter represented an opportunity to satisfy the demand that was out there. In her wisdom, the welfare woman informed me that the couple had given Jeanette a lovely time and had told her how much they'd love to have a baby of their own. She also strongly advised me that if I didn't make the right kind of choices, my own life was going to go downhill fast. "You could give that child a beautiful life with a couple like that," she said. At first I was horrified by the idea of giving my child away and I resisted it, but she chiselled away at me and chiselled and chiselled – and eventually she talked me into it, convincing me it was the best thing to do for my girl.

So they invited me to bring Jeanette to a place in Didsbury, a suburb of Manchester, a sort of convent, to hand her over. It's a dreadful feeling, taking your precious baby out for the very last time and giving her to strangers, knowing you would never see her again. My soul was aching as I walked into that convent holding her, feeling all the eyes inside looking through the windows, watching me and judging me. I knew there was no alternative, yet with every fibre of my being I struggled to think of a way of keeping her, but it was not to be. It truly broke my spirit, walking forlornly away from the place, no longer able to hold and cuddle and love my beautiful daughter.

I was convinced back then, and still am, that the Catholic Church was in effect selling babies for adoption. Money was changing hands. I suspect they got up to £10,000 from adopting couples, not that I, or any mother in my circumstances, would ever have received a penny of it.

I never actually met the couple who adopted my daughter. She was less than two years of age when I gave her up for adoption. It was the couple themselves who changed her name from her birth name to Philomena after me – a lovely gesture on their part. On her birthday every year since then I would get this strange feeling, an ache that was almost like period pains. Often, I would cry my heart out, wondering whatever might have become of her, hoping that maybe sometime in the future we might meet again, but accepting that it was never going to happen. It is a very lonely feeling.

Back then I'd no time to think about whether I was pretty or not. These days, girls can spend so much time on their appearance, but it wasn't something that occurred to most of us back then, especially girls in my circumstances, single and with a child to look after. I still had to eke out a living, as well as looking after Philip, and there were more earth-shattering developments just around the corner.

I've already explained my affair with Jimmy Angel and how it ended when he had to return to the USA. But what I have kept hidden for all these years was that I had a son with him, the lovely man I now know as Leslie.

I feel like a child all over again writing this down now. I'd already been pregnant twice. I'd had two kids. I should have known the score. Or so any reasonable person would say. But I was also still young and strangely innocent, and I didn't know anything much about sex.

In the modern era, there's nothing wrong with a girl deciding that she is happy to sleep with one boyfriend after another – and I agree. As long as people take the necessary precautions, then there's nothing wrong with being sexually active. That was probably my own instinct all those years ago – I didn't see anything wrong with having sex or being loving with a new boyfriend like Jimmy. But unfortunately I didn't know how to go about finding out what I'd needed to do to protect myself. I'm not going to claim there was anything epic or beautiful about it, but we made love more than a few times and the predictable happened. I was pregnant for the third time!

It might seem like some kind of black comedy, the way these different strands of the saga unfolded, but I can assure you that it was no laughing matter at the time. In fact I was mortified. I was frightened. And from the minute I heard the news, I was constantly fretting in case I'd never see my Mammy and Daddy or my sisters ever again. I had risked turning myself into an outcast. I felt sick to the pit of my stomach, wondering what was going to become of me? I was going to have my third baby in less than three years! It was as if I only had to glance at a man and I'd get pregnant.

Looking back, Jimmy was good about it, but I can't say that he was thrilled. He was an American living temporarily in England and I suspect he knew in his gut that he wouldn't be staying there forever. But he didn't run away or disappear like a lot of men do when a girl gets pregnant.

Philip was less than three years old when my second son, Leslie, was born, in June 1952. I went home to the digs and Jimmy did his bit to make me feel better. But it wasn't long before time caught up with us. The word came through. Jimmy's stint in England had come to an end. He could conceivably have stayed – or better still I could have gone to the US with him. Instead, he was shipped back home to South Carolina, a deeply racist part of America at the time and where the Ku Klux Klan were very dominant.

I wasn't aware of the politics of all that back then, but he did tell me that it was no place for a white lady. Or maybe it was his way of fobbing me off. Because I was very fond of him, and he had been good about bringing our son Leslie into the world, I'd harboured the thought that we might actually make a go of it together. I know that if I'd gone there with him it would have been hard for a black man and a white woman to live in peace together, but I felt a depth of love that was new to me and while he was with me Jimmy made me believe that he felt the same way.

He promised he'd be in touch with us, but the truth is that I never heard another word from him, ever again. He left not long after Leslie was born and never looked back. I have no idea why. Maybe he was married or had a fiancé there. I always tried to give him the benefit of the doubt, and in a way I still want to. Perhaps he was full of good intentions and circumstances got the better of him. I like to think of him planning to call and then putting it off, since he might have better news tomorrow or next week or whenever. We are all capable of letting things drift – only suddenly to realise that two years or three or four have passed. The whole world has changed. What would be the point of making contact now or even trying to?

I like to think that Jimmy Angel loved me and missed me as much as I missed him. But he left me and Leslie, who was only a couple of months old, and once again I had to fend for myself, with two babies to look after. Was this to be the story of my life, getting pregnant with one man after another who would then abandon me? When I eventually wrote to Jimmy I received a letter back from his grandmother, more or less calling me white trash and telling me not to dare to write to him again. To this day I pretend to myself that he would have sent for me had it not been for the racism that was rife where he lived and the attitude of people like his grandmother. But maybe that is just wishful thinking on my part.

In the meantime, there was no space for daydreaming or fantasising about what might have been. I had the frightening reality of my situation to deal with on a daily basis. I kept things going reasonably well, but that was hard during a period when tuberculosis was rampant both in Britain and in Ireland – and fate intervened in the most horrible way. My darling Leslie was diagnosed with TB and was taken from me and put in a sanatorium in Abergele in Wales. I felt that this development somehow reflected on me, and I suspect that the doctors and the nurses did too. Was I feeding him properly? Was he getting enough nutrition? And what about sleep? I was doing my best, but the truth is that I just didn't know.

I used to visit Leslie in the sanatorium, but it was a long, arduous trek there and back, and so I could only go at the weekends. But it was worth it just to see the little fellow and to know that he was alright, although I was only too aware of the fact that I was going to find it hard to nourish him back to full strength when he was eventually given the all-clear to come home.

It is hard to convey the confusion and isolation that a woman feels when she has been left alone, to mind a new child. I don't want to portray myself as a victim. I did what I did and I enjoyed myself while I was doing it, and I can't simply pretend that the responsibility was someone else's. But it is shocking to think that, back then, we could go through school and never hear even a single word about the physical functions of a woman's body, how people had sex and the basic precautions we could take to avoid becoming pregnant. When you mature and get a bit more sense it seems strange to look back and to wonder: how could I have been so careless or silly or apparently lacking in basic intelligence? Three times I made the same mistake. Three times. All I can do now is apologise to those who were, in different ways, hurt as a result of my profound ignorance. But life has a funny way of confounding us: for all that it was hard for my children, in the end the love that is at the root of all our passions and our joys has come shining through.

. . . .

The welfare nun, the one who had been around after Philomena was born, had kept in touch with me, and so she knew that I had given birth again and was under renewed pressure, especially with the little Leslie's illness.

She then told me that a couple she knew, a white lady and a black man, had fallen in love with Leslie. I had been through it before and so now I knew the drill. I was half-beaten before she even started, and so she was able to walk all over me pretty easily. As she had done with Philomena, she persuaded me that Leslie would have a far better chance of living and enjoying a good life with this other couple than with me. There are hundreds of thousands of women who went through this over the years. Millions, in fact. You feel like you are betraying something in yourself. And you know that you are, in some obscure way, letting the child you brought into the world down. And yet, the picture has been painted for you in a way that makes it almost impossible to say, "No, I insist, I'll keep my child." Only a bad mother, a selfish mother, a sinful mother would do that! They play on your weaknesses and your insecurities and you give in. Well, I – and a lot of women like me – did.

So Leslie was over two years of age when I reluctantly endured the torment of parting with my beautiful baby. I felt a powerful sense of confusion, pain, loss and worthlessness, having to give up my baby for the second time. But I think I knew in my marrow that, the way the deck was stacked against unmarried mothers at the time, the alternative might have been even worse.

. . . .

"Uncle Peter was writing a book
and his Mama was starting to cook."
from 'Saga Of The Ageing Orphan' by Philip Lynott

Philip was back in Dublin, and there was no doubt that he was happy there. When he was disobedient, he was disciplined by my parents like any other child, but they got on extremely well together and he liked being part of a big family. Inevitably, he suffered racial prejudice in school. Yet, despite the inevitable difficulties caused by his colour – which, in fairness, to some children was merely an innocent source of novelty – he was popular in the neighbourhood. As soon as he learned to write, his letters to me were an added comfort. He had a natural way with words and he shared many of his highs and lows with me through his correspondence.

Somebody who knew more about these things than I did might just have spotted the gem of a poetic talent in those letters. In the meantime, Philip had also begun to exhibit signs of being a confident showman. He used to clown around a lot, putting lampshades on his head, pulling funny faces and generally play-acting. My father, who used to encourage him, often said that he reminded him of Sammy Davis Jnr, who was also black, and one hell of an entertainer.

One thing was certain. Philip was never shy, although I cannot imagine he got that confidence from me. I had been reared through the war years and, like most working-class people, we never thought we had anything going for us. Indeed, personal confidence only grew in me in later life.

Apart from his developing gregariousness and his entertaining tomfoolery, there were other early signs that music would become his life – though I'd never have made the connection at the time. I remember that I caught him one day with a bunch of his pals in the house in Crumlin, giggling and whispering. After much probing, he admitted he was going to a concert in a small wooden hall near Mount Argus, not far from where he lived. What he didn't tell me – though one of his pals did secretly – was that he was going to sing at the concert.

So, unknown to Philip, one of my sisters and I decided to attend, and I hid behind a tall priest in the audience to prevent him from seeing me. He came on stage with his band as if he had been born to it, wearing a single glove and singing a pop song of the day. That was the first time I saw him performing on stage and I was genuinely amazed at his self-assurance. I won't claim that I spotted straightaway that he was a star in the making – but I was impressed.

As he grew older, he had become greatly taken with his Uncle Tim's record collection, and they often went shopping together for the latest releases. Philip would avidly listen to whatever they bought – Tim was a fan of black American soul music, of British blues-rock bands like John Mayall's Bluesbreakers, Cream and American west coast artists like The Mamas and The Papas – and Philip was influenced by all of these different types of music. Indeed, Tim may have later regretted fostering this love of music because when Philip moved to London, he took much of Tim's prized collection with him!

Apart from Tim's record collection, Philip's musical interests would also have been stimulated by his uncle Peter, who played guitar and sang in a band called The Sundowners. When Peter (who eventually made it into rock music history when he was mentioned in Philip's song-poem, 'Saga Of The Ageing Orphan', recorded for Thin Lizzy's first album) turned down an invitation to join a local band, Philip jumped at the offer in his stead.

However, the first real indication that his musical ambitions might be serious and long-term came when I saw Philip singing in a band called The Black Eagles who, unknown to me, had become really popular all over Dublin. They played at venues like The Five Club, The Flamingo, and Club A Go-Go, as well as gigging outside the city. By all accounts,

Philip – who was just fifteen at the time – was beginning to revel in the modest level of local celebrity he had earned.

Back in Manchester, I took on three jobs, working in a dress shop, barmaiding at night, and selling at markets at the weekend. I had no choice but to do all this to earn enough money, not just for my own food, clothes and lodgings, but to send some over to Mammy in Dublin to help her look after Philip.

But my personal life was on the up, as I had a new male companion in Dennis Keeley – although I didn't know then that we would end up spending the rest of our lives together. Put it this way: our first meeting was far from auspicious! I went with a crowd of girls to a nightclub one night, but the man on the door stopped us going in. Dennis was at hand, and, for no obvious reason, he asked the owner to let us in. He wasn't long in letting me know why he had intervened. As I walked up the stairs Dennis said to me "I'm going to have you!" When we were leaving the club later, Dennis got into the taxi that was taking me and my flatmate back to Didsbury. It was hilarious. When we got to our digs I couldn't find the keys – but, fortunately, the gallant Dennis helped us to break into our own place through a small window. How could I resist him? To celebrate we opened a bottle of wine, and that's how our wonderful relationship started.

And there were more life-changing events just around the corner. One of my regular jobs around that time was as a cashier for the Jewish businessman Mr. Harold Marsden, who ran an open market trading business on Saturdays. He was a bit of a gangster, but I didn't have a problem with that. Instinctively, I was a bit of an outlaw myself. There was a well-known clothing factory called Dannimac and Harold had the concession to buy all their seconds. There were rumours that one of the managers was bent, as in criminal, and gave Harold a load of perfect coats as part of some sort of back-door deal.

Harold used to pick me up at 6am on a Saturday morning to take me to the market stall, where me and another girl would sell these Dannimac coats for £5, way less than they cost elsewhere. Yes, the money was rolling in for Harold, and he ended up owning yachts and living in luxury. Although he also ended up in prison because he got found out!

And he wasn't the only one who was capable of pulling a fast one. Me and the other girl on the stall used to wear tight jumpers with tight sleeves and we'd stick fivers up the sleeves when nobody was looking. We were robbing him, but as far as I know he never suspected anything.

But I loved Harold. He was one of those rogues you can't help liking. Every Saturday, he would treat his son Peter and myself to a beautiful meal after we had finished our work for the day. During one of those dinners in a nearby nightclub, a Mr. Kent, who owned The Clifton Grange Hotel in Manchester, confided to Harold that he would have to sell up because he was becoming increasingly concerned about the way it was being managed. I have no idea what inspired him but Harold interjected, saying, "Why not let Philomena run it for you?" I knew nothing about hotels – but I talked it over with Dennis and we agreed that it'd be worth looking at the set-up. The Clifton Grange Hotel, we discovered, was a detached old Victorian house on the corner of Manchester's Wellington Road. The house had been converted for use as digs, specialising in a showbusiness clientele. It had a somewhat rundown appearance, but inside it had a character and charm all its own – never mind the characters who stayed there!

When we sat down to discuss things, Mr. Kent threw me a little off balance by inquiring whether I had any money to invest as a partner. I told him that I didn't have those kind of resources and thankfully he wasn't put off. He decided to appoint me as manager of the business. Needless to say, I was thrilled. It was a lucky break and, what's more, he had no objection to Dennis working with me, so that we could develop the business and earn a living while also getting on with our relationship. It was such a unique opportunity that we both determined to work our fingers to the bone and to do whatever would be necessary to make the business work. We gave it everything, so that when the owner, who was himself a qualified accountant, reviewed the situation after a few months, he was so impressed by my scrupulously accurate bookwork that he bought me an enormous box of chocolates.

Then he took me to his solicitor and made me joint owner of the business on the spot. Can you imagine how astonished I was, after all I had been through since Philip's birth? We settled down at the Clifton Grange and, for a long time, it was a great place to be…

5. BIRTH OF THE ROCKER

On Thin Lizzy's debut album, released in 1971, there is a song called 'Clifton Grange Hotel', inspired by the hotel and its unique atmosphere, lifestyle and clientele. And boy, was it unique. Graham Cohen started working for me at the hotel shortly after I began to act as manager. He was aged eighteen when we first met and he is still one of my closest friends and confidantes. Percy Gibbons, another dear friend to this day, was already firmly ensconced there with his band, as were a troupe of Maoris from New Zealand, a young couple called Shirley and Johnny, a whole menagerie of cabaret singers, dancers, magicians, strippers, ventriloquists, comedians, a whole parade of colourful outsiders – among them a drag artist who always insisted on using the ladies' toilet!

The hotel was situated in the Whalley Range area of Manchester, and I grew very fond of the people who lived around us because they were essentially ordinary folks like ourselves, with no pretensions. The bar was a glorious hotchpotch, a mix of antique decor and all kind of knick-knacks, with dolls and flowers and other stuff hanging from the beams that crossed the low ceiling. On the walls, we displayed mock-autographed photographs of film stars like Gregory Peck and Sammy Davis Jnr. To be honest, I really loved the place right from the start and enjoyed running the business so much that after just 18 months working there, I took my courage in my hands, arranged a bank loan and bought the Clifton Grange for the price Mr Kent had originally paid for it himself. That's how Philomena Lynott from Crumlin, Dublin, became the proud owner of a hotel in Manchester, virtually overnight!

No doubt about it, the tide was finally turning in my favour, after years of poverty, struggle, abuse and dejection. By the time I had finalised the purchase of the hotel, I was also enjoying a deeply loving and stable relationship with Dennis. Of all the white men I have had friendships with, Dennis was the only one who never exhibited any jealousy of Philip. In fact they struck up a rapport right from the outset. Dennis and I had been happily living together for quite some time when I announced that my son, whom Dennis knew was black, was coming over from Ireland to meet him. I explained to Dennis that it would be improper for us to sleep together while my innocent, by-now teenage, son was in the house, so a separate room was arranged for the two males.

Of course, Philip wasn't nearly as innocent as I imagined. Dennis recalled waking up during the night and seeing Philip sitting up in his bed very sheepishly, but when they looked at each other in the morning they both burst out laughing – conscious, I suppose, of the absurdity of the situation. Philip later admitted he knew only too well that we were sleeping together, and could not understand why I had chosen to pretend otherwise. I explained that it was a question of respect, though what I actually *meant* by that, I'm not too sure. He and Dennis were later to become really close buddies and they would regularly go shopping together, despite Philip's irritating habit of spending ages chatting up all the girls who worked in the shops!

It was around the same time that, during a visit to Dublin, I noticed that Philip's teeth had badly deteriorated. So I flew him over to Manchester for three successive weekends to a great dentist I knew called Hans Kurer, on whose wall hung a motto, "Pain Is Forbidden In This Room." Young Philip told him he was the greatest dentist in the whole world, and he was not far wrong. Doctor Kurer was later honoured with an O.B.E. by Queen Elizabeth II.

Overall, however, Philip was a very healthy, wiry teenager, who kept himself fit playing football. The first time he was in hospital was in 1969. Philip was in Skid Row at the time, and probably as a result of the rigours of singing against a very loud and noisy backing band, his tonsils had swollen to a phenomenal size. Again, I flew him over to Manchester, to a private hospital called St. Joseph's, where they removed the tonsils. Brush Shiels, who was the leader of Skid Row, had apparently been troubled by the deteriorating quality of Philip's voice. While Philip was undergoing his operation, the band did some gigs without him and then decided to dispense with his services permanently. Or, to put it more bluntly, he was sacked. As you can imagine, that decision hit him pretty hard, but he had enough confidence in his own ability not to let it get him down, and he remained friends with Brush down the years.

Because Philip and I were apart most of the time, we made the most of our occasional get-togethers, no matter what the circumstances. In some respects, our relationship was more like brother and sister than mother and son. We behaved as if we were best friends, sharing all our joys and at least some of our heartaches. Philip often came over to us in Manchester with my own mother, who was, not surprisingly, overwhelmed by the weird and exotic characters she would bump into in various parts of The Biz or The Showbiz, which were colloquial names for the Clifton Grange Hotel. In virtually every respect, it was a world that was completely removed from her conventional upbringing in conservative, guilt-ridden Ireland, but she liked it all the same.

During one visit, we took Philip and my brother Peter to a popular cabaret club in Manchester and secretly arranged for the compere to introduce Philip as the night's special guest performer. Despite Philip's obvious surprise, not to mention embarrassment, he did a pretty impressive version of 'I Left My Heart In San Francisco' in a style that could not have offered a greater contrast to his subsequent international tough-guy image as 'The Rocker'.

My immediate circle of Manchester friends included Percy Gibbons, whom I've already mentioned – he was a member of a highly successful three-piece all-black Canadian cabaret act called The Other Brothers. He was already entrenched in his favourite psychedelically-decorated attic room at the Clifton Grange Hotel, long before Dennis and I first moved there. When Percy's band went on the road, he insisted his room had to be either closed up, or only let to people he approved of – and that included Philip, with whom he had developed a close relationship based on their mutual obsession with music.

Predictably, Philip was in awe of Percy, who had been living in Manchester since 1964, and was a really striking character. While it has to be acknowledged that Brush Shiels played a major role in Philip's early development as a musician, I have a feeling that Percy was an equally significant influence, not merely in the artistic sense but because he made such a terrific impression on Philip's personality and behaviour as well. Philip practiced incessantly on Percy's guitar and they would discuss music, politics, racism and show-business non-stop at every available opportunity.

The two of them would sing, play guitars and bongos and write songs together in Percy's room. Some of the ideas that later turned up in Thin Lizzy songs had their origin in those jam sessions, and I believe Philip was heavily inspired by the fact that a band like The Other Brothers could get on in the UK, in spite of the fact that they were black. For his part, Percy has also admitted to me that he, in turn, learned a lot from Philip's determination and commitment. When he later saw Thin Lizzy in full flight, he encouraged his own band to modernise what he came to acknowledge was a somewhat dated style.

In the song 'Clifton Grange Hotel', Philip refers, perhaps with some degree of poetic license, to the place as *"a refuge of mercy"* but there's no doubt that he loved coming over to us. He also referred to *"Old Lou the Jew who will takes your bags from you"* – Lou was a real character, and a nice man with whom Philip got on very well. Percy also gets an oblique mention when Philip sings about *"another brother."* I think I even get a namecheck myself!

Rock 'n' roll trivia fans may be interested to know that I had earlier, if a little misguidedly, attempted to persuade Percy to take Philip into his band which, in the wake of the Beatles' revolution had been given the more psychedelic name of Garden Odyssey. Percy may have recognised that Philip's long-term musical ambitions lay in other directions and in a different musical style. Either way, that particular musical marriage was never consummated.

Such were the close ties of friendship that had grown up in and around the hotel that, when Christmas came, Philip, Percy, Roy and Dennis would all compete with great gusto to see who could buy me the best present, which one year included a mynah bird! I was a lucky woman, surrounded by such good, close friends in such a wonderful, family atmosphere. I don't recall ever hearing harsh words between any of them. Even I, his mother, only had one serious row with Philip in my life. That occurred years later when I discovered he had given away, to a roadie, a very expensive suitcase I had bought him, a green leather Antler model with his initials specially engraved on it. Perhaps the nature of that single disagreement best explains the closeness of the relationship we enjoyed.

. . . .

"It's three o'clock in the morning
And I'm on the streets again
I disobeyed another warning
I should have been in by ten"
– from 'Dancing In The Moonlight' by Philip Lynott

My brother Timothy was getting married in 1967 and Dennis, Percy and another musician by the name of Roy Ellis, and I, all headed over to Dublin for the wedding in Malahide, a picturesque seaside suburb to the north of Dublin and not far from where I live now. Philip was about 17 at the time, and he pleaded not to be forced into singing at the wedding because he had a gig in a Dublin nightclub that same night.

After the wedding, all four of us went along to the club, which I remember was in a cellar. I can recall relaxing nonchalantly against a pillar until my reverie was interrupted by a large group of girls screaming. I looked up and realised that they were screaming for Philip who had just come on stage. It was only my second time to see him performing and I was stunned by how good he and his band were. Percy, who really knows his music, turned to me and said in amazement: "Isn't Philip brilliant!" I said, "Percy, you took the words right out of my mouth, but because you might think I'm biased, I didn't want to say anything." I was convinced then that Philip had something special. For me, that was a night to remember.

Within a month or two, Mam rang me in Manchester to ask me to come to Dublin again because Philip was now proving to be a bit of a handful. She was convinced he was heading for trouble with the police, hanging around with what she felt was a rough lot of young lads and staying out until three or four in the morning. The final straw, it seemed, had come when he arrived home having lost one of his expensive new shoes.

Most teenagers go through a rebellious phase, and Philip was probably no different, but even his uncle Peter – who was only a year older than my boy – was becoming increasingly disenchanted with Philip's behaviour whenever they went to a club together. His grandfather having passed away, there may have been an absence of an authority figure who could control Philip's wilder impulses, and so poor Tim was cast in that role. On one occasion he became so frustrated with Philip that he locked him out of the house when he did not arrive home by the appointed hour. Afterwards, he gave Philip a serious ticking off, but to no avail, apparently.

It's curious how these things work. This was a really traumatic period for everyone else in the family. They were worried, probably unnecessarily, about Philip. But for him it was to become the inspiration for one of Thin Lizzy's best and most successful hit songs, 'Dancing In The Moonlight', with its references to the narrator being out on the street until three o'clock in the morning, disobeying warnings and being kept indoors as a punishment.

But however much he was enjoying being the rebel, I felt that the problem needed to be tackled and, being now a little more flush with funds because of the success of Clifton Grange, I flew over to Dublin immediately. Of course, when I challenged him about the lost shoe, I got all the predictable excuses a mother usually gets from a son in a situation like this. His story was that the band had been down the country doing a gig and the manager had arranged for them to sleep in tents, presumably to save money on hotel bills. They were a bunch of lads enjoying a teenage adventure together and they behaved accordingly. During a bout of typical, boyish play-acting one of his shoes went missing, never to be found.

And then he told me that he had his own grievances – he was genuinely upset because his grandmother thought his friends looked like gypsies on account of their style of dress, and she would not allow any of them into her house. And it's fair to say that a lot of parents and teenagers were experiencing similar conflicts at the time, and not only in Dublin.

One of those who was being excluded from the Lynott household was Brian Downey, who later turned out to be a loyal friend to both Philip and to myself and who stuck by Philip throughout more or less all the highs and lows of Thin Lizzy's career. Philip had first met Brian, who was a little younger than him, when they both attended the Christian Brothers school in Crumlin. (Incidentally, while attending that particular school, Philip had been insensitively given the chore of collecting money from the schoolboys for what was called "the Black Babies", but in reality was for the Catholic Missionaries in Africa.) Anyhow, although I had some sympathy for Philip, my mother was entitled to run her house the way she saw fit, and she was certainly entitled to have her wishes respected by Philip, to whom she'd given so much.

Philip himself was intelligent enough to understand fully why his Gran was upset and how, as long as he was living under the same roof as her, she'd be constantly worried about him. So, it was eventually agreed that the best solution all round would be for Philip to move out of the Crumlin house and live on his own. He and another guy moved into a lovely flat in Clontarf on the northside of Dublin with a superb panoramic view of Dublin Bay and with the majestic Dublin Mountains off in the background. The song 'The Friendly Ranger At Clontarf Castle', on the first Thin Lizzy album, was inspired by the time he spent in this lovely part of the city. The palm trees, which were planted just before Philip took up residence in that flat, are still there, although now fully grown, of course.

One time, when we were over in Ireland, Philip invited Dennis, Percy, Roy and me to stay at the flat, an invitation we happily accepted. No doubt it was part of my motherly instinct to want to find out if my young man was capable of taking care of himself while he was free of adult supervision. I was thinking how mature he'd become until, in the process of admiring the tidiness of the rooms, I inadvertently stumbled upon a cupboard where the two flatmates had, in obvious haste, hidden their rubbish in anticipation of our arrival. That discovery gave us all a good laugh!

On another trip to Dublin, he took me out to an Italian cafe near one of his favourite haunts, The Bailey pub off Grafton Street – it was probably the Coffee Inn, where he used to hang out quite a bit. I heard him asking the waiter, who obviously knew him, for, "My usual order but can you put it on two separate plates?" Two plates of piping hot Spaghetti Bolognese duly arrived and I spotted Philip slipping the waiter a half-crown (twelve and a half pence in today's money). My heart secretly went out to him when I realised how much he wanted to treat me to a nice meal – but that that was all the money he had left.

Of course, I felt sorry for him, and he was cute enough to know that such a gesture would soften me up. Sure enough, when we the left the restaurant and he was basking in the glow of having bought me a meal, he asked me to treat him in return. I couldn't have resisted, even if I wanted to, and so we went straight to the open-air Iveagh Market where, after meticulous deliberation, he chose a 1930s-style gent's evening suit with long tails. The front was worn shiny with age, but that didn't matter – he was convinced it was the business. He also chose three or four shirts with detachable collars, which would prove useful no matter which direction fashion might shift. As soon as he could, he took the suit to the cleaners and I washed the shirts for him, and when I saw him all dolled up in the new gear I thought he looked marvellous.

In all, I spent about five pounds that day, a sizeable sum at that time, but it was worth every penny just to see his unrestrained delight with the purchases. I guessed that he must have been a regular customer at that market because I noticed that the old ladies there knew him very well, as did the flower women on Grafton Street.

By now, Philip had become very conscious of his image. He was beginning to pay the kind of close attention to his clothes and to his appearance that is characteristic among rock stars. Not that he was a star yet. In fact in a way, his almost dandyish look reminded me of his father The Duke, who always dressed as stylishly as funds would allow. Most of the time, Philip looked the part, and as he achieved greater success and affluence he could afford to wear pretty much exactly what he wanted to. Later in life, most fans probably thought of him as a really sharp dresser with a wardrobe always full of carefully-chosen clothes. But that wasn't always the case, and I saw him several times over the years, in a beautifully-tailored expensive suit with a pair of cheap pumps on his feet. Given how fashion has gone since, I suppose you could say he was ahead of his time!

I have to be honest and say that there are areas of Philip's life that remain a mystery to me even now. We were great friends and, compared to most mother-son relationships, he was very honest and truthful with me. But the lengthy period we spent apart meant that there would always be significant gaps. On the other hand, the occasions when we *could* be together were so precious to me that they remain ultra-vivid in my mind. For whatever reason, when Philip was around the place, something out of the ordinary was bound to happen. It might seem odd to people who weren't around in the 1960s but these things often related to his unconventional appearance.

I remember when he was about seventeen or eighteen, Dennis and I invited him and his then girl-friend, Gale, to join us in Ibiza for what was his first real overseas holiday. He packed his clothes in a very shabby hold-all, which looked decidedly out of place beside my brand-new luggage. Before going for a spot of swimming one day, he left this somewhat unsightly object on a sunbed, which was being used by another tourist. She turned out to be an insufferably overbearing woman. When she came back to her sunbed, she threw his bag on the ground in disgust and harangued me when I began to offer an apology. Thankfully, her tirade was abruptly interrupted by Philip's return from the beach – when she saw him with his big, bushy hairstyle, she fled! At times he had that effect on people.

Generally, I was aware of Philip's musical adventures in Dublin, and all the changes in the various bands with whom he worked – but only through his regular phone calls and the copies of newspaper clippings he sent me, since I was myself busy with my own hectic schedule running the Manchester hotel. Only gradually did I become aware of the depth of his determination to make it as a rock star. I missed a lot, as a mother, not being in a position to be with him all the time – and I guess that he missed a lot too, not having me around. Certainly, I will always regret not having been a first-hand witness of the goings-on of his teenage years, including all of the details of his involvement with earlier bands like The Black Eagles, Skid Row and The Orphanage. Obviously, it would have been very gratifying for me to have been a privileged insider at the birth of the rock 'n' roll legends that Philip Lynott and Thin Lizzy were later to become. I know they can be desperately troublesome, but there's a kind of tragic vulnerability about teenage boys, and I'd like to have been in a better position to help Philip through these difficult years.

In a general sense, I knew that music had become the main focus of his life. I proudly read of him being voted one of the top 20 Irish rock performers by the readers of an Irish pop magazine in 1968, when he was still in Skid Row. That poll, incidentally, also featured Brush Shiels and the late Rory Gallagher. After his departure from Skid Row, Philip had begun writing his own material, a comparatively rare activity in Ireland at that time, since up to then most bands – whether they were showbands, cabaret acts or even the more credible rock acts such as The Black Eagles – concentrated almost exclusively on cover versions of tunes by The Beatles and other chart acts of the time. I took a keen interest in how Thin Lizzy's first single, 'The Farmer', fared when it was released in Ireland, but little did I dream of what it would ultimately lead to. Of the songs on Thin Lizzy's first LP, all bar one of them, were written by Philip, no mean achievement for a man of just twenty-one years. In the context of his music, Philip Lynott's vivid freewheeling imagination was at last given the free reign it had craved for so long, and he thrived on it.

The success of Jimi Hendrix, another flamboyant black musician with a liking for colourful clothes and progressive rock'n'roll, must also have been a tremendous inspiration to Philip. The striking similarity between the two was later reflected in rumours that Philip was to play the part of Hendrix in a film. But there was great satisfaction to be derived, nevertheless, from the fact that my boy's reputation was growing. It wouldn't be long before Thin Lizzy – and Philip Lynott – would achieve lift-off, before soaring into the rock stratosphere.

While the musical revolution of the so-called swinging '60s had transformed the entertainment scene in Britain in a way that few could have thought possible even a decade before, the culture of official Ireland, even in the early 1970s, was still extremely conservative, buttoned-down and conventionally-minded. Musically, the domestic scene was dominated by the showbands, groups of eight or ten musicians in neat suits who played set routines comprising note-perfect versions of the latest British and American pop hits. At their height, there were as many as six hundred showbands travelling up and down the roads of Ireland, among them the likes of Dickie Rock and The Miami Showband, Brendan Bowyer and The Royal, and The Capitol Showband.

Such was the power that these outfits and their managers possessed, that all other types of music were effectively marginalised and frozen out to peripheral beat clubs, tennis clubs and backstreet shebeens. Given the kind of original, progressive rock that Thin Lizzy wanted to pursue there was little point in putting down permanent roots in Dublin. At that time, there was only one Irish radio station, the State-run Radio Éireann, whose musical policy was by and large restricted to light pop, easy listening music, Irish ballads and traditional Irish dance music. From what I can remember, the main outlets for live music were the dance-halls and ballrooms (which only used showbands), ballad sessions for Irish folk groups and variety shows which at best might have a ten minute spot by a pop group in the middle of all the comedians, jugglers and magicians. Most serious Irish rock fans had to listen to Radio Luxembourg to hear their favourite artists and their favourite songs.

In the light of that, it is ironic to note that, all these years later, despite the proliferation of radio stations throughout the country and the massive worldwide acclaim for original artists like Thin Lizzy, Snow Patrol, Glen Hansard, The Cranberries, The Script, Van Morrison, Clannad, Sinéad O'Connor and U2, young Irish rock bands and singer-songwriters still have had to mount public protest campaigns because they still find it so difficult to have their music played on Irish radio. What a strange little country we are.

So, like many Irish artists before them – from The Bachelors to Rory Gallagher's Taste and Van Morrison's Them – Thin Lizzy moved to Britain in search of the career their own country could never offer them. Of course, not many of their predecessors had access to a hotel where they could stay and eat for little or nothing, and the members of Thin Lizzy were smart enough to stay with us in the hotel as often as was convenient. If they were gigging within driving distance, they would automatically head back to The Biz after the show. That gave me the welcome opportunity to keep an eye on them and ensure that they ate properly, at least every once in a while! They could eat and sleep and do their laundry in the hotel, an advantage enjoyed by very few bands at the time. So, in my own small way, I suppose I assisted Philip on the rocky road to rock stardom.

In the wake of the success of The Beatles, and the beat group explosion that followed, the hotel had become a regular stopping-off point for many of the country's hit-making groups: I remember acts like The Searchers, The Troggs, The Bonzo Dog Doo-Dah Band, The Temperance Seven, The Flowerpot Men, The Ivy League, backing musicians for Val Doonican and Frankie Vaughan, and indeed loads of others who tried but sadly failed to scale the dizzy heights of fame, all staying with us.

I also remember one guest who was part of an act of identical twins. Believe it or not, it was Rick Parfitt, eventually to enjoy enormous success with Status Quo, and when Philip met him many years later, he remembered his time at The Biz. The hotel was a popular place for musicians to stay, partly because I had developed an understanding of their attitudes and the particular requirements of their profession, but also because it had a great atmosphere. It was a fun place to stay and, in spite of shouldering the responsibility of running it, I enjoyed it enormously, particularly since – contrary to the public perception – most of the musicians who stayed with us were genuinely nice, down-to-earth, if eccentric, people. Indeed, we actively discouraged anyone who was difficult or unpleasant, but then that was hardly extraordinary. Sports stars such as Hurricane Higgins and George Best, who actually became a really good friend of ours, were also regulars, as indeed was Geoff Hughes, who played the part of Eddie Yeats in *Coronation Street*. I was "Auntie Phyllis" to most of them, including "Bestie", as we knew him.

Philip himself loved football and he later told Liam Mackey, then a music journalist with *Hot Press* magazine, now a sports writer with *The Examiner*, that he preferred his band's fan club to be known as the Thin Lizzy Supporters Club.

Brush Shiels had, in his own inimitable way, remained on good terms with Philip, even after Philip had been dumped from Skid Row. When Brush was planning to get married, Philip knew he could not afford a proper honeymoon, so he persuaded me to invite Brush and his wife-to-be Margaret to stay in our hotel. As we were fully booked at the time, we improvised some mattresses on the floor for them, so at least they got away from Dublin for a half-decent break. The happy couple arrived wearing the most flamboyant clothes imaginable, in keeping with the hippy mood of the times, and I gave them a portable radio as a present.

During their stay, a member of The Ivy League was suddenly taken ill, putting their next few gigs in doubt. Any cancellation would have meant them going without wages, and they might not have been able to pay me for their rooms or food either – so I had, you might say, a vested interest! After some thought, I came up with a brainwave: I asked Brush if he would like to earn some money, and he jumped at the chance, gamely deputising for the stricken musician after some hasty rehearsals, even overcoming the inconvenience of having to use a borrowed guitar which was set up to be used by guitarists who played left-handed. Or so the legend goes!

Between one thing and another, I never got the chance to find out what his new wife Margaret thought of this rather unusual interruption to her first few days of married bliss, but Brush still tells the story of him getting paid for a gig during his honeymoon. In many ways, I think life has been somewhat unfair to Brush. His talent is widely recognised, but for my money he deserved far more success internationally than he achieved. He appears to have fallen foul of some of the more unscrupulous charlatans who inhabited the music industry at a vital time in his career, and never to have fully recovered the momentum which drove him onto the scene in the first place. It's worth saying that, after Philip died, and I was suffering from grief on a terrible scale, some people were mischievously spreading rumours, and Brush somehow got the impression that I disliked him. A bit later on we talked it over and cleared the air. Some Irish people have a regrettable habit of spreading unfounded tales, often with no deliberate malice, but with no understanding of the difficulties they may cause either. This was a case in point, because I've never had anything but the highest regard for Brush.

The way in which he helped out The Ivy League was typical of the eventful life that revolved around the hotel, and a by-product of our policy of only encouraging guests whose company we really liked. In a way, The Biz almost took on the character of a club, through which people made contacts and got to know one another. The Radio Luxembourg DJ, David "Kid" Jensen was one of the first in the British media to show an appreciation for the music of Thin Lizzy. As a result, Philip used to stay with him in the Grand Duchy when he visited Radio Luxembourg. Jensen was largely responsible for the first Thin Lizzy album reaching the number one spot in the station's Hot Heavy 20 and so – needless to say – he was always welcome at the hotel.

As time passed, it made increasing sense for the Clifton Grange to concentrate, almost exclusively, on showbusiness clientele and it became affectionately known as "The Biz". Because showbusiness people generally work late and might go for a meal after completing their night's work, breakfast was a moveable feast, more likely to be set for midday than mid-morning, so it would have been inconvenient to have had guests with conflicting lifestyles. The hotel management, staff and clientele were often described as one big showbusiness family. Most of the time, we had great fun, often sitting up into the small hours of the morning, listening to one band telling us how well they had gone down at their gig and another admitting they had died a death – although sometimes you knew the reality was the reverse. Such can be the insecurity of showbusiness; it's often hard to be absolutely sure what's for real and what's not.

Whenever Philip arrived, he would immediately renew his contact with Percy. If a band with a record deal was staying at the hotel, he would pump them for information about their contract, their management set-up and other details. In his fascination with the whole music scene, he would often be first up and last to go to bed, always relishing the stories he heard from the various characters who came and went. He was as cute as a fox too, his ears always open for useful advice or information, and he would especially observe the various personality problems and conflicts inherent in any set up where there are four or five talented people competing for attention. He noted the number of times musicians arrived with us as part of one group and left aligned to another. That early attention to business details explains why I never had concerns about his ability to take care of himself financially.

The music scene in the late 1960s had a reputation, which had inevitably intensified with the passing years, for fairly conspicuous drug use, but we did our best to keep a tight rein on these things at The Biz. In view of the tragedy that overtook Philip later, I must quite categorically state that I never had any inkling that hard drugs were being used in the hotel at any time, and I still believe that they weren't. In spite of, or maybe even because of, its illegality, pot was the most popular and trendiest drug at the time, and I must admit to having enjoyed it a few times myself, partly out of curiosity. I presumed that many of our guests regularly indulged in the privacy of their bedrooms, and that wouldn't have been a major problem for me.

But anything harder was definitely out of the question as far as I was concerned, and anyone suspected of having any connection with hard drugs was made most unwelcome. The social climate of the time indicated that pot was okay, but I think there was a genuine fear of the harder stuff, and thankfully it just did not seem to intrude on our scene at all – though clearly it would have an appalling impact on Philip's life, and by extension on my own, in the longer run.

While I was generally as innocent about drugs as I had been about sexual matters, I could usually detect from a person's shifty behaviour that they might be using something. I regularly came upon groups of musicians giggling and behaving oddly, and they would try to pretend there was nothing going on, but I was a little more savvy than they suspected, and sometimes I would feign ignorance just to add to their hilarity! Some might see that relatively lax environment as having sown the seeds of Philip's later involvement with hard drugs, and they may even argue that, somehow, I should have prevented Philip setting off on the drug trail that was eventually to kill him. But, in showbusiness, the softer drugs like cannabis were assumed to be part and parcel of everyday life, and I had no reason to assume that they had any long-term effects.

Besides, cannabis use was so prevalent among musicians that any attempt on my part to prevent Philip using pot when he was with me would not have stopped such a very determined and increasingly confident young man doing exactly as he pleased when he was out of my sight. I gave him the usual motherly talking-to about drugs and other matters before he moved permanently to London but, just like the rest of our showbiz guests, I knew he smoked pot now and then, and I also knew there was nothing I could do to stop him.

And when you think about it, for every casualty like Philip, there were hundreds and hundreds of people involved in rock 'n' roll and showbusiness who used cannabis and never went near heroin. What takes people over that threshold I'll never know, but I really don't think that me confronting him about using cannabis would have made a blind bit of difference. Since he never lived with me in his adult life, in most respects I had almost as little influence over his lifestyle as I had on the other musicians passing through. The curious thing is that he often tried to persuade me to give up smoking cigarettes and drinking, and I did so once, for a while, just to please him. He was probably the only man I ever obeyed!

. . . .

With the hotel going so well, I was much more content in my life than at any time up to then. I was responsible for a successful business, in receipt of a regular income, secure in a stable relationship with Dennis, and taking enormous pleasure from observing Philip's enthusiasm for his increasingly successful music career. I was also proud of the fact that he had also become so observant about whatever was going on in the world about him. He had to be tough to progress in music but he was also sensitive and hugely likeable.

As Philip's fans will be aware, those qualities are evident in his lyrics and poems. As he drove along the motorway, or waited at an airport, an advertising hoarding might catch his eye, and a phrase or an idea would go straight into the notebook he carried with him at all times. He was a highly intelligent young man of considerable depth, and possessed of a real creative drive. Even his own mother could see that.

'Whiskey In The Jar', that brilliant ballad of passionate love and romantic highwaymen, has gone down in rock history as the single that first catapulted Thin Lizzy onto the world stage, but only die-hard fans know how close it came to not becoming a single at all. If it hadn't, who knows how different so many lives would have turned out?

The song was originally recorded as an impromptu filler track, merely to be used as the B-side of their next single. But to the band's initial

The eye has it: Colm Henry portrait of Philip.

(Left): Easy Rider Philip;
(right): Philo always liked to
party; *(below)*: brother Leslie
as a child.

Form of Inquiry and Notification of Baptism

From The Parish Priest

St. Lawrence's

3, Malvern Street

Manchester, M15 4FL

Date ....15th January, 1980

Please certify to the Baptism of
Philip Paris Lynott

Son or (Daughter) of ....Philomena Lynott........

Baptised at St. Edward's, Selly Park, Birmingham

Born ....20th August, 1949..........

Certificate

The above-named ....*Philip Lynott*....

was baptised at ....*St. Edward's, Selly Park*....

on ....*4th September 1949*....

(Signed) ....*T. W. Dennison*....

J. E. Mulligan & Co., Ltd., 34 Victoria Crescent, Eccles, nr. Manchester. (D)

· COISTE GAIRM-OIDEACHAIS CATHAIR BHAILE ATHA CLIATH

TECHNICAL SCHOOL, CLOGHER ROAD, CRUMLIN
WHOLE-TIME DAY COURSES

REPORT

On *Philip Lynott*   Class *J* *1st*

For Period *Sept* 19*64* To *Dec* 19*64* No. in Class *21*   Practical = 60%   Other Subjects = 50%

SUBJECT	MARKS %	PLACE IN CLASS	PROGRESS	CONDUCT
Religious Instruction	81		E	E
Physical Training	82	8	E	G
Mechanical Drawing	85	3	G	G
Woodwork	84	1	E	E
Woodwork Drawing	98	1	E	E
Metalwork	—			
Irish	65	10	G	G
English	65	8	G	G
Mathematics	71	9	F	F
Mechanics & Heat	—			
Magnetism & Electricity	—			
Art	83	4	G	G

E — Excellent   G — Good   F — Fair   U — Unsatisfactory

Punctuality: *E*   Attendance: *E*   Possible: *69*   Actual: *69*

Remarks: *A satisfactory, all round student*

School re-opens: *4-1-65*

(Signed) *P. J. Mulholland*   Headmaster

Date: *18-12-64*

The Headmaster will appreciate an acknowledgement of this report

W.W.A.S.LTD.VEC88

(*Above left*): Philip's baptismal certificate was required in 1980, to allow him to marry in a Catholic church. It was posted to the house in Kew Road.
(*Below left*): School report from the Technical School in Clogher Road, Crumlin (now Clogher Road VEC). His punctuality and attendance were excellent! (*Below right*) Philip and Brian Downey.

Opposite page: Philomena Lynott, in her early days in England.
This page: (*above*) My Boy: Philomena and Philip. (*left*) Philip's sister Philomena, originally named Jeanette, as a bridesmaid at the age of 14

A striking portrait of Philip in the early days of his involvement on the Dublin scene, by Roy Esmonde.
Opposite page: *(above and bottom right)*: early days on the road with the three-piece Thin Lizzy; *(bottom left)*: Philip, Brian Downey and Eric Bell.

Mother and son: Candid shots of
Philomena and Philip together.

Two Irish heroes: Philip with George Best of Manchester United and Northern Ireland.
(*Below*): Philip's shares in his beloved Man U.

CERTIFICATE NUMBER	TRANSFER No.	DATE OF REGISTRATION	NUMBER OF SHARES
000484	200827	5 FEB 79	10

CERTIFICATE FOR ORDINARY SHARES

MANCHESTER UNITED
FOOTBALL CLUB LIMITED

(INCORPORATED UNDER THE COMPANIES ACTS, 1862 TO 1900)

This is to Certify that

PHILIP LYNOTT ESQ
THE WALLED COTTAGE
184 KEW ROAD
RICHMOND, SURREY

is/are the Registered Holder(s) of   TEN *

Ordinary Shares of £1 each in the Company, subject to the Memorandum and Articles of Association thereof

Given under the Common Seal of the said Company

Exd_____

NOTE: NO TRANSFER OF ANY OF THE SHARES COMPRISED IN THIS CERTIFICATE WILL BE REGISTERED UNTIL THE CERTIFICATE HAS BEEN SURRENDERED TO THE COMPANY'S REGISTRARS, NATIONAL WESTMINSTER BANK LIMITED, REGISTRAR'S DEPARTMENT, PO BOX 82, 37 BROAD STREET, BRISTOL BS99 7NH

CE/874/A/

(*Above*): Scott Gorham, Brush Shiels, Philo, Brian Robertson, Tim Creedon and Eric Bell.
(*Below*): Ay Ay Cap'n!: Lizzy go messing about on a boat.

LEFT: LIAM QUIGLEY

(Above): In terms of cool, Phil shades it.
(*Below*): Treasure on the wasteland: Philo in Dublin in the late '70s.

CHALKIE DAVIES

(*Above*): Phil, Gary and Brian; (*below*): Brian, Eric and Phil, on the road again.
Opposite page: A perk of the job: Philo judges Miss World competition, 1978; (*top right*):
extract from a short essay by the teenage Philip, on what he'd like in a girl (courtesy
Terry O'Neill).

MISS WORLD

I NEVER REALLY THOUGHT ON GETTING MARRIED BUT I'VE THOUGHT ABOUT KIDS, I'D LOVE SOME. So, I SUPPOSE, SO WOULD THE WIFE. SHE'D BE A FLIRT, CAUSE ~~ITS THE~~ ITS THE ONLY WAY TO KEEP ~~HER~~ ME INTERESTED. SHE BE DOMINANT, BUT LET ME WIN MOST ARGUMENTS. NICE LOOKING PREFERABLY BUT DEFINATELY NOT UGLY, SHE'D LOVE MUSIC, OR ELSE WE COULDN'T COMMUNICATE AND SHE MUST LOVE ME WITH ALL MY FAULTS.

PHILIP SEX LYNOTT

IN AID OF CHILDREN'S CHARITIES IN ASSOCIATION WITH THE VARIETY CLUB OF GREAT BRITAIN
CHAIRMAN ERIC D MORLEY EXECUTIVE DIRECTOR JULIA E MORLEY DIRECTOR JON OSBORNE

The World's Most Coveted Beauty Title
MISS WORLD LIMITED, REGISTERED OFFICE
22-24 SHAFTESBURY AVENUE LONDON W1V 8AP TELEPHONE 01-734 9211 TELEX 27654 CABLES MECCA WORLD

MISS WORLD REGISTERED IN ENGLAND REGISTRATION NUMBER 963565

15 November 1978

Mr Phil Lynott

Dear Mr Lynott

We are delighted that you have agreed to join our Panel of
Celebrity Judges for the Miss World Contest, which, as you
are aware, is held in aid of Children's Charities as
nominated by the Variety Club of Great Britain.

You are required to be at the Royal Albert Hall tomorrow
evening by 7.30 for a Briefing, and the show commences
at 8.00 pm with the programme being transmitted live by
the BBC from 9.25 until 10.10.

We will arrange for a car to collect you and your guest
from the above address at 6.45 pm.

The contest is followed by a Coronation Ball held at the
Grosvenor House to which you and your guest are invited,
and the car will transport you from the Royal Albert Hall
to the Grosvenor House and return you home later that
evening.

Dress for the night is black tie.

All judges and guests enter by Door 1 - Artistes Entrance -
and are escorted to the East Arena Bar to receive
instructions prior to the show. The host for the judges
and their guests is Mr Oliver Grant-Crichton.

We look forward to having you with us on this occasion,
and thank you for the part you are playing in helping
under-privileged and handicapped children throughout the
world.

Yours sincerely

JULIA MORLEY
Chief Executive
Miss World Limited

(*Above*): The identical triplets who made a special visit to Philip.
(*Below*): Philomena with Dennis Keeley (left) and Graham Cohen.

Philip with his daughter Cathleen.
Next page: Iconic silhouette of Philip by Liam Quigley.

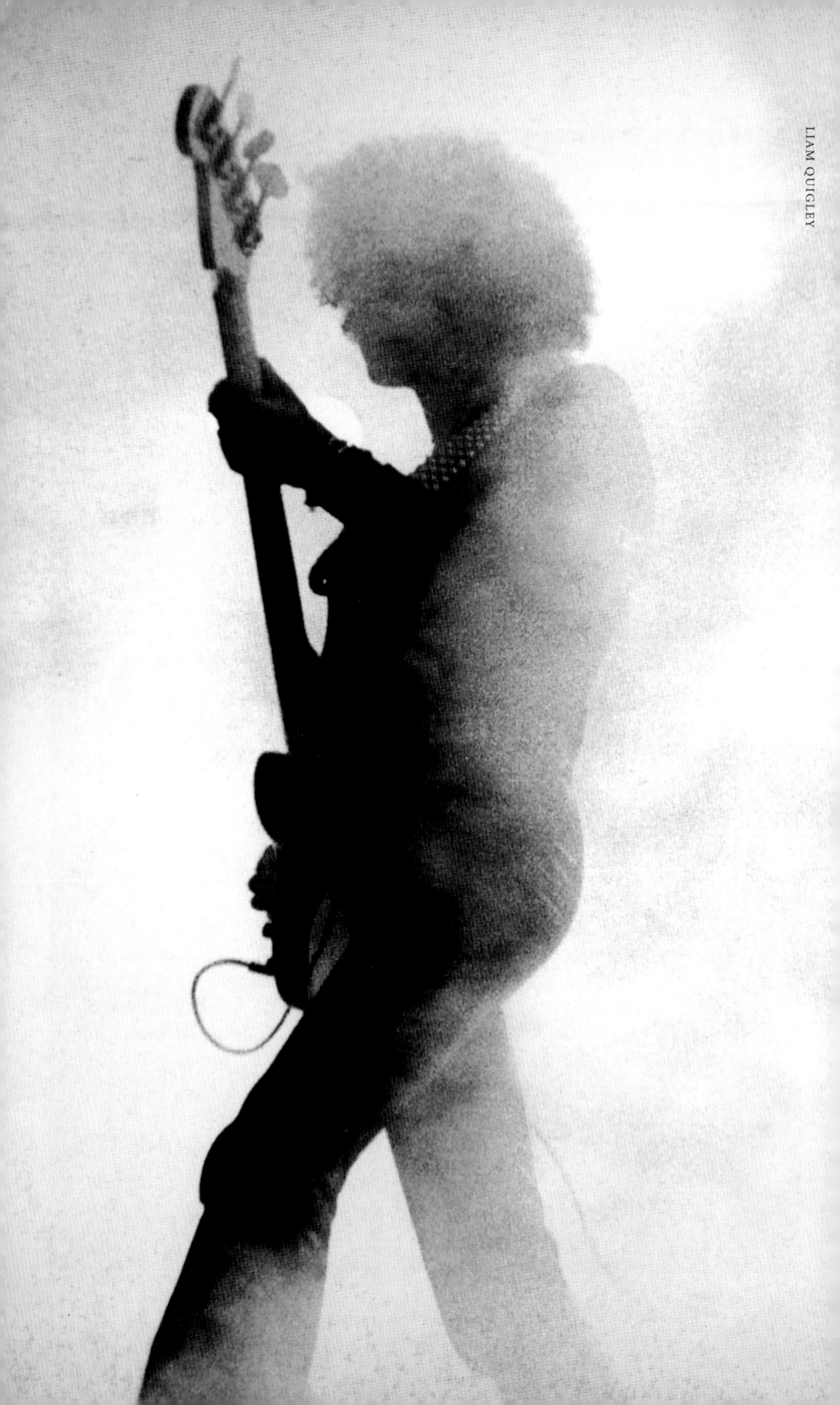

LIAM QUIGLEY

displeasure, their label Decca insisted on making it the A-side. For once, you might say, someone in a record company got it right. Released in November 1972, the single got off to a slow start and did not enter the British singles chart until 20th January, 1973. As you can imagine, this was a tremendously exhilarating time for us, and everyone in the hotel eagerly followed its progress as it moved slowly, week by week, up to the number six spot. All told, it stayed in the charts for a total of 12 weeks.

It was wonderful to see this kind of success happen to my own son. In Ireland, it went to number one, of course, confirming the band as national heroes. I was so proud of Philip. What made the feeling even better was the fact that it was a great record. To this day, I love the way it opens with Eric Bell's ringing electric guitar and Philip's distinctive voice howling out at you. I knew that Philip was writing good songs himself, but the fact that this was an old Irish folk song appealed to me. Indeed, in 1993, I was delighted to hear it again on the soundtrack of Jim Sheridan's superb film, *In The Name Of The Father*, about the disgraceful injustices heaped on the Guildford Four by the British "justice" system. But I think we'd better not go into that here.

Before the release of 'Whiskey In The Jar', of course, Thin Lizzy had recorded two other albums. The first, called *Thin Lizzy* was released in April '71, and the second, *Shades Of A Blue Orphanage*, in March '72 – this album has a cover photo of Philip, Brian Downey and Eric Bell walking through St. Stephen's Green in a typical Irish downpour. I love that picture – it captures not just the spirit of the era, but also Philip's love of Dublin, which is something that he never lost.

Neither album had sold well enough to dent the British charts, although they had been reasonably well received by the more discerning rock fans and had earned a solid reputation for the band all over Europe. As their career was developing, Thin Lizzy had been to Germany to play club dates and to perform on German television, so they were beginning to spread their wings successfully.

To me, the boys seemed to be permanently busy, working nearly every night, whizzing all over Britain and Ireland for tours and festivals. Up to the time that first album came on the market, I had still been sending Philip the money I had promised when he first moved into his flat in Clontarf. Like most rock bands, they had often pretended to be more successful than they actually were, and gigs back in Ireland, where they were obviously far more popular, were initially used to subsidise some of their dates in Britain and on the Continent. Now that Philip no longer needed to be subsidised, I felt that things were really beginning to happen for him.

The first real personal involvement I had in Thin Lizzy's career after they had started to take off was the recording of a television programme, which Dennis and I attended in Manchester in early '73. Lulu and an impeccably-dressed Joe Dolan were also on the bill. When Thin Lizzy arrived at the hotel before the recording, I insisted that they each have a bath. I wanted them all to look spotless for this important appearance on national television. Needless to say, my fussing and mothering gave them a good laugh.

At the time, Philip used to wear what I can only describe as a disgusting woolly Rastafarian-type hat. I suppose you could say that it was in keeping with the new untidy style of the time. To me, it was more like a tea-cosy, with his hair poking through the various holes in it. Anyway, that afternoon, I washed their clothes and ironed their jeans, much to their disgust, since it was considered old-fashioned then for men to wear a crease in their trousers, and I darned all the holes in Philip's ugly hat.

So when the band came on the studio set to perform 'Whiskey In The Jar', which was hitting the charts by then, I was really proud to see the son for whom I had walked the streets, trying to find work in order to clothe and feed him, up there in front of the cameras. There he was, with a record in the charts and starring on television with his band. Even noticing that the hat on which I had done such a thorough repair job during the afternoon now had as many holes in it as ever didn't faze me! They obviously thought of me as a boring, old-fashioned mother, whereas they wanted to portray a devil-may-care, hip image. Fair enough. Judging by the reaction in the studio at the time, they'd clearly got it right.

It was equally exciting for me, attending my first real Thin Lizzy gig, when they supported Slade at the Free Trade Hall in Manchester. Slade were so popular that the streets were full of police and the kids all wore hats reading, "I'm Slayed". Slade had a reputation for attracting a skinhead audience with racist tendencies, and when we arrived backstage before the concert, I noticed Philip and the band were very nervous about the ordeal ahead.

When Suzi Quatro finished her set, we took our seats just in time to see Lizzy arrive on stage. They were greeted by a chorus of abuse, with louts shouting slogans like "Get off the stage, black arse" and "Get back to Africa." I wasn't used to the intense atmosphere at concerts, that air of barely controlled tension. I reacted emotionally, attempting to run over towards where some of the most vociferous offenders in the audience were gathered. I shudder to think what might have happened if Dennis and my friends hadn't succeeded in restraining me – those guys looked thoroughly nasty, and I doubt if they'd have been intimidated by a middle-aged woman losing her temper. Philip, meanwhile, was pleading with the audience in his broad Irish accent, "Ah, come on, give us a chance, just give us a chance." Somehow, his pleas got through and most of the audience listened, but I think the band were relieved when their spot was over and they could retreat to their refuge backstage, bruised but not broken.

That night, we threw a party at the Clifton Grange and decorated the place with balloons and promotional material supplied by the record companies. Suzi, Noddy Holder and Philip were there, with the other members of the band, and they had a great time together. Needless to say, there wasn't even a hint of the unpleasant racism evident in the audience – my own impression was that Noddy was a very decent fellow.

About a year later, Thin Lizzy were back at Manchester Free Trade Hall – only this time, they were top of the bill. It was another memorable night for me. It began with a police escort through the centre of Manchester in the limousine Philip had arranged for us – but that was just the start of it. Lizzy had deliberately reserved a space in the centre balcony for me and my fifty personal guests. I felt like the queen, being able to preside over such a brilliant occasion.

It was an astonishing gig, like nothing I had ever seen in my life before. By this stage Lizzy had put together a real show, using amazing lights, and there were loud explosions from their smoke bombs that frightened the life out of me – I thought they were real bombs, because there was a lot of violence in Northern Ireland at the time, and there was always the threat of bombing in England as a spill-over from the Northern troubles. Needless to say, the crowd, who were more used to that kind of thing than I was, went berserk – the band made such an impact that they were called back to the stage again and again, till I lost count of the encores. I remember being struck at the time by how *loud* the music was – it took three days for my hearing to recover, but that didn't matter. It was the start of my love affair with hard rock.

What a turn-around it was, when you think about it, for a band to play a venue in front of a bunch of mindless racist hecklers one year, and the next to be greeted with the kind of hysteria I thought was reserved for The Beatles and The Rolling Stones. Thin Lizzy's growing stature was even bestowing some reflected glory on me, as people arrived in Manchester to seek out 'Phyllis's place' because of the Lizzy connection.

As their success grew, I took advantage of the occasional opportunity to snatch a glimpse of the inner workings of the record industry. I was taken to meet Frank Rodgers at Thin Lizzy's record company Decca, and I was terribly impressed at seeing a real gold disc on the office walls there! Decca were a very big record company then – with many famous hit artists on their books – people like Vera Lynn, The Bachelors from Ireland, Mantovani, David Whitfield, Lonnie Donegan, Tommy Steele, Billy Fury and Dickie Valentine, most of whose music I had heard on the radio and some of whom I liked quite a lot. When I looked at the gold records by some of these celebrities adorning the Decca offices, I was struck by the possibility that, before too long, my own son and his band might be joining such an elite collection.

Frank was a brother of the Irish singer, Clodagh Rodgers, who had had hit records with some nice pop tunes such as 'Come Back And Shake Me' and 'Goodnight Midnight'. The fact that I admired her and her music, and that they were both Irish, helped break the ice. I really got to like Frank. I have to admit that being part of all this made me feel just a little bit special. How many other rock 'n' roll stars' mums were happily admitted to the inner circle? But I was very privileged because of the kind of close relationship I had with Philip. That he made me feel involved in things was one his lovely qualities.

There were other occasions when I would be called upon to help out over one problem or another, because I got on so well with most of the band members, the management and crew. For example, at one stage an acrimonious row developed during a tour of Germany and the situation became so critical that the group were on the verge of splitting up. Their management company, led by Chris Morrison and Chris O'Donnell, had taken over the band's management from their old Dublin friend and mentor Ted Carroll, and they relied on me a lot in those days. So, when there was trouble brewing in the camp, they pleaded with me to fly out to Germany, at their expense, in an effort to keep the group together.

Fortunately, the disagreement – whatever the cause of it – was resolved and my flight was unnecessary, but the occasion proved how tenuous the survival of a band often is. When one considers the clash of personalities and the inevitable squabbles that arise when people have to spend so much time together, often working under intense pressure in strange circumstances, you could argue that it's a miracle that rock bands last as *long* as they do. Needless to say, Thin Lizzy were no more exempt from such traumas than any other band on the road. Far from it.

When I originally queried Philip about the kind of people who were looking after his music business interests, he reassured me that the 'two Chrises' were two genuinely nice guys who attended church every Sunday. He jokingly promised me that the day they stopped going to Mass, he would start worrying about them.

Of course I knew that was just a load of old baloney – but overall I had the feeling that Thin Lizzy were in good hands. There was a bit of an anti-climax after 'Whiskey In The Jar' when their next single 'Randolph's Tango' didn't work but that was before Chris O'Donnell and Chris Morrison were involved. Besides, it's not altogether unusual, and overall the band were continuing to make good progress. From my perspective as a mother, Thin Lizzy's spiral of success was so overwhelming that I hardly had time to reflect on it, as one highly-publicised incident was swiftly followed by another. Philip regularly sent me pre-release acetates of their new records, but I was probably too close to him in a personal sense to appreciate fully how popular they were becoming all over the world. Sometimes one of their songs would come on the car radio and I would nearly crash with excitement, particularly when I reflected on all we had been through, together and separately, and how we were now enjoying the fruits of our separate careers.

My own life had settled down to a level of contentment that would have been unimaginable when we were evicted from the Catholic Home in Selly Oak. Racial abuse was something I now rarely encountered. I never allowed it to affect me anyway, always putting it down to a combination of fear and ignorance. I have always freely associated with black people, and proudly number several of them among my closest friends, including Roy and Percy, who was like a son to me, and who became a regular guest in my Dublin home in the grief-stricken years that were to follow Philip's death. When they wrote to me, they would sign their letters: 'Your son', and Percy often referred to me endearingly as his 'Irish Mammy'.

Because Philip was now abroad a lot, touring and promoting his records, I was not aware of him having to deal with overt racism, but I believed that he was sufficiently strong to cope with it in his own way. Some of his best friends, like Percy and Roy, were black, yet he played in a white rock group.

Not surprisingly, it was sometimes impossible for me to distinguish the real events of Philip's life from the inevitable hype that surrounds celebrities in all walks of life, and probably even more so in the flamboyant, anything-goes rock business. There was the occasion when he was shot at in America, for instance. The first I learned of it was when he rang to warn me that the media would probably be reporting it, and he wanted me to know he was safe. Naturally I was extremely shocked and upset, and even now I have no idea what was going on at the time or what the real background to the incident was.

There were also the now-famous stories of him allegedly going deaf with tinnitus, stories which, to my knowledge, were totally without foundation, and which Philip claimed had originally been dreamed up by a record company PR bigwig as a publicity stunt. Whatever the truth of the matter, I could not avoid becoming extremely concerned, especially when television companies ran programmes about the dangers of loud rock music, using Philip's alleged problems as part of the evidence to support the theory. But, of course, such publicity served to enhance the image of a band eager to portray themselves as taking major risks by playing dangerously loud for the sake of their music. And maybe in that perverse way, it was somehow good for the band. But for an outsider, it can be deeply disturbing to see not just the lengths people have to go to achieve success, but also to realise that this kind of media manipulation actually works.

Another blast of publicity, which did my own nerves absolutely no good at all, centred around a violent incident in a bar. Supposedly, Philip was just talking to a girl who had asked for an autograph. Whatever was going on, her guy obviously didn't see it that way and smashed a pint glass over Philip's head, with the result that all the Lizzy roadies piled in and created a dreadful ruckus. Afterwards, he phoned me to warn me that the media were going to run stories along the lines of: "Lynott loses an eye in bar-room brawl." He wanted me to know that there was no foundation to the speculation. Again, looking back, I have no idea to what extent the Lizzy PR machine had actually fed the media a line and it suited the newspapers to run with it. I do believe that Philip himself was conscious of how these kind of bad-boys-of-rock stories might benefit the band, but I was never fully sure to what extent his calls were merely bravado or truthful reassurances.

Philip was astute enough to realise that the comparative novelty of a black Irishman was another exploitable angle that had built-in media appeal, and he was capable of cleverly using his colour to good advantage as part of the band's and his own image. But at the same time, he was unquestionably genuinely proud of his Irishness.

Every year, he would endeavour to be at Clifton Grange for our annual Saint Patrick's Day party which would inevitably turn out to be a real humdinger and at which George Best and other celebrities were regular, and generally boisterous, revellers.

On a trip to the States, Philip bumped into a New York cop, who was amazed to find that this tall black guy had such a thick Irish accent. He phoned me afterwards asking me to send the guy a complimentary T-shirt and a copy of his first collection of poetry. In due course, the cop became one of his best friends in America.

When Philip's first book of poetry was published, I, like a lot of other people, including some of the hippest rock critics, was pleasantly surprised and enormously proud. Until then, it was unusual for a songwriter in a heavy-rock band to have poetic ambitions, but when you explore Philip's song lyrics, it becomes apparent the extent to which his work transcends the run-of-the-mill rock song. I got the lovely feeling reading the book that I was entering into Philip's world and sharing in his inner life. The songs, teeming as they are with references to Ireland, Dublin, his friends, and aspects of Irish culture and history, seem to me to possess a genuine poetic flair.

I have to admit that it was only after his death that I began to study his poems and lyrics in depth, and slowly began to understand the extent to which his lyrical work bore a direct relationship with his life. I regretted not listening to them more attentively while he was alive and exploring their deeper meaning with him – but I must say that it's one of the problems with the kind of hard rock that Thin Lizzy played. At times it's so difficult to make out what's going on in the songs that I do think, in Philip's case at least, a lot was lost as a result.

One of the things that does come through in the songs is that Philip loved Ireland. He never felt in any way alienated from the ordinary people of Ireland, despite being black and having been born in England to an unmarried Catholic mother. I have often suppressed a wry grin when I hear people winning prizes in quizzes by wrongly answering 'Ireland' or 'Dublin' to the question, 'Where was Philip Lynott born?' But irrespective of the *place* of his birth, Philip always regarded himself as Irish and was deeply proud of Ireland and his Irishness throughout his life. It must have added a real sense of achievement for him that someone from an underprivileged background in Dublin could compete with the best the music world had to offer. I suppose a significant number of the world's most successful rock stars do come from deprived, working-class backgrounds, underlining the extent to which great talents are undoubtedly lost in other areas of human endeavour. Because one of the great things about rock 'n' roll is that it does offer an escape route for working class kids with artistic leanings. Sadly, it's one of the few.

6. GLORY DAYS – PASSING BY

"Then somewhere from the north
This Gale I knew just blew in
and I am afraid."
– from 'Look What The Wind Blew In' by Philip Lynott

When Philip, then still in his teens, had moved into his first flat in Clontarf in Dublin, he had a girlfriend called Gale. I am reasonably certain that she stayed in the flat with him, although she would discreetly move out whenever I came to visit.

I can't say I'd have been utterly shocked if I'd known, but there's no doubt that it was a typically unconventional thing to do at the time. In those days in Dublin, it was rare for couples to be as open and frank about their sexual affairs as they might be in the Ireland of the 21st century. Today, a very high percentage of households might have at least one person in a sexual relationship outside marriage. But the widespread scale of this is quite a recent development.

It was much less common for young people in Ireland to have sexual experiences in those days as well. Before Philip moved to London, I would have assumed he was probably less experienced sexually than a young person in similar circumstances would be today – as indeed I had been when I left Dublin. But perhaps not. Between my departure from Ireland and Philip's move to Dublin, the 60s revolution had occurred and had resulted in enormous worldwide changes in young people's attitudes towards sexual morals. Ireland had not escaped those influences.

Television had become a fact of Irish life by the mid-1960s. Teilifís Éireann had been launched with great fanfare at the end of 1961, and was now broadcasting five or six hours a day, of which well over 50% were featured programmes brought in from abroad, mainly America.

Gradually, even on home-produced programmes such as Gay Byrne's *Late Late Show*, matters relating to sexuality were being more openly discussed. Even in Manchester I'd get word of what was going on, reading the Irish newspapers, talking to my family or indeed when I visited. At last, there were signs that the Irish people were beginning to shake off the stifling fears and anxieties of Catholic repression.

We had been so cushioned from the realities of life during my own pre-television, teenage years, that when I emigrated I had no knowledge of a lot of issues that today dominate the news and the magazine programmes – issues like homosexuality, for example, or abortion. So Philip and I were probably quite similar in that we both underwent a process of awakening after we left home. It is, of course, a necessary process and, if it's well managed, a very beneficial one.

Looking back now, I suspect that the main reason for him wanting to have his own flat was that he was beginning to build relationships with girls, and there were definite limits to how far he could go while under his Granny's watchful eye in Crumlin. The house was too small and offered little in the way of the privacy you might need for even the most innocent sexual exploration. In the Clontarf flat he was obviously free of those restrictions and it must have been shortly after his move there that he met the young, green-eyed beauty Gale. It must also have been around that time that he wrote 'Look What The Wind Blew In', a song which appeared on the first Thin Lizzy album, and in which he sings about how, *"somewhere from the north this Gale I knew just blew in."* In the printed version of the song, the word *'Gale'* has a capital letter, whereas obviously, if the word were being used as simply indicating a 'wind', it would require no capital letter.

Philip and Gale were to enjoy a very close relationship for nearly six years, later living together in a nice flat in Embassy House at the junction of Cleve Road and West End Lane in London. At one point, they were engaged to be married, a fact very few people know – I remember her selecting a ring costing £4 in a second-hand shop, a poignant image when you put it in the context of the scale of Thin Lizzy's later success and the amount of money Philip made.

I thought Gale was a fabulous person, and both Dennis and I worshipped her. She was the highly intelligent daughter of a dentist from Northern Ireland and had three lovely sisters. We enjoyed her company so much that she often came on holidays with myself and Dennis to places like Ibiza. She had a strong personality and was always perfectly capable of holding her own on every level with Philip. Although they would have their occasional rows, they were very much in love and he seemed very fulfilled by their relationship. After they had moved to London, she often came to stay with me in the hotel in Manchester. Despite their six years together, she refused any suggestion that they might have a baby unless they were married first, which of course was her prerogative. And in the context of what happened later, I'm convinced she was right.

After they had enjoyed a steady relationship for about five years, she told me she was unhappy about the direction in which they were going. By that stage, Thin Lizzy had become quite popular, and Philip was becoming a star in his own right. That level of celebrity in itself brings its own pressures and temptations, since it usually attracts the opposite sex in droves, like bees to a honeypot, such is our perpetual fascination with fame.

Since I was busy in Manchester and he was in London when not travelling extensively with the band, I was hardly in a position to know how he was behaving one way or another. As far as I could tell at the time, both he and Brian Downey, who lived near him, in Greencroft Gardens, and who had an Irish girlfriend called Terry, were in steady partnerships. I was not so naïve as to assume that Philip was a saint, and I did know that he would not want me to find out if he stepped out of line, because he knew of my high regard for Gale.

In retrospect, I have no reason to imagine that Philip did not respond willingly to the increased sexual availability of young women attracted to him as a rock star. Gale certainly suspected he was beginning to have extra-curricular relationships of one kind or another, and this was leading inevitably to frequent, unpleasant arguments. So, she felt a break from him for about six months, during which she would go travelling abroad, might clarify his true feelings and help make up his mind as to whether he was sufficiently committed to her or not.

"After all," as I said to her, "if you go away for a while and it turns out that he doesn't miss you, then at least you'll know where you stand." I told her that I loved her dearly and that I would understand and support her no matter what decision she came to. I was really on her side in the matter, as I was disappointed by Philip's attitude.

While she was away, Philip moved out of the London flat into a rented house. When Gale came back, I pointed out to him that she now had nowhere to live, and so she moved into what had been their flat on her own. From a sexual point of view, it seemed Philip wanted to have Gale around when it suited him, but he also, unfairly, wanted his freedom to have other women too, even though Gale had stuck with him when they struggled to live on cans of beans and virtually nothing else.

I have to admit that his attitudes were clearly contradictory and somewhat chauvinist. He would complain to me if any of his "spies" reported that she had been meeting other male friends. He often became extremely upset at the thought that she might take a fancy to other men, whereas he wanted to play around with no restrictions. His behaviour really irritated me and I remember even at one point suggesting to Gale that she should investigate whether she could sue him for breach of promise. I wasn't often critical of Philip, but in this instance it went further. I was so enraged, the thought crossed my mind that I'd give evidenceagainst him in court, on her behalf! Of course, I wouldn't have but I was really upset.

Either way, Gale was too proud to go down that road and, much to my deep regret, she faded out of his life. Although they remained friends right up to his death, inevitably Gale found a new man, whom she later married. She also carved out a very successful career with Sky TV. I know that a mother has no hold over her children in this respect, and it was probably a selfish reaction on my part, but I was extremely upset when I lost her as a future daughter-in-law – just so that Philip could play the field and enjoy the rock 'n' roll lifestyle with what were probably groupies and hangers-on a lot of the time.

As her parents had passed away, Gale had no family in Ireland and she often referred to me as 'Mother'. I'm happy to say that her husband Colin and their two children Zoe and Jamie, all stay with me in my house on their regular visits to Ireland. Like they say, true friendships never die.

I suppose I knew too that, in the long run, Philip would develop a curiosity about the absence of a father in his life. It happens in most single-parent families – some choose to tell their children as little as possible, but I never felt that that would be fair. A child has, I believe, a right to know and so I had decided to keep him as fully informed as possible. As time went by, I filled in as many of the missing pieces as I thought he could handle. Of course, I couldn't help fretting and wondering whether not having a father made him feel odd when he saw that nearly all his school pals had so-called 'normal' families. When he was still young, I explained to him the background to his birth, convinced him that his Dad loved us both and had wanted to marry me – and I told him that Cecil had since married a nice lady, whom he introduced me to at a dance, and that he was raising a family of his own. I never wanted to badmouth his father or to make Philip feel that he was somehow unworthy.

I never really held anything back from him in this regard, but it didn't seem to preoccupy him too much either, perhaps because his upbringing was so full with all the people in Ma's house and he was part of the gang in what was a busy neighbourhood. On the face of it at least, Philip just got on with his own life. In the meantime, I also let Cecil get on with *his* life and we had been totally out of contact, more or less, since the court hearing.

When Philip was about ten, he asked me a lot of questions about his Dad. Then he enquired if I would forward a letter he had written to Cecil. I said yes, because I didn't see any way that I could refuse – but I later decided, unknown to Philip, not to post that letter. It was not an easy decision for me to be deceitful to Philip, but I knew that Cecil was happily married with a family of his own, and I thought that such a letter from Philip might arouse old feelings in him, or even cause some discomfort to his wife and family. I'm not saying that that was the right decision, but I felt it was at the time. To put it simply, I suppose I reasoned that it was best to leave well enough alone, because, quite genuinely, to have met Cecil might have had a hugely disruptive effect on a boy who was happy at the time. But it is still a tough call for any mother or father to have to make, and my heart goes out to anyone who faces that particular dilemma.

But I knew deep down that, sooner or later, curiosity would almost certainly get the better of Philip's apparent indifference and that he would want to meet his Dad face to face. I had resolved that if he wanted it, I would be wrong to obstruct him in something so important – but I had a feeling that the older he was at the time, the better he'd be able to handle any emotional turmoil that might unfold. And so it transpired – genuinely, there was no rush on it from Philip's side.

After the first flush of success, there had, of course, been all sorts of turmoil in the Lizzy camp. Eric Bell walked off stage one night and never came back. Gary Moore, Philip's old friend from the Dublin scene, stepped in. But Philip had other plans and, after a period when there was a temporary twin guitar set-up, he brought in Scott Gorham and Brian Robertson to complete what was widely considered to be the classic Thin Lizzy line-up. Their first record together was called *Nightlife* and it marked a new departure. There was a lot that I liked on it, but I wasn't expert enough to comment on why there were no hit singles.

Their second album was called *Fighting*. Shortly after its release in 1975, a popular magazine – some might classify it as a scandal sheet – called *Titbits*, published a rather fanciful article about Philip, emblazoned with the headline, "Thin Lizzy In A Tizzy About His Dad!" Cecil's wife accidentally spotted it and drew it to his attention saying, "I think this is about your son".

When Cecil read it, he went straight down to the Thin Lizzy management office and spoke to Chris Morrison – and announced there and then that he was Philip's father. Philip was recording at the time in Soho, I think. The people in Philip's management office were perplexed as to how to deal with this new drama, so they telephoned me for my advice. I asked them not to put Cecil in touch with Philip until I had thought the matter through and spoken directly to Cecil myself. After all, I had no way of knowing if Philip, by now a grown man, actually wanted to meet his father. Would he want whatever illusions or mystique he had built up to be shattered? And might he interpret – or misinterpret – Cecil's interest in meeting him as being merely a product of his success as a musician?

I was just beginning to mull things over when the phone rang and I was amazed to hear Cecil's voice: I recognised it straight away, although we hadn't spoken for years. He was calling from the management office. He asked if I could arrange for him to meet his son – and to be honest I just couldn't refuse. I then confirmed to the office that this man was indeed Philip's dad. After a series of phone-calls back and forth, during which my heart was doing a crazy dance, a meeting between them was arranged for the following evening. I offered to accompany Philip if he felt he would like someone there, but he quite firmly and confidently said, "No Ma, I'm grown-up enough to do this on my own." He promised to phone me after the meeting to tell me how it had gone.

Next evening I waited anxiously – and more than a little impatiently! – by the telephone, yet no call came through from Philip. I was simultaneously furious with him but also concerned that the meeting might have gone badly. It was classic Philip. He was an incurable romantic and could be extremely solicitous – but he could also be thoughtless and forgetful. When I eventually could hold off no longer, I rang the office to be told that he was still engrossed in a recording session and had skipped the meeting. I knew this must have been bitterly disappointing for Cecil, but a second appointment was made.

This time Philip did show up. I don't know how he was feeling at the time, but I'd have assumed that his first meeting as an adult with his natural father would have been a momentous occasion for him. Maybe he didn't take to Cecil, or they just didn't really know what to say to one another after all those years, but he seemed far less excited afterwards than I had expected him to be. I rationalised this to myself, concluding that they were two adult men with utterly different lifestyles and attitudes, and with very little, if anything, in common – and that was probably about the size of it. At the very least we can conclude that Philip Parris Lynott wasn't very impressed with Cecil Parris – and maybe, just maybe, the feeling was mutual.

That day Philip met not only his father but also Cecil's wife and their daughter, and his sister Sarah, who had also come along. One can imagine that such an encounter must have been stressful for all concerned, and this may have inhibited any kind of in-depth discussion between the two central characters in the real-life drama. I have often wondered whether, had Philip not lived the whirlwind life of a rock star, he might have had more time to get to know his father more intimately, and perhaps explored his father's background, political views, culture and so on.

But these are not things that can be forced by anybody – such relationships must grow naturally or not at all. As it transpired, Philip rarely mentioned his father after that meeting and, as far as I know, that was the only time they ever spoke face to face.

Who can really know what went on in the minds or hearts of either of them?

· ·

Although I always loved Philip dearly, and he was rarely far from my thoughts at any stage in my life, I could not help observing a marked change in his personality over the years as he became more successful, more powerful and more affluent. Particularly as a result of all the torment we went through together when he was a child, as a mother I still find it difficult to be really critical of him – but there would be no point in denying that he had his share of failings like any other human being, and that these were sometimes exacerbated by the circumstances of his life. Yes, he was romantic and generous and sentimental, but an unpleasant and unnecessary aggression sometimes crept into his manner, more particularly towards the latter part of his life.

Some people have suggested that that change in his personality was a direct result of his use of cocaine, but I had no way of knowing that then, and I can't say that I know it for certain even now. I did notice him beginning to talk very sharply to people and, because I did not like what I saw, I pulled him up on it many times. He didn't argue when I scolded him, and afterwards, I would remind myself that I often behaved likewise under the pressure of the moment and I too would need to apologise later. But the bottom line was that I didn't like to see him treating people badly, no matter who they were. And if he was capable of doing it while his disapproving mother was around, was it not probable that he was behaving even more boorishly when there was no-one to answer to, except the flunkies and yes-people who inhabit the fringes of the rock world?

My old friend Percy had encouraged Philip to project the more aggressive side of his nature, which he felt the fans would respond to very positively, and while in commercial terms he may have been right, there is a possibility that such posturing only served to allow a more unpleasant side of Philip's character to assert itself. Not that he had undergone a Dr. Jekyll and Mr. Hyde-like transformation. I firmly believe that Philip was more consistently generous and attentive to me in his adult life than many sons are to their mothers. Dennis and I were taken on various Thin Lizzy tours overseas and treated like royalty. We had a very good relationship with the band members in general, and it was a terrific treat for Philomena Lynott, from working-class Crumlin, to be taken free of charge to stay in some of the most luxurious hotels in the world and to meet countless world-famous celebrities. I often had to pinch myself to confirm that it was really happening. We shared many close, fun times together, all of which have become even more precious and memorable to me since he passed on.

There is no way that Philip was mean or miserly with his money. He enjoyed spending it having a good time with his friends – like the time in 1977 when he invited nearly 300 guests, among them Bob Geldof, Graham Parker and other stars, to what was a lavish 28th birthday party amid the grandeur of Castletown House in Celbridge, County Kildare. He would also have thoroughly enjoyed being invited to be a judge for the Miss World event in 1978 – he had absolutely no inhibitions about that sort of thing. He was in his element when he was partying. But of course that can sometimes get in the way of the work, which happened I think increasingly over the following years.

He was one of a select number of celebrities invited on Virgin Atlantic's inaugural London-New York flight and he later featured in advertisements for Virgin Atlantic and Maxell tapes, which were useful at least in bringing the money in. And despite the fame, adulation and wealth, he had an endearing ability to laugh at himself. Once when we shared an Aer Lingus plane-trip after he had achieved a degree of celebrity, he began laughing aloud at an article in their in-flight magazine which listed him in a chart of the worst-dressed men. He loved all that and, in my opinion, probably played up to it, and I took enormous satisfaction in seeing that he never seemed to allow any of that fame to erode his sense of humour. In moments like that I felt that he had, early on in his career, learned the happy knack of separating the real Philip Lynott from the star, and that he successfully kept the different personae separate most of the time, though certainly not always.

He often complained that the combination of his skin colour, his big bushy, black hairstyle, his gangling, six-feet two inch frame and his very individual stride – all difficult to disguise or hide, even if he had wanted to – meant that he could never become inconspicuous in public. And it was true. Unlike other rock stars who can – and do – become anonymous by wearing different clothes or a wig or other disguise, he could never escape so easily.

When Dennis and I arrived back in Dublin one afternoon after a tour of the Irish countryside, we immediately spotted a distinctive figure walking along the pavement as we drove up O'Connell Street – it was Philip. On another occasion, I went to the Brown Thomas store in

Dublin's fashionable Grafton Street to buy him a black Stetson hat which I knew he would really appreciate. To cope with his hairstyle I asked the elderly shop-lady for the largest hat in stock. When I rejected the one she first offered, she insisted that there was no larger size available and began to look at her colleague pityingly, as if the hat must be for a person with an abnormal head. It was only while taking my name for a special order she realised the hat was for Philip, a regular customer, she told me, whose measurements she already had!

In a small but vivid way, that illustrates how difficult it had become for him to maintain any real sense of privacy as his reputation grew, and I know he craved, just occasionally, to in become anonymous and to melt into the crowd. But if the hat doesn't fit, I guess you can't possibly wear it.

After all the racial abuse we had endured when he was younger, he now occasionally had to deal with people who saw us together on the street thinking we were dating and muttering equally outrageous insults. One of the worst instances I can remember occurred after I took him to visit the dentist.

Philip was suffering the effects of the anaesthetic as we walked out from the dentist's residence, and I had to hold him up because he was so groggy. Even when I managed to get him into a cafe to sit down, I could hear the unkind tongues wagging, expounding on what was obviously a crass misunderstanding of the situation. But we never made any attempt to hide or apologise for our closeness, and he once described our relationship as more brother and sister than mother and son, so some people inevitably got the wrong idea. That might have been avoided had an obvious father-figure been around, but what the hell! The fact that we loved each other was much more important than any slings and arrows that narrow-minded busybodies might throw at us.

Although Philip became an astute businessman who was very conscious of the need to avoid being short-changed in an industry where sharks flourish, I never felt him to be unduly money-conscious. He knew when someone was not pulling his or her weight for the band, and he would openly remonstrate in no uncertain terms, because he wanted everyone associated with Thin Lizzy to be as committed as he was. And, as I indicated earlier, there were rows, with Eric Bell, Gary Moore and Brian Robertson in particular – occasions when egos clashed and the future direction of the band had to be sorted out. But Philip was the leader and the creative focus of Thin Lizzy, and while I am certainly not saying that he was always right, in the end there can only be one leader.

But in my experience he was neither greedy nor a hoarder of pointless possessions. Nor was he ever attracted to worthless baubles merely to impress others or to excite envy. He was not one for wearing ostentatious jewellery, diamond rings or Rolex watches just to show off. He had no flash car, for example, and never learned to drive. Plain pieces of silver attracted him. Gadgets also fascinated him and he enjoyed picking up an unusual bargain. He would proudly show me some watch that you could use underwater and do all sorts of fancy things with, and then he would admit it had cost a mere £13.

In London, or on trips overseas, he tended to wear more outrageous clothes, but he would be less ostentatious back in Dublin, partly because there is something in the Irish character that reacts against that kind of behaviour. Whenever he returned to Ireland, he was conscious of the possibility of meeting old friends who might not be doing so well, and he was always careful not to make them feel that they were missing out. Nor did he ever try to disguise his broad Dublin accent, because he always identified with the genuine down-to-earth Dubliner and, in some ways, getting back to those people was his way of maintaining contact with his real roots.

Such contacts may also have provided him with the best opportunity he'd have of fading into the background for a while. Of course, when asked, he would frankly admit to thoroughly enjoying fame, and there is an inherent contradiction in his enjoyment and his desire to escape from it when it suited him. But a lot of musicians are like that! He remarked to me, on more than one occasion: "When we were kids, didn't we all want to grow up to be famous, and aren't I lucky to have been one of the few granted that wish?"

And you know, he was. On balance, I suppose he did revel in being the star, but he also harboured an inherent suspicion of the falseness that attaches to fame. And, as I say, he could always relate to the everyday, hard-working guy or girl, and their dreams and ambitions. I generally thought of him as very down-to-earth, though others may have felt otherwise. One of his so-called friends accused Philip of being so vain that he would walk up Grafton Street in Dublin constantly looking at his reflection in the shop-windows. But I do that myself. Who hasn't? And either way, it's hardly a major crime, is it?

If Philip thoroughly enjoyed being the star, I have to admit that I equally enjoyed being the mother of the star. If he was a notorious party animal, then I enjoyed that side of the life too – it'd be dishonest and hypocritical of me to suggest otherwise. And the truth is that when Philip had the opportunity, he treated me amazingly well, inviting me to tour with the band whenever I was free to go. And I loved it.

In 1974, along with Brian Robertson from Glasgow, a young Californian called Scott Gorham had joined Lizzy. Scott and Brian played together first on the *Nightlife* album and it was a musical marriage that was made if not in heaven – for neither of them hid the fact that, like Philip, they were 'bad' boys in that very rock'n'roll meaning of the word – then in some special musical spawning ground. Those who know Lizzy's music will be aware that they operated as twin guitarists, replacing Eric Bell with a new and distinctive sound after his departure. It was the patented Thin Lizzy style which would mark the band's greatest records and bring them to the brink of megastardom. On one of the band's U.S. tours, Scott introduced Dennis and me to his wealthy parents. They in turn invited us to be their guests, and to stay in their breathtakingly beautiful home in the mountains around Hollywood, surrounded by many of the mansions that Scott's father, a master builder, had built. My eyes were attracted to a magnificent coffee-table which they casually informed me had cost $10,000. Well, hello! I liked both parents and we got on well with them. They were so phenomenally rich that they could fly virtually anywhere by private plane at a mere whim. Needless to say, all that wealth and privilege had rubbed off on Scott, who would regularly regale me with stories about all the famous old film stars, like Red Skelton, who were regular house guests when he was growing up.

When Scott had originally announced his intention of moving to Europe, his disapproving father had given him a wad of money and told Scott not to expect any more hand-outs from him. Obviously, the elder Gorham had worked hard to earn his fortune and did not appreciate the possibility that Scott might be turning his back on all that to adopt the rock'n'roll lifestyle. Thankfully, Scott was successful enough not to have to feel embarrassed about the career he'd chosen, and he was a lovely, warm, genuine guy – in fact the general camaraderie between Scott and the diverse personalities around the band was a key factor in making touring with Thin Lizzy such a bundle of fun.

Being on tours, particularly in the USA, made me realise what a mammoth task it is putting a major rock band on the road, with so many people involved, and with trucks, limos, sound gear, lighting equipment, merchandise, promotional material and so on, not to mention the complex business of hotel bookings, media interviews, personal appearances and a thousand and one big and small problems that all have to be considered if the show is to be successful.

One of the highlights of my travels with the band came during a visit to Chicago for a major concert. On arrival at O'Hare International Airport, I naturally headed towards the luggage carousel to collect my bags. When Philip told me that all of our luggage would be taken care of by somebody else, I could hardly believe him. To me, this was the height of luxury, not having to worry about such normal chores as taking care of your baggage. But that was only the start of it!

The first sensation I experienced when we arrived in Chicago's Hyatt Regency Hotel, was the scent of expensive perfume, which seemed to be wafting up from the luxurious carpets. Even the porters were magnificently attired and walked with a very stately bearing. Or that was how I perceived them anyway. After showing Dennis and I to our sumptuous room right next to Philip's, the porter stood stiffly to attention with his hands as good as out-stretched for a tip. Unfortunately, having just arrived directly from the airport after our flight from England, we didn't have even a dime between us. So he turned and walked out in disgust, much to our embarrassment as the guests of a rich celebrity!

I was preoccupied with taking in the opulence and the dizzying view out over the city when someone came and discreetly placed packages on either side of our bed. When Dennis opened them he discovered an ounce of dope in each package! In a panic, he ran down to Philip, who nonchalantly explained that the stuff was meant for some other room, not ours. But whose room? That was the unasked, and therefore unanswered, $64,000 question.

That night, the record company drove us in elegant stretch limousines to a top-quality Mexican restaurant. Soon the tequilas were being distributed and, amid the goings-on, I spotted Philip and the rest of the band larking about and trying to make me laugh while an overweight Mexican in an enormous sombrero was attempting to serenade me. Philip then departed for some pre-arranged television and radio interviews, while we were whisked off to a huge theatre for a Genesis gig. Unfortunately, jetlag was finally catching up on me, and I suspect that I may have fallen asleep during their set. But it was a wonderful night all round.

Dennis and I travelled the length and breadth of America, to such places as Maryland, Washington, Las Vegas, Galveston, Miami and Atlanta. And, as I said, we loved every moment of it. On our way through Maryland, we took the opportunity to visit my sister, Irene, who lived there with her husband, Don. Then, when we reached Los Angeles, we went in search of our friend Georgie Best who was living in the USA by then, his English League football days behind him. As it happened, he was not at his house when we called, but we found the place occupied by his friend Bobby McAlinden, another legendary footballer, who was George's best man and long time friend. Bobby, who shared a birthday with George and was really close to him, kindly asked us to make ourselves at home, told us there was beer in the fridge and left us to our own devices. Sometime later, when Georgie himself telephoned the house, he was amazed to hear the voice of his "Auntie Phyllis" on the line.

When George came back, he took us out to Fat Face Fenner's Saloon on Hermosa Beach, and we then transferred into a hotel right next to the shore. For our entire four-week stay in LA, we socialised nearly every night with Bestie and his friends and we had great crack. When Philip arrived in Los Angeles, he checked into a hotel on Sunset Boulevard and sent a limousine to take Dennis and myself to meet him. As we rode in this beautiful chauffeur-driven limo through the LA traffic, passers-by stopped and stared into the car. On such occasions, I could not help reflecting on how my new lifestyle contrasted with my early days in an oppressive English work-house. Would you blame me for enjoying myself, now that the good times were well and truly rolling? I certainly never felt any pangs of guilt – and why would I?

In 1977, Thin Lizzy undertook an extensive tour of the USA, supporting Queen for more than 40 shows. The tour had begun in disaster – the night before the band were due to travel to the States, Brian Robertson had become involved in a brawl in the Speakeasy in London with fellow Scotsman Frankie Miller. Robertson was rushed from the premises with his hand pumping blood and there was no way he could travel. In fact the verdict was that he would be unlikely to play again for a couple of months, having ripped tendons in his hand. Cancelling the tour would have been a desperate blow. Luckily, Gary Moore was free and sufficiently familiar with the Lizzy scheme of things to be able to slot into Robertson's place – and so it was onwards and upwards, for the moment at least.

Philip took me on board on this occasion as well, and I remember being whisked to a post-concert party in Los Angeles at which I met the late Freddie Mercury and Brian May, with whom Philip got on particularly well. The guests included a huge variety of celebrities including Alice Cooper and a daughter of Errol Flynn's – all surrounded by burly security guards armed with guns.

Before arriving at the party, Philip gave us all strict instructions to drink nothing except from cans we opened ourselves. He insisted that rather than leaving a can down, even for a moment merely to visit the bathroom, we must take our drinks with us to avoid anyone putting foreign substances into them while we were away. His concern was heightened by the tragic death of a drummer in a band he knew, apparently as a result of something someone had slipped into his drink in similar circumstances. This was strange territory but there was an extent to which it added to the bizarre allure of it all.

No matter where you looked at this party you could see incredible glamour, but Philip was unimpressed with Hollywood – or with this taste of it anyway. "They're all plastic," he said dismissively. When I later spotted the biggest roll of dollars I had ever seen lying unattended on the floor, my eyes popped and I picked it up and handed it to a security guard – who swiftly stuffed it into his pocket, as if finding the owner was not going to be his number one priority.

Not surprisingly, the pressures of touring – and let's be honest, the lifestyle surrounding life on the road – wreaked havoc on Philip's health. In an incident which in some ways presaged the circumstances of his death, he took ill with hepatitis during the tour, and the final leg had to be blown out. It was regarded by business insiders as a mortal blow to Thin Lizzy's prospects of breaking America big-time. Finishing this tour, they might have pushed the album they were promoting into the higher reaches of the charts. But it was not to be.

Hepatitis is a horrible, debilitating infection and, as a result, most of the following album, *Johnny The Fox*, was written while Philip was recuperating. Shortly after he began his hospitalisation, I took advantage of one of my visits to play a practical joke on him which I'm glad to say he enjoyed as much as those involved in the prank did. Knowing only too well at this stage how keen an eye he had for an attractive girl, I roped the hospital Matron and three beautiful young women, who were friends of mine, into the scheme. In fact the girls were identical triplets, who performed in a cabaret group as Looking Glass and so I asked Matron to fit them out in nurse's uniforms, and she duly obliged.

As I sat by Philip's bed, I pretended not to notice when the first girl

Cindy, came in and did a bit of tidying up around the bed. When she left, Philip was clearly agog at seeing such a stunner. Next came Yvonne on the pretext of asking Philip for some piece of information for his wall-chart. Once more, Philip could hardly believe that the hospital had not one but two extremely attractive nurses who, it would seem, were likely to be working on his floor. Then the third girl, Valerie, came in and when Philip saw her he was absolutely flabbergasted. Before he had time to figure out that something might be going on, "Nurse" Valerie said she needed to examine his private parts. At that, we could keep the pretence up no longer, and we all collapsed in a heap of laughter, including Philip!

There were also more threatening risks which came as part and parcel of the rock tour lifestyle. In August 1978, in Memphis, USA, Philip's car, driven by his chauffeur, was involved in a minor accident. Whatever happened, several shots were fired by the irate driver of the other car, during a ten-mile chase through the streets but, fortunately, none hit either Philip or the car. In June 1980, he was detained overnight in Southampton General Hospital for treatment to a damaged eye, after a glass was thrown at him while he was signing autographs following a concert at The Southampton Gaumont – not the kind of news you want to receive about your son a couple of months before your second grand-child is due.

Fortunately, the eye was not permanently damaged and, in typical rock business style, the incident was used for publicity purposes. It was in Philip's nature to turn such events into jokes anyway, and I can remember him making fun of the whole episode by crawling around on the ground pretending to look for his "missing" eye.

But those rare difficulties apart, I loved every second I spent travelling with the band, and I will always appreciate the opportunity I had to see so many fascinating people and exotic places because of Thin Lizzy's success.

7. LOVE AND MARRIAGE

Gale and Philip were still living together in the Embassy House flat when he started his relationship with Caroline Crowther. As far as I know, he met Caroline at a party organised by the well-known Thin Lizzy publicist, Tony Brainsby. At that time, she was working in Brainsby's office, and someone from the Thin Lizzy office had escorted her to the party. He may have known her beforehand, but it was on Philip's arm that she left that night, and that, as I understand, was how their relationship began.

It would be unfair to imply that Caroline stole Philip from Gale. I think, looking back, that the time may really have been right for him to move on – and Caroline clearly was the woman he wanted to move on with. There are times when we all come to a fork in the road and this was one for Philip. And I daresay for Caroline. Clearly they were both following their hearts, which is what people tend to do.

My first awareness of her came through one of Philip's almost daily phone-calls, when he happily announced that he had a new girlfriend. I distinctly recall him laughing as he told me that she did not have dark hair and green eyes like both Gale and I had – a reference to his habit of joking that he would only marry a girl who had both of these attributes.

I was a little stumped for a response to the news, partly because it most likely sounded the death-knell for his relationship with Gale, but I accepted that his new partner must be important to him since he was taking the trouble to tell me about her. And so it proved. Another phone-call brought the news that his new woman was pregnant, although there was no mention of marriage at this time. Of course, given my own history, I was hardly in a position to lecture him on that issue.

I met Caroline personally for the first time in the house in Anson Road in the Cricklewood part of London, which I believe Philip must have rented while Gale was away, and which was full of lively young people. I could not help wondering to myself whether or not Gale still hankered after Philip, and if she would be hurt by the latest turn of events. But with Caroline expecting Philip's first child, I realised there was no foreseeable way back into his life for the long-term girlfriend towards whom I still felt a deep loyalty.

Caroline was a tall, willowy blonde, born into what you could describe as a conservative, if hardly entirely conventional, English family. She was very different in both appearance and personality to Gale, and I was sufficiently worldly-wise to accept that what I felt wasn't important. Any mother who thinks they can or should dictate to their children in these matters is mad. Philip would make his own choices. I was, I admit, a bit thrown by the fact that I was going to be a grandmother for the first time. I still felt I was so young! And I suppose it complicated things even further that the woman who was carrying my son's child was still very much a stranger to me and a recent and unexpected arrival in my life.

While I was probably instinctively sympathetic to Caroline, having a baby out of wedlock as I had done, there was some comfort in knowing that her circumstances were certainly nothing like as deplorable as mine had been. The father of her baby was with her and he was quite flush, if hardly secure, by this time. There was no likelihood that she would have to suffer the torment and the pressures I had endured – Caroline's own background was also far more affluent than mine had been, and in such matters as education and job opportunities, she was in a higher league than I could ever have realistically aspired to. But the fact that there might be stormy waters up ahead for Philip, for Caroline and for their daughter-to-be, could not be discounted. My only role would be to help all three of them in whatever small way I could.

After we got to know each other a little, Caroline invited me to her parents' house in London for tea. There, I met her father Leslie Crowther, the well-known television personality and presenter of shows such as *The Price Is Right*, her mother Jean and the family. They were very respectable, eminently friendly people. They made a lovely fuss over me and we all got on very well together. Caroline was the third of five children and, on various occasions I met her brother, Nicholas, and her sisters, Charlotte, Lindsay and Elizabeth.

Caroline later told me of an incident which occurred early in her relationship with Philip, but prior to her introducing him to her family. One night, she took a cab driven by a black – or at least, dark-skinned – man to her parents' house. When Leslie saw the cab arrive, he noticed the driver and, assuming it had to be the new boyfriend Caroline had told him about, he came out and greeted him most effusively, shaking his hand and inviting him into the house for a drink. It was only the cabbie's astonished reaction that made him realise his embarrassing mistake! In later years, he was reported to have made some very offensive remarks about Philip, but I think they were always meant as harmless jokes. Anyway, he was always courteous to me whenever I met him, and I found it difficult to accept that the views ascribed to him by the tabloid press actually represented his true feelings.

Not least because Caroline was going to be delivering my first grandchild – the more I thought about it, the more excited I became – I wanted to make a fuss of her too, so I took her on several shopping expeditions and treated her. We got on very well at that time and seemed to enjoy each other's company, which was encouraging. Soon afterwards, Philip bought the house known as the Walled Cottage, at 184 Kew Road, Richmond in Surrey. I was a regular visitor there, sometimes giving Caroline driving lessons in my car. When he was away, she would sometimes visit us in Manchester. Life for all of us proceeded calmly towards the birth of his first child, whom Philip was adamant must be born in Ireland and raised as a Catholic. Despite my own disenchantment with Christian society in general, I welcomed his strong views on these issues since they indicated that he was taking his impending fatherhood seriously, and that he saw Ireland as his real home.

As I have already mentioned, Ireland always loomed large in Philip's life. References to the country are scattered throughout his music, even as far back as the debut Thin Lizzy album, which contains titles like 'The Friendly Ranger At Clontarf Castle' and 'Éire', and a song entitled 'Dublin' appeared on their first EP *New Day*. 'Fool's Gold' on the *Johnny The Fox* album refers to the Irish Famine, which was hardly even on people's radar at the time, though it was hotly debated later. Apart from those references to the Dublin that he knew from his own experiences, he developed a deep interest in Irish mythology, and that in turn fuelled his friendship with the artist Jim Fitzpatrick, whose highly elaborate and distinctive designs inspired by Celtic mythology adorned some of Thin Lizzy's most memorable album covers and posters.

Philip's view of Ireland, though it had a Republican tinge, was heroic and romantic rather than political. Like most of us, he loved the Irish community and felt at home among the Irish people, and he would have kept himself reasonably informed on the political turmoil in which his adopted country was engulfed, but I never really probed his private political leanings. What was not in doubt at all was his yearning for all of us to settle eventually in Ireland when his days as a rock star were over, preferably in the Dublin he wrote about in the eponymous song, or the city he lovingly portrayed in *Shades Of A Blue Orphanage*. Perhaps the first step towards realising that ambition came when, towards the end of her pregnancy, he persuaded Caroline to stay with his friends Gus and Maeve Curtis and family in their house, Glyde Cottage, on the magnificent Hill of Howth, which overlooks Dublin Bay.

Caroline, a non-Catholic, had already begun taking instruction in the Catholic faith from a priest attached to Richmond Parish Church in London where Philip often attended Sunday mass, and where they planned to get married – but, as far as I know, she did not formally convert. To describe Philip as deeply religious would be misleading – he certainly didn't take the teachings of the church seriously in relation to sex. But he was certainly God-fearing, no doubt on account of his Irish education which was far less liberal than a similar education today.

On his death-bed, in his final hours, Philip was to request the presence of a priest, and I don't think he could be accused of being hypocritical in doing so. At the worst, you could say that he was hedging his bets as he had always done.

Caroline had agreed that their children would be baptised into the Roman Catholic faith, and, in fairness to her, that promise was fulfilled after both Sarah and Cathleen were born. She also deferred to his desire to have the baby born in Ireland, and while she was staying in the Curtis household, he arranged for her to look around for a suitable permanent family home for them in Ireland. In a million years, I could not have envisaged the fluctuating periods of contentment and turmoil, from one extreme to its opposite, which that house would bring to all of us.

. . . .

"When you came into my life, you changed my world
My Sarah . . .
You are all I need to live
My love to you I'll always give."
– from 'Sarah' by Philip Lynott

With the birth of their first baby now imminent, Philip asked Caroline to attend an auction where she purchased a house, known as Glen Corr, for them. Located near Howth, a popular coastal resort north of Dublin, it cost them £130,000. It's a lovely house with a gorgeous, big garden, and is surrounded by protective trees and pleasant greenery, on a quiet road sandwiched between the Dublin-Howth railway line and the beach – and thus, on the face of it at least, it was the ideal place to set down roots as a family. Looking back, it was hardly fair of Philip to heap the responsibility for making the purchase on Caroline. She was only 19 years of age at the time, and she was pregnant and living in a strange culture but she took the challenge in her stride and got the result they wanted. And there is little doubt that it was a good purchase: in the long run it would certainly have been seen as a very good investment. And so they moved in for the final countdown to the birth of their first child.

When her time came, I collected Caroline at Glen Corr and drove her to Holles Street Maternity Hospital in central Dublin. En route, I stopped to furnish myself with a plentiful supply of foodstuffs, as I planned to stay with her in the hospital overnight, and then spoke by phone to Philip who had arranged to fly in from London.

He arrived in an excited rush directly from the airport, taking the stairs in the hospital two at a time, but his anxiety had not affected his playful sense of humour. As he leaped past a hospital worker scrubbing the stairs, she looked up and said, "Hey, don't I know you? Aren't you somebody famous?" When Philip replied, "Yes, I'm Red Hurley," she said, "That's right. How's it goin' Red?" How anyone could have mistaken a tall, thin, black man like Philip for Red Hurley, a decidedly white, red-haired, male cabaret singer, is beyond me, but it satisfied the woman, who probably got a buzz from meeting a celebrity no matter who she thought it was.

Reassured that the birth was not likely to occur for some hours, Philip insisted on treating me to dinner at Jury's Hotel, where we accidentally – I assume – bumped into Lizzy tour manager Frank Murray and the gang. Philip came in for a lot of slagging along the lines of, "Hey, Philip, I've just seen three camels and three wise men heading for Holles Street hospital!" (Christmas 1978 was only about a week away). The good-natured banter from his friends helped him to relax.

Prior to Caroline's move to Ireland, Philip had confidently boasted that he was going to have a son, hence the irreverent teasing – but his sheer delight was apparent when he came out of the ward lovingly hugging his first child, a beautiful healthy daughter. When Caroline passed in a wheelchair on her way back to her room, she burst into tears because she felt Philip was disappointed by her not giving him a son. But his adoring behaviour, then and later, was proof of his devotion to his daughter, and the next time together they were busily selecting a name, opting for Sarah Philomena in honour of his grandmother and mother respectively.

Money was not a problem for Philip by this stage. He owned the house in Kew in London, the Embassy House flat, also in London, Glen Corr in Dublin, and a little later he bought me White Horses, for my fiftieth birthday, the house situated not far from Glen Corr, and just a short distance from the Sutton cemetery where his body lies today. But to keep the money flowing in he had to work extremely hard.

Philip still shouldered the lion's share of the responsibilities for the band – a fact that is often overlooked – writing the songs, working on the production, dealing with the management and the record companies, tour planning and, since he was the lead vocalist and principal songwriter, he was also the preferred target for most media interviews.

So, despite the purchase of Glen Corr and his intention that the children would be reared in Ireland (not to mention his fervent wish that, in time, he might himself retire there too), Philip spent comparatively little time at the house because he had to maintain London as his business base. Objectively speaking, there were too few opportunities for him to get back to his wife and child. He visited as often as his work commitments allowed, I'm sure, but never as often as he, or we, would have wished.

While Caroline was pregnant with their second child, I suggested to Philip, half in jest, I suppose, but probably wholly in earnest as well, that it was time that he and Caroline got married. So, when plans for the wedding were announced, I was genuinely happy for them and had my dreams of Philip eventually settling down as a family man renewed.

I can still recall a newspaper article at the time in which the journalist wondered what Leslie Crowther thought of his public-school educated daughter marrying a black, illegitimate, Irish rock star. That angered me. I wondered why the question was being asked about what Leslie Crowther thought of the marriage, and not what Phyllis Lynott thought? All of the press speculation centred on Philip's suitability as a potential son-in-law, but never on how good a daughter-in-law Caroline might be. But I suppose that's just another version of the British media's snobbery about Irish people coming into play.

Leslie was also reported to have made an offensive remark about Caroline at a Variety Club lunch, allegedly quipping that when Philip asked for Caroline's hand in marriage, he replied, "Well you've had everything else" – a reference to the fact that they had already been sleeping together. In fairness, it was also reported that Leslie had phoned Philip to apologise but, given the nature of the publicity that celebrities constantly attract, there may be scant truth in either report.

Inevitably, there was considerable press publicity about the forthcoming wedding, with few reporters failing to remind their readers that they already had a 14-month old child, that Caroline had been fined £200 for possession of drugs, that she had posed nude for a girlie magazine, had worked as a topless waitress in Soho and was now pregnant with their second child. As if any of that was news worth bothering with, either way.

Like many mothers, I cried more than a few tears when I saw my son and his bride kneeling at the altar in the Saint Elizabeth of Portugal Church, in Richmond, on St Valentine's Day, 14th February 1980. Scott Gorham performed the role of Best Man. He and Philip were great friends and shared a similar sense of humour and attitudes about a lot of things. As with most marriage ceremonies, it was a happy, emotional occasion, and I was proud to have so many of my friends present. And yet, as is so often the case, silly things intrude. On the way out of the church after the ceremony, the pair of new shoes I had purchased especially for the big occasion were cutting into my feet and giving me a lot of grief. As I walked alongside Leslie Crowther, I confided to him how my shoes were killing me – and how I would love to just fling them off to relieve my feet. Leslie is genuinely witty, and he took my mind off my problem by cracking a couple of jokes, which made us both laugh.

There were many photographs taken that day which caught that moment, with the two of us looking so jolly together – and which thankfully do not reveal the mundane torment I was suffering over those new shoes! Another photograph, also taken that day, as we shall soon learn, was to play a role in my life that could never have crossed my mind at the time. But I digress.

Looking back, I can only think how stupid I was taking the risk of ruining the day for myself by wearing a pair of shoes I hadn't even broken in, and yet this kind of thing probably happens all the time to people who are trying to look as swish as they can for the big day. Maybe wedding invitations should carry a government health warning!

Later, at the reception which was held in the Kensington Hilton Hotel, I asked Leslie what he thought of the marriage, and he astonished me by his somewhat off-hand comment: "Oh, it's taken a while to get that one off my hands." I'm sure he meant it as a little joke to lighten the mood, but it bothered me all the same.

Philip and Caroline honeymooned in Rio de Janeiro, Brazil, while I took care of Sarah in the Kew house, content in my illusion that we would all live happily ever after.

. . . .

"This kid is going to wreck and ruin
I'm not quite sure of what I'm doing, you see
It all happened a little to soon . . .
I'm a little sick, unsure and unstable
But I'm fighting my way back."
– from 'Fighting My Way Back' by Philip Lynott

I really didn't know until quite late in the day that Philip had been using hard drugs – which I always believed to be a mug's game. The first serious inkling for most of us, outside of Philip's inner working circle and the hangers-on at his house in Kew Road, Richmond, had come via a telephone call from Caroline alerting me to the fact that there were likely to be stories all over the media concerning a drug raid by policemen from the British Special Patrol Group on their house, at 8am on 13th November 1979. Apparently, the police had gained admission to the house at dawn, convincingly disguised as gas board workers and accompanied by two sniffer dogs. They later claimed to have found two quantities of cocaine in a jacket beside Philip's bed, some cannabis in his Mercedes car, and a cannabis plant growing in the conservatory.

At Kingston Crown Court, Philip, who was represented by George

Carman QC, claimed he had given up drugs completely since Sarah's birth. One of the band's former roadies helpfully admitted that some of the drugs may have been his. I was particularly disturbed by the presence of cocaine, irrespective of who owned it, but my queries were dismissed by Philip's insistence that he and some others had tried cocaine once, merely as an experiment, and that the raid was a total over-reaction by the police to a non-existent problem. Whatever the truth, he got off – but, however you cut it, I knew that Philip was lucky to escape a jail sentence.

The police had, by this time, earned an unpleasant reputation for harassing rock stars for drug offences, and they were not above planting evidence in some cases, so it had become difficult to know what exactly was going on in such situations. High-profile stars like ex-Beatle Paul McCartney, Keith Richards of The Rolling Stones and Pete Townshend of The Who had openly admitted to having indulged in drugs of one kind or another, but there was no reason to assume that every single rock star was on drugs, and Philip's denial convinced me. The realisation that he might have developed a lethal drug habit did not hit me until it was far too late.

I suppose there must have been some inkling at the back of my mind that all was not well when he was busted a second time for possession of drugs at Dublin Airport, on his arrival on a flight into Ireland in May 1985. It was alleged that some incriminating needles were discovered in his suitcase. His explanation on this occasion was that he had grabbed the first suitcase he found when hastily packing for the flight, and that the one he had chosen must have belonged to one of the numerous people who passed in and out of his London home. He was cleared by Justice Gillian Hussey, vehemently denied any culpability, and I had no option but to believe my own son.

But looking back now, I have to admit that I was being gullible. It had surprised and disconcerted me somewhat that, after the court hearing, he dashed back to England without stopping off to visit any of us in Howth. I probably excused his hasty departure at the time by assuming he wanted to escape from a media pack ever-anxious for any scandal involving celebrities and drugs, or that he was embarrassed about the case among his Dublin friends – but I realise now, sadly, that I might have been simply trying very hard to avoid accepting the grim reality that was slowly creeping up on me and, lethally, on him.

My reaction was not helped by my own vast ignorance of the insidious nature of heavy drugs, and my misplaced, motherly confidence in Philip's ability to avoid doing anything so stupid as to use cocaine or heroin. I had constantly warned him about the dangers of addictive drugs in the early days of the band and, later, I recall him admitting on more than one occasion that he had more or less tried them all, was not interested in any of them, and implored me to stop bothering him about the subject. I never had any reason to say to him, "Philip, I do not believe you," and I am not sure whether I would have had the courage to do so either, even if the truth had started to crystallise for me.

I was later to learn that he was so determined to ensure that I would never discover the depth of his problem that he had warned all around him never to breathe a word about it to me, and when Philip laid down the law like that among his inner circle, he really intended it to be obeyed. All of the lads knew that I had not the slightest suspicion of the extent of his drug problem. He knew I would be horrified by such revelations and would probably go berserk. In the event, I never got the chance.

Even when he was living in Glen Corr, he lived a mainly night-time existence and probably did all his buying in the clubs while I was innocently asleep upstairs in the house, or over at White Horses. After a late one around the Dublin nightclubs, his friends would join him next day in the master bedroom where he watched a lot of television. I would always knock, out of respect, before entering the room, and that probably gave him sufficient time to cover up anything he did not wish me to see. In hindsight, deep down I probably did have an instinct, which I suppressed, that something sinister was going on and I have since had to live with the consequences of my own naïveté. It eventually dawned on me why, whenever we went on holidays with the children, he would arrange a suite for me and the two girls, while he had his own separate bedroom which he kept very private.

In 1984 he formed Grand Slam, his next band after Thin Lizzy. They were a loud hard rock band, playing music that was very different from the far more personal and funky material on his solo albums, *Solo In Soho*, which was released in 1980, and *The Philip Lynott Album*, which followed two years later. The group rehearsed in a Community Centre near my home in Howth for their 1984 tour, and I suspect that everybody must have been under the strictest orders not to let anything slip about his drug habits to me. There was a report that during a row, one of the musicians threatened to tell me everything, but nobody did, and I continued in ignorance. Here is one case that very definitely contradicts the proverb that "ignorance is bliss".

Of course, it has been relatively easy, particularly with the benefit of hindsight, to put forward the argument that some of those who claimed to be his friends should have had the courage to tell me – or if not that, at least to do something concrete to alert somebody about the deteriorating situation. Unfortunately, anyone who knew Philip well will vouch for the fact that he was a determined, strong-willed person, and that he would have been fiercely intolerant of the merest hint of disloyalty. Maybe that instinct to control is a characteristic of the drug-abuser, a reflexive means of protecting their habit.

It is possible to interpret the song 'Fight My Way Back' on the 1975 album *Fighting* as either a prophetic warning of troubles ahead, or as a track about a battle, even then, against drug-dependence. Other songs, like 'Opium Trail' and 'Sugar Blues' on the *Bad Reputation* (1977) album, have obvious drug inferences, as does 'Got To Give It Up' on *Black Rose* (1979). Philip himself claimed that the song 'Warriors' on the 1976 *Jailbreak* album was about heavy drug users, and he sometimes talked almost in tones of hero-worship about people like Jimi Hendrix and Duane Allman making conscious decisions to see how far they could go. But it is always difficult to know how much of that attitude was a contrived image for the media, exaggerated macho talk, or the truth.

Perhaps, in a way, it was a bit of all three.

I must also concede the possibility that others close to him may have suffered from the same drug dependence. Some may now have to rest uneasy at night with the uncomfortable thought that they might have contributed indirectly to his demise, by helping him to keep his addiction a secret from those who were not dependent, and who might have done something about it.

By some bizarre twist of logic, Philip did not want to tolerate having anyone else around him who might have a dependency on any drug, even alcohol. It seems outrageous now, and more than a little hypocritical too, but he asked me to inform the parents of Thin Lizzy guitarist, Brian Robertson (Robbo, as he was known), that their son had a drink problem. For all I know, Philip may have suspected that Brian had a drug problem too, and wanted to have that sorted out, but it defies logic that he would have been so concerned about another's addiction and done so little about his own.

On one occasion, I was told that he had actually struck a roadie called Studs in anger – with an umbrella of all things! – when he found traces of marijuana in the house, after he had been left to take care of it while Philip was away. Perhaps, since it was his band, he may have felt a responsibility to those involved, especially if they were younger, like Robbo and Studs. However, it's more likely that, in this instance, he was conscious that it could have been the police rather than himself, who discovered the drug traces.

I noticed during this time that Philip was putting on a lot of weight and that it did not suit him. I had always assumed that a serious drug habit would have had the opposite effect, that a user becomes haggard and gaunt, so I merely thought he was losing interest in his appearance. He had developed a particular fondness for Courvoisier brandy and had a tendency to drink quickly, but other than that, I noticed no tell-tale signs of strange behaviour. Admittedly, I would only see him for three or four days intervals and then he'd be gone, so I could not be aware of his every move or anything like it. You reach a point where your interest in the minutiae of someone else's career or their daily life diminishes, and you simply allow them to get on with it. And besides, there wasn't any great new ground being broken. After Lizzy split, Philip did some good solo work, but I couldn't tell you even now whether or not he did solo gigs after the demise of Thin Lizzy.

I recognised that he had to work to earn his livelihood, support his family and whatever musicians were in tow, and I had to give him the space to do so. No member of a rock band wants a mother, no matter how well-intentioned, fussing around all the time, interfering in things she knows little about. Through my experience in the hotel trade, I was accustomed to having a lot of people around me, but I was also used to allowing them the privacy they needed.

By this stage, I was in effect acting as the de facto housekeeper there, and I have to emphasise that there was never any evidence of hard drugs in Glen Corr, but at that time my attention was fully occupied taking care of Dennis, Philip, Sarah and any of the band members or their wives who stayed with us. Their lifestyle allowed them to sit up through the night, but I would be exhausted from cooking, cleaning, ironing and other daily household chores.

They may of course have indulged in all sorts of drugs behind my back, but Philip never once used a hard drug in my presence. Not once.

As it transpired, Caroline also had her own problems with drugs, but to give her credit, she had the discipline and determination to overcome them. I can recall a visit she and her mother made to Dublin, during which the three of us went for a meal in the King Sitric restaurant near Howth. During the meal, Caroline excused herself, and when she returned to our table she was noticeably drowsy, and Jean Crowther had to take her home. The explanation I was given subsequently was that her new contact lenses were hurting her eyes, and, in my innocence, I swallowed that story, but Jean was obviously less naïve than I was, and more aware of the darkening shadow on Philip and Caroline's lives. During a later visit to the Crowther house, she made a remark to me to the effect that she was taking care of hers and I should take care of mine. Although her words stirred something in me, I did not think to ask her to explain them more fully. I was too innocent or stupid or out of touch to comprehend that she was gently trying to alert me to a major problem. Had I responded to her comments, maybe subsequent events would have taken a much different turn. Unfortunately, all of our lives contain innumerable 'could haves' and 'if onlys'. But there are times when I think that this seems especially acute in my own case.

In due course, I learned that Caroline, who was fined by the courts for possession of cannabis, had courageously taken the crucial step of admitting her problems to her family and was receiving counselling for her alcohol and drug problems. I even accompanied her to a drug-counselling clinic in Bristol, without ever suspecting for a moment that Philip might need similar attention.

At the risk of sounding like a cracked record, when these developments led me again to ask relevant questions of Philip, he vehemently repeated his denials, told me that he wasn't using hard drugs, and since I had always believed he would never lie to me over a serious matter, I accepted his word completely. When I found him staying on in bed in Kew, I presumed he had either been out partying or working late in the studio. That those who knew the truth and seriousness of the situation conspired to avoid telling me, only added to my exclusion, and I don't mind saying that it took me a long time to forgive them. Equally, some will argue that it was not their responsibility to become informers since, after all, society has little time for those who tell tales behind another's back.

8. REMEMBERING PART 2 (NEW DAY)

Over the years, since I'd given my baby girl up for adoption, whenever I was in the deepest despair I'd think about trying to track her down and see how she was getting on. There is a longing inside that never dies, once you know that there is a child of yours out there. What does she look like? What colour is her hair now? How did she get on in school? Is she interested in music? What might she be doing for a living? At different stages the questions take on varying shades of nostalgia, concern and deep yearning. But I'd always have to remind myself that this was totally against the rules of adoption. Besides, I was also concerned to avoid doing anything that would upset either her or the parents who had kindly taken her into their home.

It is no secret that Philip's marriage began to fall asunder while he was living in Howth and so I had moved into the house permanently, minding the kids while he and Caroline dealt with their own demons. Philip had produced the single 'The Ballad of Sandy Denny' for an Irish band called Clann Éadair, and Snowy McLoughlin from the band was in the house doing some plumbing work for me. The phone rang and he kindly answered it and, as agreed with all calls from people I didn't know, told the woman on the phone that I was busy. But the caller persisted. "Tell her that it's Jeanette calling," she said. Snowy turned around to me and passed on the message word for word.

It was as if he had slapped me in the face. *Jeanette*. I felt the blood drain from my cheeks. My mouth went so dry I had to swallow hard. Once. Twice. Three times. My heart skittered. I went to the phone and lifted it to my ear. "Hello," I said. It was all I could say. A voice tentatively said, "Hello, my name is Jeanette and I think you could be my mother."

I was stunned. I swallowed hard again. I must have sounded strange because I felt it. "Yes, Jeanette," I said. I felt my voice cracking. "You could be my daughter. Tell me more." I was so excited to hear her voice as she spoke to me, and yet I was aware too that this was the kind of bombshell that can turn a life upside down. I was full of trepidation in particular because my Mammy was still alive at the time and she still knew nothing of my two other babies. It could have been a hoax too, someone who had found some old documents and decided that there was a story of some kind in it. I didn't know. But the more she spoke the better I knew that this was my daughter and that she had found me at last.

Overwhelmed with emotion, I started crying and she did too. It was strange and intense and lovely, all at the same time, that first phone call. But of course you never know how these things are going to go, and so there is an element of fear too that you might not get on, or that the fact that you gave a child up for adoption will be held against you. All of these thoughts were rushing through my head while I was on the phone. But I wanted to see her and she wanted to see me. I couldn't possibly think of rejecting her, now that she was reaching out to me. We agreed that we'd have to arrange to meet, to talk about things face to face.

Jeanette – or Philomena as she had been renamed by her adoptive parents – had read a story in a magazine that included a photograph taken at Philip's wedding. I was in the picture and my name was in the accompanying caption. Looking at the photograph, it hit her that I might be her mother, and that Philip's father Cecil could also be her father. But of course Cecil wasn't her dad at all. She had begun the process of tracking me down, eventually making the phone call to Glen Corr. I travelled over to meet her in Derby in England. She'd already sent some photographs across, so when I got off the train I immediately recognized her husband – and then her, and their three children. As her husband led the line, he got the first hug!

And then I saw Philomena coming towards me – and it was such an exciting moment, the truth is that I'll never forget it. I had known her only as a baby – and now, thirty years later we were looking at one another again for the first time. She had beautiful long hair, a gorgeous shade of brown, flowing down her back. She had a lovely soft face too, and I was struck straight away by how closely she resembled an aunt of mine who had died in Manchester. We hugged each other for so long I thought we'd never let go.

For years and years, I had cried so many tears over the loss of both Leslie and her, and now she and I were there together, on the platform, safe in one another's arms. It was like a miracle. No, it was a miracle, something I never would have thought possible. I'd suffered so much anguish about having to give her away, and she had suffered too. Nothing can ever totally take away that pain for either of us, but to have her back in my life was an undiluted joy.

They then brought me from the railway station back to their house, my head buzzing madly with all that was happening. I talked excitedly to her and her husband and the children, and we tried to find out as much as we could about each other, filling in the gaps in the missing thirty years since I'd last seen her. I can imagine someone else saying it was surreal, which I suppose it was. But there are probably better words to describe it if only I could find them.

The conversation flew on and on, but there was so much to tell, and I didn't know how to convey emotions that felt gigantic, like nothing I'd ever experienced before, a great stew of happiness, sadness, tenderness and love all rolled up into one massive sense of release. I think I know now what the phrase 'I was beside myself' actually means. It describes that unique place I found myself in. I was, it seemed, literally beside myself, watching what I was feeling and feeling it all at the same time.

There was so much to absorb. I remember her house had a fine piano and I discovered they made their own wine and jams. They had an organic garden too. I was also surprised to find that she was quite religious, one thing I can assure you she definitely did not inherit from her birth mother! But it was a joy to be there and to listen to her story and to discover a whole new branch of the family. And to know that they were – I really mean *are* – lovely and loving people.

From then on we met as often as we could and spoke regularly on the phone too, as we began to learn everything we could about each other.

Although in a way she was a stranger to me at first, I was pleased to find that I quickly began to like her as a person and was happy that she seemed to like me too. I was so relieved, as you can imagine, to hear her tell me that she did not resent being given up for adoption, and she was kind enough and intelligent enough to accept that I'd had no real choice.

We also finally got around to discussing the question: whom would we tell about her birth and adoption? But, unless you've experienced such a dilemma, and computed all of the various implications, it is hard to imagine how tricky a question that can be. There might be a temptation to rush out and broadcast the news, but it isn't as straightforward as it seems. I won't go into detail about all of the issues that were raised by one or other of us because they aren't that important all these years later, but the upshot was that, after much discussion, we made a solemn pact to tell only a select few. In particular, while I was hesitant about telling my mother, she wanted to keep it a secret from her adoptive parents.

I understood why. They had been brilliant and generous and loving to her. They had sheltered her, raised her as an only child, educated her and given her real love. She truly idolised them as kind and good people. Every situation is different, and there is no 'one size fits all' right move to make in circumstances like these, and she felt that it might hurt them to know that she had sought me out.

Her adoptive parents went to their graves not knowing that she had found me, and I am proud of her fortitude and selflessness in seeing that original determination through. Sometimes it really is better to say nothing. Of course, I told my partner Dennis, as I had always told him everything about my private life before I met him, and I told my sisters. But I never told Philip, which is something I am sad about. He never, ever knew that I'd found his sister again. I am always scratching around for things that might have made a difference to him, or that might have given him sufficient cause to turn back before the going got too rough – and this is one of those that niggles inside me. What if he had known about Philomena? But in all likelihood nothing would have prevented the downward spiral when it did happen. I know that there is no going back, but I'm afraid there is what we might call 'going back over' – and I still do it, though not as much as I used to.

When Philomena's adoptive parents died, they left her a beautiful big bungalow in Blackpool. Her father was a keen stamp collector and he left her a valuable collection too, which generated about £18,000 when she sold it – which is a lot of money for stamps! But what they gave her in terms of love was far more important.

Her parents didn't just give her immense happiness growing up, they gave her a great education and complete security. The family life Philomena described to me made me appreciate that there was a good outcome to what the welfare nun did, in arranging the adoption in the first place. Life can be complicated, and a lot can be irretrievably lost if a young woman feels pushed into handing over her baby without enough time to really think it through. Similarly, a child can imagine he or she was unloved and abandoned by a mother when that is, more often than not, so very far from the truth. There are times when an adoption just doesn't work, for any number of possible reasons. But Philomena was blessed and to the extent that she was, in the long run, I was too. I'd be lying if I tried to say that I had fully escaped the guilt and the shame that still haunted me over having given her away to begin with, as well as having to lie about her existence for so many years, but now those feelings have been tempered with the sheer unadulterated delight we both feel at our reunion. I am very fortunate and I know it. It was like a whole new chapter had, totally unexpectedly, been opened in my life.

9. BLOOD ON THE TRACKS

"But my home is where my heart is
And my heart is not at home."
– from 'Sweet Marie' by Philip Lynott

G iven the inexorable way in which time passes and the fact that so many turbulent events took place along the path, it can be hard to piece all the memories together. To what extent might I be blanking things out, my mind playing whatever tricks it has to, as I tried to come to terms with my grief over Philip's death? To what extent was I, at the time, deliberately not acknowledging something that I must have felt in my heart of hearts?

Sometimes I think, as his life fell prey to increasing turmoil, I must have been a fool not to have copped on to what he was going through. Other times I ask myself, how could I have known? And then I recall that as far back as 1980, Caroline was having problems with drugs to an extent that put her relationship with Philip under terrible strain. I remember the date because it was marked by one particularly traumatic and horribly unforgettable experience, which almost brought everyone's world collapsing in on top of them – including Philip's.

Shortly before Cathleen was born, in 1980, Thin Lizzy were scheduled to play a homecoming gig at the RDS Simmonscourt Extension in Dublin, as part of a massive world tour. It should have been one of those triumphant emotional occasions, which Thin Lizzy's Dublin bashes tended to inspire, and an excited group of family and friends met before the show at a nearby pub called The Horse Show House, in a decidedly celebratory mood. While the rest of the company prepared to enjoy themselves at a gig which was expected to be as exciting as any of Thin Lizzy's previous concerts in their home town, I noticed Caroline seemed out of sorts. Initially I put that down to her pregnancy, but I became a bit more concerned when she had not improved by the time we went backstage, to the caravan which was normally reserved for close friends of the band.

The gig went ahead, and we all went out to watch, but Caroline clearly wasn't in good shape. Inevitably, when Philip left the stage at the end of the main part of the show and was preparing for what would have been the first encore, he saw Caroline was in distress. I presume he was worried that she might be about to go into labour, and I remember him frantically clearing the way for her to get back to the caravan, and ordering someone to call for an ambulance to take her away for medical attention. Meanwhile, the crowd were still demanding an encore, with increasing restlessness.

In the middle of all this, someone in the entourage informed me that Caroline's condition was actually the result of having taken some drugs. Emotions were running high, and in the circumstances I probably behaved badly. I remember screaming at Philip that Caroline was not going into labour at all, and that she should return to the stage and do his encore for the fans. I really don't know what Philip knew about Caroline's drug use at the time, but I had the impression that he was enraged that, whatever the cause, she had been so careless as to get herself into this kind of predicament. On the other hand, maybe he knew everything, and what we saw was sheer blind anger at the fact that all this was going on in public. Either way, Philip's concern turned to fury, and he lashed angrily out at all the people around him. Back inside the hall, the crowd understandably continued to demand an encore – totally oblivious, naturally, to the intense drama that was taking place backstage. The ambulance was cancelled, and Philip himself accompanied Caroline home to Glen Corr.

My own immediate reaction was that Caroline had ruined an important Thin Lizzy gig in Philip's home-town, which was in itself inexcusable. Worse still, if she had used drugs while carrying his child, I felt that she could no longer love my son, despite what she might have said. On reflection, that was a one-sided judgement, but I was still unaware that Philip's own entanglement with serious drugs was even more lethal than his wife's.

Worse was to follow. Philip telephoned me later that night at White Horses in Howth, to tell me that Caroline had been taken to hospital in Dublin because he had slapped her. He claimed that she had threatened him with a poker. Naturally, I was horrified at this dreadful turn of events, but my first priority was to protect Philip. When I went into the hospital, I was probably close to a nervous breakdown. I accused her of ruining a very important night for Philip and of putting his position in jeopardy. I was probably blind to any right which might have been on her side, and so I am not proud of my own reaction, which should probably have been more sympathetic to someone who was clearly addicted. But she didn't help when she admitted quite openly that she had peed in her clothes to convince Philip her waters had broken. I know that this was just to get out of a violent confrontation, but she really screwed his brain that night, whatever was going on between them.

I was also concerned in case she might tell the doctors that her bruises had resulted from Philip being violent with her. Imagine how that would have looked in the press – a famous, rich rock star beating his pregnant wife after his band's homecoming gig? At the time, that seemed to matter more than anything else, so I reminded her of the things I knew about her, and threatened to reveal all if she did anything to ruin Philip's reputation. I know now that this was deplorable behaviour, and that I was wrong – but the situation was out of control, and I wanted to put some kind of brake on it so that at least no further damage could be done.

On the spot, Caroline agreed to stay silent about the incident, although she did later tell some relatives of mine that he had beaten her. I think most people, knowing the truth of their situation, would have understood that any person can only take so much of that sort of behaviour from someone who purports to love him or her. On the other hand, I cannot condone any man, son of mine or not, being violent to a woman at any time, never mind during pregnancy. What he did was wrong in every way, and it cannot be justified by reference to the emotional turmoil they were going through.

It wasn't just about drugs either. I don't know how the dates relate, but Caroline later confessed to me that her real love was an extremely handsome man who used to work as a lifeguard on the beach near Howth and who was a frequent visitor to Glen Corr. Caroline admitted that she was in love with this man for quite some time, and I believe that their friendship continued after Philip died. I cannot say if they ever actually had an affair. He has personally denied to me that there was ever any sexual relationship between him and Caroline.

Philip and Caroline's second child, Cathleen Elizabeth Lynott, was safely born on 29th July 1980, like Sarah, in Holles Street Hospital in Dublin. But shortly after the child's birth, Caroline had another serious bust-up with Philip and I took her to White Horses where she stayed with me until they both cooled off. There was little I could do to prevent the deterioration of their marriage, particularly when I assumed there must be fault on both sides. In fact, I was conscious that any additional interference from me might only worsen their difficulties, and I was particularly concerned that two young children, innocent bystanders in all of this, should be protected from any side-effects of their parents' problems.

It was also important for me to retain Philip's trust, and – sympathetic as I might have been to Caroline as a woman – I couldn't do anything to undermine or erode that. By 1980, Philip and I had gone into business together. Having missed out on purchasing our first choice, the nearby Royal Howth Hotel, we bought the Asgard Hotel overlooking the bay in Howth for £235,000. We needed to be close to make this venture work, and the domestic havoc wasn't helping at all.

The decision to buy the Asgard came about after some typical manipulation on Philip's part. While I was still in Manchester, he called me in a panic about a kitten that he had bought for Sarah – and which had apparently been attacked by a rat. A confirmed animal lover, Philip had even named his publishing company Pippin The Friendly Ranger after a kitten. He was concerned that any injury to the kitten might upset little Sarah, so I rushed to Glen Corr, only for the kitten to die in my arms. Caroline and I buried it in the garden.

Why I would be needed for such a straightforward domestic incident is hard to explain. In truth, Philip would persuade me to come over to Howth on the most spurious grounds, mainly I think because he wanted me to look after Caroline, who was, after all, living in a different country than she'd grown up in, away from her own family and personal friends, and was married to a man whose work took him away from the family home for long periods. At the very least, it's a recipe for loneliness, and possibly a degree of inevitable heartache. During one such visit, Philip bought me White Horses, another fine house in Howth, and he was obviously convinced that since I had managed a successful hotel in Manchester, I could do likewise in Dublin.

Initially, Graham Cohen and Dennis looked after our affairs in Manchester while I was engrossed in sorting out the arrangements for taking over the Asgard. Eventually we decided to sell the operation in Manchester. We wanted to make our future in Dublin, so Dennis moved over to Howth. We worked incredibly hard, day and night, and in a fairly short time managed to establish the hotel as a lively business, and a popular out-of-town spot for Dubliners. In many ways, I was sad to leave The Clifton Grange Hotel with all its memories, but I was pleased to learn that it was subsequently turned into an old person's home. Maybe I can head back there in a few years!

Whenever he paid a visit to Dublin, no matter how fleeting, Philip spent a good bit of his time at the Asgard, and his regular presence undoubtedly provided a boost for the image of the hotel as we tried to build up its reputation. On one occasion, some guests at a wedding reception spotted him and started making a fuss, so following much persuasion from me, he agreed to dance with the bride. He found such occasions a little demanding and more than a little embarrassing. He often admitted his admiration for Brian Downey's ability, at the end of a tour, to set off on a fishing expedition with his son. He was aware of his own inability to sit and relax for any lengthy period, but the fact that Philip carried the responsibility for running the band's affairs, and subsequently his own, contributed to him burning himself out.

Sometimes, perhaps when he thought everything was going smoothly and he could finally afford to take a break, some fresh problem would arise. Indeed, Thin Lizzy's history is littered with dramatic crises, including Eric Bell's early departure, Brian Robertson's hand injury, Gary Moore's surprise exit during an American tour, Philip's ear problems and the shooting incident – not to mention all the normal personal conflicts that arise when people have to spend so much of their time in close proximity. Philip has been described as an approachable genius who demanded one thousand per cent from everybody in his organisation, including himself, and who would get into a fierce temper if anything went awry. But that kind of intensity, while it may bring success, sometimes also carries a price with it. In fairness to Caroline, I think you have to view all the problems which afflicted their marriage in that light. There are worse fates, I know – but it isn't easy living with a rock star.

While Philip departed on yet one more protracted tour, this time to Australia, Caroline, Sarah and Cathleen continued living in Glen Corr. At the time, Graham Cohen was managing the Asgard, and he had agreed to take on the added responsibility of looking after Philip's family when asked to do so by Philip himself – so he moved into the house to keep a watchful eye on things and to provide any back-up that Caroline might need.

Each night, we would finish in the Asgard at about 2.30 a.m. after enjoying our usual drink with the staff. On our way to our own house at White Horses, Dennis and I would lodge the day's takings in the bank's night-safe and drop Graham at Glen Corr.

This routine was followed on numerous occasions without anything untoward happening. So we were more than surprised to arrive at Glen Corr at about 3 a.m. on one particular morning to find all the lights on in the house and rock music blaring out into the night air – a most unusual situation, especially as we had no knowledge that a party of any kind had been planned. Thinking that perhaps Philip had arrived home unexpectedly, and that a celebration might be in progress, Graham and I ran into the house only to be met by an astonishing sight. The house was full of kids of both sexes, in their teens, drinking, kissing, partying and lying around everywhere. And there was absolutely no sign of Philip.

My first concern was for Sarah and Cathleen, and I made straight for the nursery where I found Sarah, who was then about four, and Cathleen a year younger, completely unattended. Thankfully, they were sleeping like angels, oblivious to the mayhem going on around them. When I found the door to Philip and Caroline's bedroom ajar, I called out his name, but getting no answer, I pushed it open slightly and went in, as I had done many times before.

Noticing two people in the bed, I went past Caroline, towards two male feet protruding at the other side. Assuming they were Philip's, I started playfully tickling them. But when I pulled the covers back, instead of finding Philip I discovered a total stranger in bed with my son's wife, who was by now swearing at having been caught red-handed and red-faced in an adulterous situation by her own mother-in-law.

Disgusted, and in a raging fury, I rushed from the bedroom past an astonished Graham and towards the kitchen in search of a weapon to use on the man who was occupying my son's marriage bed. I probably would have done something violent if I'd got the chance – and doubtless lived to regret it. Fortunately, Graham wrestled the knife from my hand. Meanwhile, the guy made his escape through the bedroom window and was spotted by Dennis, who had stayed in the car outside the gate waiting for my return, running up the drive struggling to put his trousers on.

When I endeavoured to clear the house of the kids who were partying away, they protested that they couldn't go home because they had told their parents they were going to an all-night party. Had the situation not been so serious, it would have seemed like a scene from a West End farce.

I spent the next day working at the Asgard and trying to come to terms with the situation. I refused to respond to several attempts by Caroline to reach me by telephone. Her calls continued the following day and, eventually, I reluctantly agreed to meet her – though I really had no idea what was the right thing for me to do in the circumstances. I went to Glen Corr, and when I sat down in an armchair to talk, she sank down on her knees, threw her arms around me and, with her body racked with sobs, begged me not to tell Philip. She kept repeating how much she truly loved him and how sorry she was to have been unfaithful.

I asked her how did she think Philip would react if he knew what I had discovered. She said: "He'd kill me." That was what the voice inside my own head had also been saying, over and over. I knew that *he'd* take it terribly badly and that he might do something he'd regret forever. With that in mind, I told her that I had no intention of reporting her treacherous behaviour to him – because in my eyes she was not worth the possibility that he might end up in prison.

At this, she hugged me and thanked me. With considerable difficulty, and more than a little guilt at the duplicity involved, I managed to avoid telling Philip anything of the incident until much later. But it is another of those incidents that revolves in my mind: I have asked myself over and over whether telling him the whole story sooner might have brought him abruptly to his senses, and, as a result, altered the course of his life – and who knows, perhaps even his death.

Nor was that an isolated example of strange conduct on Caroline's part while she was living in Glen Corr. One Christmas Eve, I was at White Horses when Philip telephoned me from Glen Corr inviting Dennis and me over for a chat and a Christmas drink. But no sooner had we arrived at the house than Caroline began begging me to accompany her for a Christmas drink in the Cock Tavern, a local pub. When I declined, she persisted, arguing that Philip would let her go if I agreed to go with her. Then when one of our neighbours arrived, and Caroline redoubled her efforts – I finally asked Philip if he would have any objection to Caroline, her friend and I going out for a drink. Philip said he didn't mind, as he could then have a chat with Dennis and amuse the children.

In the crowded pub, Caroline bought me a drink and I relaxed, listening to the buzz of conversation and the strains of 'Silent Night'. My son was home for Christmas, delighted to be reunited with his children, and my own relationship with Dennis was going very nicely. I suppose I was feeling reasonably content in the way that a nice Christmas Eve can induce. After a while, however, I began to notice that Caroline and her friend had gone missing. When they returned, after what was a long and frustrating wait, they told me that they had visited some other pubs and I assumed they were searching for somebody. After one final drink, I persuaded Caroline, who had driven us there in a Saab Turbo that Philip had recently bought for her, to take me back to Dennis and Philip. But, as we approached the turn across the railway line towards Glen Corr, I was alarmed to find Caroline driving on past the turning and heading further away from the house towards town. They answered my protests by convincing me that they were not going very far, and they would get me home shortly.

Caroline drove us to the north Dublin suburb of Bayside, where she abruptly stopped the car. She left the radio playing while she and her friend went off, leaving me alone and bewildered in a neighbourhood I didn't know, full of people streaming home after their night's entertainment and last-minute Christmas shopping. I struggled frantically to get out of the back seat of the two-door car and eventually managed it, hurrying off in the direction of the flats towards which I had seen them go.

I was completely at a loss to know what was going on, and why I was being treated in such a contemptuous way. I was worried sick, but also I have to admit, in a furious temper. I called out for them at each door in turn, no doubt scaring the wits out of the occupants at the same time, until I finally heard Caroline and her friend running back to the car. When I demanded that Caroline tell me what the hell was going on, I discovered she had gone to the house of the same man (a drug dealer whose name was known to me and who since fled to Belgium) with whom I had found her in bed months previously. Presumably she wanted something urgently from him, though I never found out what the real purpose of the visit was. When we arrived back outside Glen Corr, she again pleaded with me not to tell Philip.

Inside the house, I found him, the picture of happiness with his daughters, chatting with Dennis and enjoying a drink in front of a big cosy fire while a glowing Christmas tree lit up the room. He was totally oblivious to what his wife had been up to behind his back. The contradiction between her subterfuge and his innocent happiness brought tears of anger and sadness to my eyes, and I had to retire quickly to the bathroom to compose myself – but I said nothing, rather than risk ruining Christmas for Philip, and in particular for the children.

On another occasion, while Philip was away, the unexpected appearance of a young baby and a Rottweiler pup in Glen Corr gave me further reason to wonder what the hell was going on in Caroline's head. I pointed out to her that the pup might be dangerous to have around young children, and besides, that the baby's non-stop screaming was upsetting her own children. She told me that the baby and the dog belonged to a woman who was "an initiated witch" who had gone to Spain, leaving them in her care.

I thought this was preposterous, and ordered her to pack both baby and dog into her car and find someone else to mind them. That might make me sound like an awful harridan. After all, she was old enough to make decisions for herself. But I sensed that there was something extremely odd about the situation. Caroline gave me the impression that the witch had some kind of strange hold over her, although I failed to persuade her to tell me what it might have been. I still don't know the full truth behind that somewhat bizarre relationship.

On another occasion, a two-seater couch which had been purchased as part of the furniture with the house disappeared quite suddenly, and Caroline said she had given it to the witch. My own reaction was to wonder what else might have been given away to this mystery woman and why did Caroline seem to be in thrall to her.

All of these events made me ponder what state Philip and Caroline's marriage was in, but I also knew that marriages can overcome the most extraordinary difficulties. While things were clearly awry, there was no reason to think that a breakdown was inevitable, if both people involved resolved to behave maturely and lovingly. But I cannot claim that Philip himself was any more capable of knowing what that meant than Caroline was at the time. It would be hypocritical of me to pretend that he was not guilty of similar infidelities, and I was not naïve enough to believe that Philip would ignore the endless stream of young women who inexplicably make themselves available to celebrities. But at no stage was I aware of any serious extra-marital relationship he might have enjoyed

I suppose that's the difference when someone is on the road – at least they're unlikely to become involved in relationships that cross over into what we call love. There were, however, many times when I called to the house in Kew to find some young attractive girl staying there under unusual circumstances. If I enquired about her presence, I would be informed that she was a friend of someone else. Even if I suspected he was lying to me, I probably accepted it as the way of the world in those changing times. But I didn't like it.

If personal relationships in the family were beginning to fragment badly, so too were business arrangements. Not that there was anything that could have been done to prevent the next calamity. In the early hours of an August Bank Holiday morning in 1982, the Asgard Hotel was burned down. At almost that precise moment, Philip was arriving back at Glen Corr from a tour. The blaze happened only about eight months after we bought the Asgard, and just as the business was beginning to thrive. Firemen fighting the flames were hampered by a loss of water pressure because of a simultaneous gorse fire on nearby Howth Head, and there was nothing they could do to prevent the hotel's virtual annihilation.

When we arrived at the blazing building, Philip put his arm around me and said, "Never mind, Ma, I'll buy you another one!" But the truth is that we both lost a lot of money on account of that fire. Bono later told me that his father Bobby had moved into the block of flats they built on the site. It's strange how things so often come full circle in a small city like Dublin that in many ways has all the characteristics of a village.

Between all of the stresses and strains, I have to say that it came as no great shock to me when Philip telephoned from London to tell me that Caroline had left him and taken the kids with her to a house in Corston, near her parents' home in Bath. He then persuaded me to move full-time into Glen Corr. He was obviously worried about his dog, Gnasher, named after Dennis The Menace's dog in *The Beano*, a very popular weekly comic for children – 'children of all ages', I suppose – in the 1960s and 70s. So after we moved into Glen Corr, I rented out White Horses.

But when I heard that Caroline was seeking a separation on the grounds of his alleged adultery, I blew my top. At that stage, I had no option but to tell Philip about the night I discovered her in his bed, in his own house, with another man, and he nearly collapsed. I had to apologise for keeping that incident, and others, a secret from him. Whatever else Philip thought of her and any affairs he might have suspected her of having, surely he never could have imagined that his own mother would find his wife in his house and in his bed with another man? But I suppose he had his own ghosts that were better left undisturbed, and from everyone's point of view, it was best not to become embroiled in a bitter courtroom battle.

The separation hearing was a quiet event and, in due course, a court order was issued stipulating that Sarah and Cathleen could spend time with Philip, provided I was present at all times during their visits. Caroline knew I loved them and that the children and I got on very well together. As a result, I flew over nearly every fortnight to London to see the girls, and to be present when Caroline brought them to meet Philip.

There were no overt signs of any drug-related health problems in his life, although I now know that Caroline was aware of the full extent of Philip's drug problem. In fairness to her, maybe that was the real reason for the separation, because if there's one thing that someone who is attempting to come to terms with a drug problem *doesn't* need, it's someone who's still using and flaunting the stuff in front of them. I suspect that was at least an element in Caroline's decision to leave him.

The girls generally stayed with Caroline in her own house in Bath during this time, and despite the break-up, she remained on cordial terms with both Philip and me. In fact, they were on friendlier terms now than in the period immediately prior to the split, a situation that was doubtlessly influenced by Caroline's positive efforts at cleaning up her own drug problem. Most times, she would drop the girls off at the Kew house, but I often went in a chauffeur-driven car to Bath to collect them.

Philip worshipped his two girls, so not having easy access to them was a big wrench for him. He would try not to miss being in Dublin for Saint Patrick's Day or Easter, and he would fly over with the girls to stay with me for those important occasions, but always with Caroline's approval. As far as I could ascertain, Caroline was always happy to have me there with Philip and the girls, because she was to one degree or another pre-occupied with her own personal problems at the time. She knew he loved them and she knew I would make a fuss of them and that they would return home to her in a very happy mood. That arrangement continued for the remaining years of his life, with me always present at their get-togethers, whether in Glen Corr or in Kew.

Philip and Caroline often referred to their break-up as a trial separation, and she would sometimes spend the week with her mother and stay with Philip at weekends. I often found them in Kew sitting together on a settee with her head in his lap, so there were obviously times when they might have made a real attempt to rescue the marriage. I was often confused by their contradictory behaviour and, in a strange way, it is of some consolation to me that they never actually divorced, a step which has such a dreadful finality about it.

Now that I can look back objectively, I think Caroline may have been trying to encourage him to come off the drugs, and I thank her for that. But with so many creeps hanging around him, and his own constant denials, it was virtually impossible. He never pushed them into the background sufficiently to make the space for himself to go clean which, I have to be honest, she had successfully created for herself by leaving him. In fairness, too, it would probably not have been practical for them to resume their marriage relationship while he was still using drugs and she was battling to stay off them, especially with the two girls to consider. So, much as I loved Philip, and initially felt angry at the way in which she left him, in the end I have to recognise that it was probably the right decision – for her, at least.

When you arrived at Kew, you rang a bell beside the large electric gates. One day, having dropped by unexpectedly, I spotted a blonde girl on the premises. Yet again, Philip told me that she was with one of the other chaps, although by this stage I was too disillusioned to be taken in. I assumed that Philip had normal, healthy, male sexual appetites, but he would generally try to prevent me from knowing about specific relationships, and therefore I had no real notion as to how he satisfied his carnal urges. I figured this one fell into that category, and no mistake. Had he still been with Caroline, I would almost certainly have given him an earful over it, but his marriage was to all intents and purposes over, and he was a free man in my eyes.

But it was still a pretty uncomfortable situation. While I was in his bedroom updating him on the news from Dublin, we caught this dreadful, greasy smell from the kitchen where the girl was attempting to cook Philip's breakfast. The smell was so bad that I had to go out into the back garden for some fresh air. She was undaunted and, despite the smell, took this dreadful mess of food up to him. I don't know about him, but I'd have gagged on it. When I again asked who this young women was, he just grinned sheepishly, and I got the picture. So there is no question in my mind that he was quite capable of lying to me during that period, particularly if he was embarrassed about something.

That house in Kew was a lovely place and I loved staying there. It was situated on about half an acre of land close to the famous Kew Botanical Gardens, and it was worth about £250,000 even at that time. While in retrospect, it is obvious that Philip was spending a lot of money on hard drugs, it never affected the pleasant atmosphere of the house – nor did it seem to create any financial problems for him. I had never quizzed him about his financial or property dealings anyway. But when he became famous first, he loved being able to give us all a good time and since 1976, when the *Jailbreak* album was a huge hit – it went to No.10 in the British charts and was a Top 20 hit in America, going on to sell nearly two million copies – he'd been in clover. 'The Boys Are Back In Town' hit the Top 10 in the UK and reached No.12 in the US, so Thin Lizzy had undoubtedly generated a lot of money.

When the band split up, the gravy train might have stopped rolling, and Philip was certainly hurt and frustrated when he couldn't get a deal for Grand Slam, the band he attempted to launch in the '80s. At the same time, his solo career had already seen him enjoy hit singles with 'Yellow Pearl', which was used for a long time as the signature tune of the BBC television programme *Top Of The Pops*, and 'King's Call', his tribute to Elvis Presley. There were even constant rumours of an imminent and potentially lucrative Thin Lizzy re-union for both an album and a world tour – in fact when you think about it, they could probably have re-grouped to go on to even greater things after a protracted sabbatical, if more momentous events hadn't overtaken them.

Since the band had enjoyed over a dozen hits in the British album charts and over twenty hit singles in Britain, apart from other successes around the world, many observers may have assumed that there was a bottomless pit of money. But if you get used to spending hard, money doesn't last forever or anything like it. Besides, the Thin Lizzy operation had been expensive to run. The uninitiated tend to overlook the fact that offices, staff and countless other expenses have to be met, and the money has to come from somewhere. But it was the general belief among those who knew him, myself included, that he still had a plentiful supply of money, and that he could easily afford to continue the lifestyle to which he had become accustomed – and perhaps, in time, find another woman with whom to build a permanent relationship and a happy home life. As far as I was concerned, he was still a young man with lots to give to the world and – potentially, at least – a long, rewarding life ahead of him.

Christmas has always been one of my favourite times of year. When you have been as poor as I had been in the early years of my life, there is an added quality to the pleasures and indulgences of the festive season, so long as you're in a position to enjoy them. I love everything about Christmas: the food, the songs, the reunions, the decorations and, most of all, the glowing, expectant faces of children as they unwrap their presents.

So Christmas 1985 should have been among the happiest of my life. Certainly, in the weeks leading up to it, I was as excited as a little girl, busily buying gifts for everybody and making plans for the holiday revelry. Little did I know that I was only days away from the worst nightmare imaginable.

Despite their separation, Philip and Caroline had agreed that they would spend every Christmas together with the girls. But with less than a fortnight to go before what would turn out to be Philip's last Christmas on earth, Caroline telephoned me to say that she would prefer not to join us this year in Kew. She asked me to persuade Philip and the two girls to go over to Dublin to Glen Corr instead.

I explained that Philip had already decided to spend only the New Year in Dublin, and that he was unlikely to be talked into a change of plan. I agreed to try to bring him round if I could, but it was to no avail, so I flew to London about a week before Christmas, knowing that Caroline would not be joining us. I knew that it would be a somewhat less festive occasion for everyone as a result – but there was no option but to get on with it. Or at least that's what I thought.

When I arrived at the Kew house, I was impressed by the sight through the front window of a beautifully-lit Christmas tree and a life-size cardboard cut-out of Philip standing beside it. Philip was in his underpants when he opened the door to greet me. As it was now mid-afternoon, he apologised for the fact that he hadn't got dressed yet. I followed him upstairs as he returned to his bed. We discussed a few minor matters and he told me that Big Charlie, as we always called Charlie McLennan, one of Philip's most trusted and loyal minders, would be joining us for the holiday, because he had recently split with the woman he had lived with for several years. He also asked me to collect Sarah and Cathleen from Bath.

I was struck immediately by how untidy his room was, cluttered with a mess of take-away food packages, empty bottles and general litter. Worse, Philip looked and sounded decidedly unhealthy, with his excessive weight, cloudy eyes, clogged nasal passages, and the sigh and rasp of his breathing. God, I know now that I should have sensed just how bad his physical condition was, but you always want to believe that everything will be OK, and I did.

When I asked why he was in bed so late in the day, he blamed a hangover from the office party the night before. I accepted this, and assumed that it also explained his sickly appearance. And he brightened up considerably when he showed me a box of small toys he had bought to put in the girls' Christmas stockings. In what was a remarkable and, in retrospect, moving reversion to his childhood, we amused ourselves for a time playing with them on the floor.

When I asked him what he would like from me for his main Christmas present, apart from the customary shirt and underpants, he described an elaborate tree-like lamp he had spotted somewhere. He pointed to a place in the room where he thought it would fit perfectly, but when he told me it would cost £330, I laughed and told him I was not paying that for a lamp. I said I would spend up to £30. He said, "OK, you're on," and we laughed heartily at the whole idea of it, in the way we often did in each other's company.

Later, I went on a shopping expedition into nearby Richmond, during which I purchased some spectacles with tinted lenses for myself. When I came back, Philip announced that the spectacles would be his present for me. I will always treasure them as his last gift to me.

On answering a ring at the door, I found a man with two large boxes, which I signed for. One of them contained a lamp – which turned out to be exactly the type that Philip had talked me into getting him for Christmas. We laughed again about the way he had wound me up. He then showed me some beautiful wrapping paper featuring Marilyn Monroe, and asked me to help him to wrap his presents.

Philip on the beach in Sutton, Dublin, with his dog Gnasher.

B-B-B-B-B-B-BABY! Lizzy take Sydney by storm...

Ballad of a thin man: On tour with Graham Parker in the US.

(Above): What's on the menu?
(Below): The axe-man cometh.

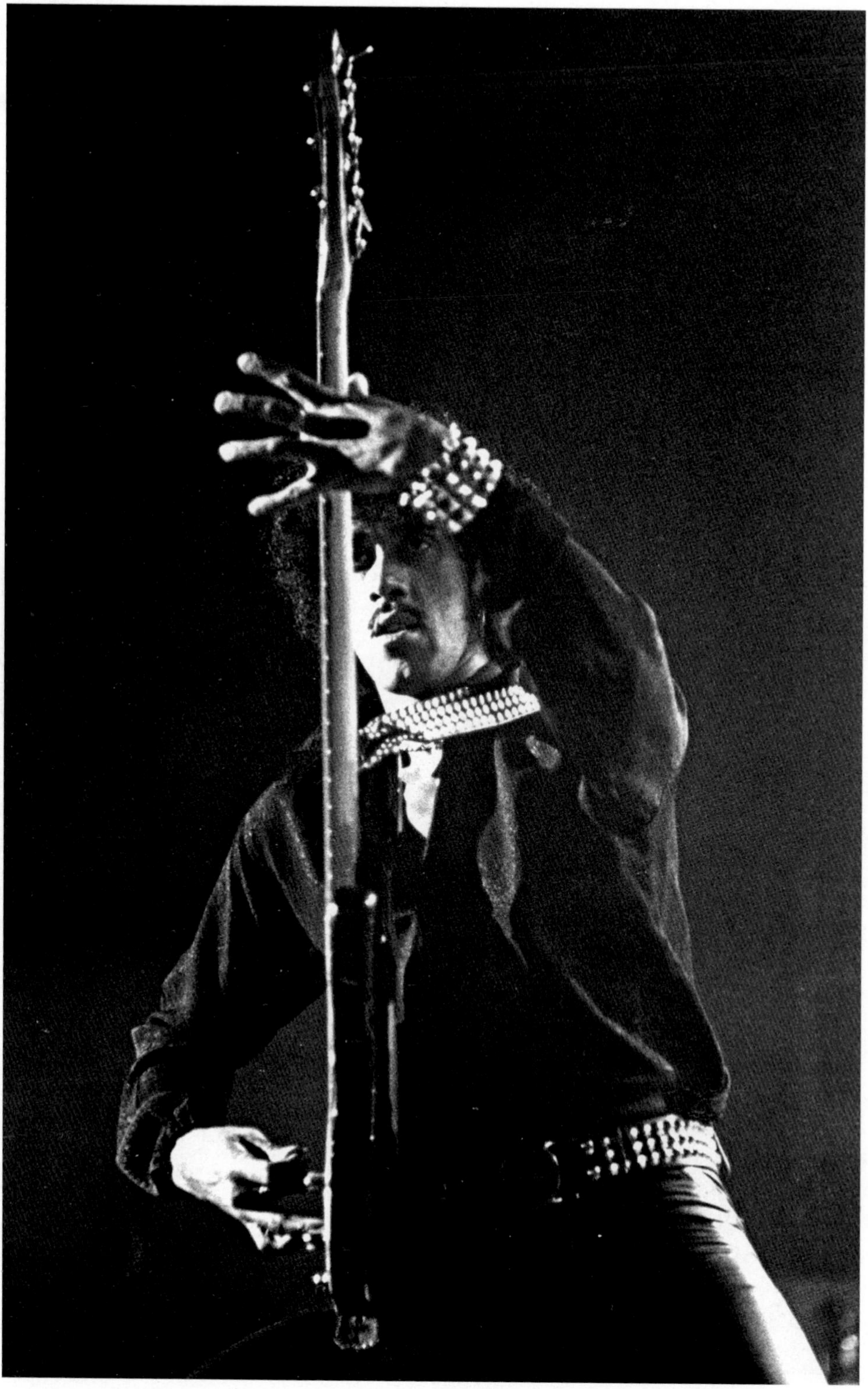

ANDRE CSILLAG

Opposite page: With these hands: Live portrait by Andre Csillag.
This page: *(top left)*: Two wheels good; *(right)*: flying high with Brian May of Queen;
(below): the classic Lizzy line-up in live action.

Everybody's crazy 'bout a sharp-dressed man: Philip in his pomp.

(Above): Artist at work; and *(below):* at play.

Philip Lynott at work in the studio. Opposite page: In unlikely promo mode...

GRAHAM KEOGH

(*Above*): Philomena with Jon Bon Jovi, holding a copy of the first edition of *My Boy*.
(Below) At the unveiling of the statue of Philip Lynott in 2005: (front, left to right) Eric Bell, the late Gary Moore, Brian Downey and Scott Gorham; (rear) Darren Wharton, Philomena and Brian Robertson.
Opposite page: (*top left*): Philomena and her son, Leslie; (*right*): with her daughter Philomena, and (*below*): Leslie and the younger Philomena.

Philip solo: Fine and dandy.

Holiday time...

Live and dangerous: Live portrait by Colm Henry.

Not long afterwards, Jimmy Bain, from the rock band Rainbow and a close friend of Brian Robertson, arrived to stay over. He had apparently separated from his wife, Lady Sophie, daughter of the Marquis of Bute. Philip really liked their daughter, Samantha, who was a perfect playmate for Sarah and Cathleen, and so they had become buddies. Jimmy was eager to show off his new overcoat and knee-high boots, which I figured were part of an obvious attempt to dress like Philip, but because he was small they frankly looked ridiculous on him. Out of politeness, and not wishing to deflate his pleasure at his new purchases, I refrained from making any discouraging comment. I immediately regretted not telling him precisely what I thought of his ludicrous get-up. When Philip called down the stairs for him to come up, Bain said to me, with real vehemence: "He thinks I'm his fucking butler." I was staggered at the idea of a man who was about to enjoy another man's generous hospitality over the Christmas period coming out with such language in front of his host's mother. I left the room in disgust, but it brought to mind a recent warning from my brother Peter.

Having visited London, Peter told me that I ought to start asking questions about the strange goings-on at the Kew house. "There's something wrong with Philip. He's not right and I don't like it," had been his very words, but I discovered too late that they had carried more significance than I imagined. The awful truth is that this was the only hint I ever had from anyone else that Philip's lifestyle had become a real worry. Many of his so-called friends knew the situation was serious, yet they all kept it quiet, and in that sense I think some of them at least can be accused of complicity in his death.

So I left to collect the girls from Bath. I don't know who had screwed up the arrangements, but when I got there Caroline told me that they had both been given parts in a nativity play in the local church hall. I agreed to stop overnight with them and enjoyed a very pleasant evening, watching my grandchildren innocently perform in a nice play before an audience that included both their grannies, their grandfather Leslie, and Caroline. In retrospect, it was like another world from the one I'd just left at Kew.

Arriving back at the Kew house on the following day, the girls were immediately disappointed to notice the Christmas tree wasn't lit, and I thought that was odd. It turned out to be a bizarre omen. When Philip answered the door in his dressing gown, I again thought this was weird, but I dismissed my concern on the basis that a lot of Philip's work was done at night, at gigs or in the studio, and that his lifestyle was utterly different from mine. Showbiz people are generally night people – or that was how I subliminally rationalised the situation.

I was even further perturbed, however, to discover the offensive Jimmy Bain wrapping his own presents using Philip's nice Marilyn Monroe paper. It was only a small thing, but it got to me. "What a cheap bastard you are," I thought to myself. "You accept a man's hospitality, make insulting remarks about him in front of his mother and you could not even buy your own wrapping paper." It disgusted me so much I could not bring myself to speak to him, so I avoided communicating with him from then on, except for the occasional dirty look.

Meanwhile, Philip and the girls were sitting on his bed watching a video he had purchased especially for them. They had great fun together, but still, I was becoming increasingly concerned by the fact that Philip showed few signs of even bothering to get up. At my suggestion, he arranged for us to go The Barbican to see a pantomime starring Frances Tomelty whom I knew from a film she had shot at The Biz and who had been married to Sting. We were joined by a son of Rolling Stone Ron Wood – apparently Philip had got to know the boy very well, because his mother was friendly with Brian Robertson.

The following day, Philip was still unable to get up. He told me that he was expecting a man to call, and asked me to give the caller a cheque, which he had hidden under a garden gnome outside the front door. This was so suspicious, that I must admit I suspected it might be payment for a consignment of drugs. When the man called, I recognised him immediately as a certain unsavoury Mr. Kelly, who had been involved with Philip before.

I asked him straight out if he worked for Philip, and when he didn't answer I tore up the cheque in anger right before his eyes and threatened to telephone the police as he ran off in fright. But not even that incident had brought home to me the depths to which my son had sunk in his addiction to drugs.

While I was downstairs taking a telephone message, I suddenly noticed water dripping from the ceiling. Assuming there must be a pipe leaking, I dashed upstairs. To my absolute horror, I found Philip fully clothed, wearing his jumper and jacket, floating in the bath while water splashed out over the sides. "What on earth do you think you're doing?" I asked him as I pulled the plug. But he just kept trying to pour hot water on himself, all the time crying out, "Ma, I'm freezing, I'm freezing. I can't get warm."

I was terrified. There was no-one else to help me – so how was I, a late middle-aged woman, trying to look after two children, to get him, a big man made even heavier with the weight of his wet clothes, out of the bath? Somehow, from somewhere, I found superhuman strength and managed to get him back to his bed. After drying him off, I tucked him in as warm as I could. I had no idea what else to do.

It is so hard thinking about all this, remembering it, even now, all of twenty five years later. I was confused and I have to admit that I probably made wrong decisions. If I had called an ambulance and had him taken to hospital, Philip might have lived, but I really had no idea of the extent to which he was physically ravaged by the drugs he had been taking.

On Christmas Eve, I took the girls into his room for a goodnight Christmas kiss from their Dad. When they returned to their own room after the usual kidding around, he called them back and hugged them both again. I can only think now that there was some kind of sixth sense at work, because a short time later he began vomiting. When I asked him what did he think was wrong, he looked at me helplessly, tears of embarrassment and pity welling up in his eyes, and said, "Ma, I don't know."

By now, my anxiety had become so intense that I telephoned Dennis in Ireland and told him what was happening. We agreed that Graham would fly over to join me, while Dennis stayed on to look after Glen Corr. Meanwhile I decided that further delay might be dangerous, so I called a local doctor whose name I had found in the telephone directory. In due course, he arrived and wrote a prescription, which I immediately took to the nearest chemist. At that point, I think the doctor thought he was suffering from gastro-enteritis or some sort of flu. Unfortunately, the medicine he prescribed only seemed to make Philip worse.

I keep thinking about ways in which things might have been done differently, and how it might have been possible to save my beautiful boy's life. I imagine, for example, that Philip might have been able to tell the doctor about his drug problem had I not stayed with him in the room. But in my distress, I didn't want to leave him – I wanted to hear every word that was being said so that I could nurse him as effectively as possible. Later, I realised that calling that particular doctor was probably another mistake. Not being made aware of any of the details of Philip's drug addiction, he may have assumed he was merely suffering a bilious attack, hardly uncommon around Christmas-time. All day long, after the doctor had left, I trudged up and down to Philip with various kinds of drinks but they mostly remained untouched. And there was no sign of improvement.

Meanwhile, Robbo arrived with some of his friends and I told him how worried I was about Philip's condition, and about the doctor and the fact that the prescription did not seem to have helped Philip at all. Without further comment, Robbo instantly told me I should have called a doctor they knew as "The Quack" or "Doctor Diamond."

Shortly afterwards Graham arrived, and the doctor Robbo recommended also came over. We took the doctor to Philip's room, filling him in about the previous doctor's visit, but, to my amazement, instead of tending to my sick son, he simply started casually looking through Philip's collection of video tapes! Maybe he was waiting for a signal because Philip then asked me to leave the room and I joined Robbo downstairs.

Ashen-faced, Robbo explained to me that Philip had a serious drug problem and that this was, almost certainly, at the root of his current malaise. While I was still reeling from the shock of this news, I was informed that the doctor had injected Philip with something. I have never been able to find out precisely what the injection comprised or what effect it was expected to have. On the surface at least, "The Quack" was still behaving quite casually, and simply told us to leave Philip for twelve hours, but to call him if his condition deteriorated. He dismissed Philip's problem as simply a dose of flu and, at the time, in my state of numb disbelief, I found his casual attitude rather reassuring, and my worries subsided somewhat.

All through the night, Robbo, Graham and I took turns tending to Philip, and I was heartened to see that at least there seemed to be no worsening in his condition. On Christmas Day, Big Charlie dropped by, and I gladly welcomed him. I remember sitting on the settee, telling Charlie how sick Philip seemed and how confused I felt about the whole situation. Since the doctor had been so casual, I temporarily disregarded Robbo's claim that Philip had a serious drug problem, but I now wanted Charlie to tell me the whole truth.

Charlie looked at me in disbelief. "Has nobody told you the full story yet?" he asked. And then he told me the horrible unavoidable truth that I had been hiding from – or that had been hidden from me – all those years. When he explained that Philip had been using heavy drugs for well over ten years, I was astounded. My son, I was now informed, had a serious heroin problem. But even as the awful truth sank in, I could not have imagined that his condition had deteriorated to the point where he had little more than ten days to live.

After breaking the dreadful news to me, Charlie ran up the stairs and burst into Philip's bedroom. "Philip, I've told Phyllis the truth. She has a right to know," he said.

All the suspicions I had been trying to avoid were crystallised by what Charlie had told me. I was shattered now that I knew what had really been going on. Just then the phone rang. By now it was 3 o'clock on Christmas Day and Caroline was calling with Christmas greetings. I was in agony, and broke down as I tried to tell her about Philip's distressful situation. I told her about the two doctors and what they had done, and she said, "Don't worry, I know exactly what to do. I'll be with you in an hour and a half, and I'll book him into a clinic."

When Charlie came back downstairs I told him about Caroline's call and we were both considerably relieved. I don't know about anyone else who was there, but I really had no idea how physically broken he was by the drugs, and I was searching for light – any kind of light – at the end of what only part of me would concede was a tunnel of nightmarish darkness.

I simply wanted all this talk of heroin and sickness to stop, and for Philip to return to his old invincible self. We began to pack his bag for the hospital trip, reassured with the knowledge that he would shortly be in the hands of professional people who I, at least, imagined would soon have him on the mend.

10. THE FINAL DYING OF THE LIGHT

"Death is no easy answer
For those who wish to know
Ask those who have been before you
What fate the future holds."
– from 'Warriors' by Philip Lynott

When Caroline arrived she explained precisely how to get to the Clouds Clinic in East Knoyle, near Salisbury in Wiltshire. She had already arranged for Philip to be admitted immediately on his arrival. She then took the two girls, Sarah and Cathleen, with her to her own place in Bath, while Big Charlie and Graham Cohen drove Philip in a separate car to the Clouds Clinic. Though sick with worry, I remained behind to take care of the house, and I waited there for news for what seemed like an eternity.

My anxiety was further exacerbated when Charlie and Graham arrived back from Wiltshire, late on Christmas night, with the bad news that Philip had only spent about forty minutes in Clouds, where he had not responded to treatment. A Dr. McCann at the clinic had advised that Philip, now almost in a coma, should be taken directly to Salisbury General Infirmary.

In retrospect, of course, it would have been better had Philip been taken from the house in Kew to the nearest emergency hospital, rather than being driven 180 miles to Clouds, but it is easy to be clever when you know these things in hindsight. At the time it seemed like the right decision. That's all I can say now.

Graham had accompanied Philip in the ambulance, with Charlie travelling separately behind, on the hour-long journey to the Infirmary, where Philip was admitted to the emergency unit on arrival. At least,

I thought, I could take comfort from knowing that he was, finally, receiving proper medical treatment. The doctors, I kept telling myself, would do whatever was necessary to restore him to health as soon as possible. Even at that stage, I wasn't considering the possibility that he could die.

Charlie and Graham promised to take me to the Infirmary later in the day to visit Philip. At about six o'clock on the morning of St Stephen's Day (Boxing Day in Britain), I was awoken from a fitful, delirious sleep by an apparition at the foot of my bed telling me that a policeman had called to say that Philip was still not responding to treatment. Such was the impact of this latest bulletin of bad news that I did not realise that the 'apparition' was actually Graham. But the implication of the message was impossible to ignore. Nausea and panic began to take hold. I desperately wanted to be with him.

I can remember little of the bleak journey to Salisbury, which began at six o'clock on a cold winter's morning. Nor did I realise that I would be with my son virtually every moment for the rest of his life. I would not leave the vicinity of the hospital for eleven excruciating, lonely, brutal, heartbreaking, cruel days.

Philip had been given a room of his own and was propped up in bed when I first saw him. A nurse was busy taking blood samples from his arm. I was delighted to find that he was conscious. I said, "Hello, love," and he weakly said, "I'm all right, Ma." We talked for a while, but he kept nodding off, and I assumed that he was drowsy from whatever medication they might have given him. I, too, was weary from the trauma of it all and would doze off intermittently.

I have one very fond memory of those first few hours. While I was sitting in an armchair with my feet up on his bed, I asked Philip for a smile and he grinned sheepishly at me.

Inevitably, word of his hospitalisation had leaked out. When requests came from friends and fans wishing to visit him, I decided that receiving visitors would be too much of a strain on him. I had to insist that no-one would be allowed in, except immediate friends or family. I wanted to give him every opportunity to recover without any energy-draining distractions – although, at this stage nobody at the hospital had told me anything about his actual condition, or how critical it might be.

Now that he was in the intensive care unit, I was totally convinced that he would recover before too long, but I would not risk any unnecessary intrusion that might hinder that process. He had no visitors at all during the first four days, apart from Caroline, Charlie, Graham and myself. Other than Graham, who stayed with me all the time, and Big Charlie who made daily visits, very few people were allowed to go near him during his hospitalisation. We kept the children away until later. Caroline's sister Charlotte, his manager Chris Morrison and his agent John Salter came, as did a chap called Paul Mauger who was already known to be a big fan of Philip's and has since been acknowledged as the leading expert on his recording and performing career. But I don't remember anyone else being admitted, and it was probably just as well.

I was struck by the fact that no members of the band came, although in fairness, they may not have known the full extent of his illness because it was Christmas-time and news took longer than usual to get through, especially in the era before mobile phones and e-mails. Lots of fans called, but I had to be resolute and explain that any exertion might hinder Philip's recovery. I promised they could all visit him when he was restored to his full health, but now certainly wasn't the time to pay their respects.

Christmas also meant that the hospital was short-staffed and, over the following days, I helped with a lot of basic chores myself, including washing him, cleaning his teeth, getting him to spit out and so on. Graham who was wonderfully loyal and a source of strength throughout, would wash Philip's body for me every single day.

There has since been much offensive and ill-founded conjecture about Philip's body being covered in open sores and marks during his final days. I can completely refute those rumours, as can Graham. The worst that could be said about his overall physical condition was that he was overweight. However, there was one utterly unexpected detail that thoroughly shocked me. I was truly staggered when I saw the state of the toes of both feet, where Philip had obviously been injecting himself. For the briefest of moments, I thought the navy blue colour of his feet was merely the result of the cold and chills, but the horrible graphic truth of the extent of his addiction was finally beginning to sink home.

Some people may, I know, object to my going into the unpleasant details of Philip's death so thoroughly. But there are two main reasons for me doing so. First, there was so much inaccurate speculation in the media about the circumstances of his death and, since I was there through every minute of his final days, I think it is important to put the real facts on the record once and for all, to avoid any further distortion of the truth. Perhaps more importantly, I would like everybody out there, particularly young people, to know that heroin addiction really does lead to a gruesome and very undignified, unpleasant end. If Philip's death can have any value, maybe a full understanding of this harsh reality might stop others following down that miserable, hellish path.

And make no mistake – these are not the words of some do-gooder who is simply out to deny people the right to live their life to the full. This is the woebegone testimony of a woman who has been there, seen that and done everything she could to help her son recover from his final illness – to no avail. I have often thought since of the irony in the fact that Philip's unexpected conception had cut short my studies to enter the nursing profession – and now, here I was, nursing him as his life slowly ebbed away.

All day every day, I remained by his bedside. Then, at night I would usually retire to a bungalow in the grounds, where the hospital had arranged sleeping accommodation for me. After a few days, Graham kindly agreed to travel back to Kew to get me a badly-needed change of clothes – I realised with some embarrassment that I had been wearing the same items since arriving at the hospital.

That Philip was very sick could not now be in doubt. I realised that he had not urinated at all since I had arrived at the hospital. When I brought this to the attention of a nurse, it immediately resulted in pandemonium, because a failure to urinate could be an indication that his kidneys were not functioning properly. He was rapidly placed on a dialysis machine, which seemed to restore some function to his kidneys. However, he had by now developed symptoms of pneumonia, and so also had to be attached to a respirator. The odds were beginning to stack up grimly against him.

In intensive care, Philip shared a room with two other patients. One had suffered a heart attack and told me his son worked on the royal yacht Britannia. The other patient was a wee baby, about a year old, whose parents had been told he might be suffering from a brain defect. The sight of his frail body took me right back to the turmoil of my son's early days, when the same Philip fought for his life in another bed, and to my other son Leslie who had been hospitalised as a baby.

The long and lonely wait was excruciating, but at least there were some creature comforts to alleviate the stress marginally. The unit was adjacent to a very pleasant rest room, equipped with a television and coffee-making equipment for which you could buy coffee in the hospital shop. I spent some time in that room with the distraught relatives of the other two patients. In my desire to be strong for them, I convinced myself that Philip was bound to recover.

During one of my brief interludes in that room, I was interrupted by a young girl who sought me out and handed me a bunch of flowers. But something about her manner made me quickly realise that she was a reporter. I refused to talk to her and she eventually departed. Little did I realise then that, for the rest of my life, I would have to cope with the intrusions of the media, a few of whom would stoop to any level, tell any lie or use any despicable trick to get their stories – which, more often than not, are then transformed into a mixture of fact and fantasy anyway.

When Caroline told me that she was bringing the two girls to see their father in hospital, I tried to dissuade her on the grounds that Philip was connected to several tubes, and seeing him in this condition might not be right for the children. But she believed they should see each other, and I accept that she was probably right. When Philip saw the two girls through the glass, he did not have the strength to do anything more than cry – the tears rolled down his cheeks. Who knows what thoughts were going through his head at this time? Did he realise that he would never again see the two daughters he loved with all his heart?

By the time New Year's Eve had arrived, TV cameras were virtually camped outside the hospital gates, and fans were sleeping rough and even hoping to be allowed in. I was feeling tired and unkempt and I needed another change of clothes. Graham found a way for me to escape undetected, and took me to a convenient branch of Marks & Spencer. I did some other shopping, but I was locked into the nightmare that was unwinding remorselessly at the hospital, and I can remember physically shaking with worry for Philip as I moved around the shops like a zombie.

My own mood was in sharp contrast to the carol singing and general air of festivity common to Christmas-time and New Year, and nowhere more so than in the beautiful, quaint cathedral town of Salisbury where my son would breathe his last. Beautiful music, including a favourite of mine by Paul Robeson, poured from loudspeakers around the centre of the town, and I could see so many happy faces. But my heart was like lead, my stomach was sick and there was a dreamlike quality to my grim detachment from the prevailing atmosphere of good humour and merriment.

At the hospital, it was difficult for me to get any clear indication regarding Philip's condition. This may have been because the staff were uncertain about whom to give priority to – to me as his mother, or to Caroline who, although they had been estranged, was still his wife. An encounter with Caroline in the hospital corridor did little to relieve my gloom. "Do you realise that there is a real possibility that Philip could die?" she said to me. For the first time, I think, I gathered that the hospital staff felt that he might not pull through and I presumed that they had communicated this appalling reality to her.

To clear up another malicious story that has been told and retold, there is absolutely no truth whatsoever in the suggestion that Caroline had callously let Philip suffer for days at home before getting him to hospital. I know because I was there and, here again, I think it is important that the truth be told. Right from the moment that she knew there was a serious problem, she did what she believed to be best for Philip. Any other suggestion is simply a lie.

My gradual comprehension that his death was a genuine possibility made it even more difficult for me the next time I went to bathe Philip's face as I had been doing regularly. I was anxious not to allow him to see any fear in my eyes, because I believe a sick person can sense that fear and it only adds to their own difficulties. So I put on my most cheerful disposition, and told him not to worry, that as soon as he was on the mend I would take him back with me to Ireland and get him right again. But inside, the emotional turmoil was killing me.

It was then that he spoke these very words to me. "Merciful Jesus, what have I done to you, Ma?" he said, in his own inimitable Dublin accent. I can still see the forlorn look in his eyes and I have carried his trembling voice, the voice of a drowning man, as it echoes those words in my head ever since. It was horrifying, truly horrifying, to sit there and know that there was, as I increasingly apprehended, no way back. I tried to put on my bravest face and kept repeating: "Don't worry, I'll get you better." I think that was the precise moment when both he and I faced the reality of his imminent death.

When I left the room, I met a man of the cloth in the corridor, and I heard him asking a nurse for directions to Philip Lynott's room. Almost hysterically, I pleaded with him not to go into the room with his collar on, for fear it might frighten Philip, but he calmly interrupted my pleas to tell me that Philip had asked for him. I just stood aside and let him pass and then rushed to the bathroom in great distress.

There was a terrible sense of impending doom in Philip's apparent resignation. I grew more sick with anxiety and fear while at midnight, the hospital and the surrounding town reverberated with the New Year celebrations. The nurses on duty popped open champagne bottles and

I did what I could to join in the festivities. It was a desperate sham, but I took some bubbly in to Philip and, wishing him a Happy New Year, I allowed three of four drops to fall onto his tongue. My heart almost burst with joy when he smiled at me, smacked his lips at the taste of the champagne and mischievously asked for more. Laughing, I told him to behave himself and, after one more sip, we sang 'Auld Lang Syne' together.

Shortly after midnight, I spoke to the doctor in charge and he gave me the good news that Philip's kidneys had started to function again. Despite the roller-coaster emotions of the previous day, I went to my room in the little bungalow with a lighter heart and a renewed sense of optimism. Maybe everything was going to be all right after all.

Over the following days I remained optimistic. Without any word to the contrary, I convinced myself that it was simply a matter of time before Philip would begin to recover. I imagined, over and over again, the moment when he would be discharged – and the world would begin to return to normal.

My fragile elation continued until the night of January 3rd. To this day, I am convinced that Graham and Big Charlie knew how grave the situation was that night but, for my own protection, they colluded to get me away from the hospital by escorting me back to the house in Kew, with the reassurance that they would send for me immediately there were any developments. In fairness, I think it was better for me, and possibly for Philip as well, that I was not around when the situation began to seriously deteriorate.

Back at the house, there was a continuous barrage of phone-calls from the media and friends, all enquiring after Philip. My niece Monica volunteered to deal with the torrent of queries and good wishes. However, I was terrified that she would get some important news and not pass it on to me immediately, so I persuaded her to follow a procedure of answering each call then telling me instantly who the caller was.

Then the call that I had been dreading came through.

Philip was dead.

The news sliced through me, from head to toe, like a scalpel-sharp blade. It did not matter that I had an inkling that he was close to death's door – now that it had happened, I couldn't believe it. In my hysteria, I ran outside and tried to get through the main gates, an impossible task since they were electrically-operated from inside the house. I was going demented, screaming and roaring for my son. When Caroline arrived from the hospital and told me again, in person, I could no longer control myself. I sank to my knees and started banging my head against the ground in utter, inconsolable grief.

My precious son, with whom I had experienced so many trials and tribulations and shared the joys and sorrows of life, was dead at the appallingly young age of 36. His ravaged body gave up the struggle on Saturday 4th January 1986, leaving two daughters, aged eight and five, a widow of just twenty-seven, a sister and brother he never knew, and a heartbroken mother behind to grieve for him.

. . . .

> *"They buried my body and they thought I'd gone*
> *But I am the dance and I still live on."*
> – from 'Lord Of The Dance' by Sidney Carter

The period immediately following the devastating news of Philip's death is still lost for me in a haze of agony and deep distress. I can remember only some of the events that were taking place all around me. Graham came to Kew to take me back to Salisbury to identify Philip's body. But I was so distraught, I could not bring myself to do it. He and Caroline bravely carried out that gruesome duty instead.

At some point, I was shown a brochure and asked to select a coffin, but I could not bear to look at the photographs. Again, Graham and Caroline chose the casket in which Philip was buried. I'm not sure that it was the most appropriate response at all, because I was clearly in a state of denial. Not only did I never see his body in death, but I even forced myself, by clenching my eyes shut, not to look at the casket either. This may have been the only way I could have dealt with his loss, by refusing to acknowledge that it had happened at all. But there is a price to pay, because you can't keep running away from reality, no matter how grim, forever.

On returning from the hospital, Graham handed me an envelope containing the jewellery, which Philip had been wearing when he died, as well as a lock of his hair which I still have in my possession. Then, Caroline wanted to know if I felt he should be buried wearing his wedding ring, and I said no. These are the kind of crazy issues people feel that they have to concern themselves with when someone dies – especially someone as young as Philip was. However trivial it may seem now, I made that decision not because of any anger with Caroline but because he was not living as a married man when he died. I have never believed in the custom of burying people with jewellery anyway.

The hospital's pathologist, Dr. Angela Scott, had announced the cause of death as a combination of heart, liver and kidney failure, and blood poisoning – Philip never did anything by halves. While his body was retained in Salisbury for the autopsy, a procession of sympathisers from far and wide arrived at the house in Kew, including Percy, who had travelled down from Manchester. As the shock-waves of Philip's death spread all over the world, more and more expressions of sympathy flooded in. I was taken, in an almost zombie-like state, to stand in a shop, crying my eyes out, while a woman fitted me with some black funeral clothes. My body started trembling from the moment I knew he had died, and continued to do so for years afterwards.

As a convenience for his English friends and fans, many of whom would have found it impossible to travel to Dublin for the funeral, it was decided to celebrate Mass on Thursday 9th January, in the Saint Elizabeth of Portugal church, in The Vineyard, Richmond, which he had attended and where he had been married only six years previously. The church was filled to capacity and the congregation overflowed into the street.

Chris Morrison read a passage from the Bible. The attendance included

Bob Geldof, his then-wife, the late Paula Yates, members of bands like Motorhead, The Boomtown Rats, John Coughlan from Status Quo and, of course, former members of Thin Lizzy. The pop group Duran Duran sent red roses. Mass was celebrated by Father Raymond Brennan, the same priest who had married Philip and Caroline. The church organist played a very emotional version of the folk tune 'Lord Of The Dance', a particular favourite of Philip's, and one which had also been played at his wedding. Sarah and Cathleen brought a personal wreath, but you could tell that they were as stunned as I was by the tragedy and waste of it all.

After the Mass, we retired to the Richmond Hill Hotel for drinks and everyone shared the sad reminiscences about Philip and their adventures with him that are the staple of occasions like this. It was all desperately depressing.

Then came the most harrowing journey I have ever taken in my life, the plane trip back to Dublin for the burial on Saturday 11th January 1986. Dennis and I and the rest of the funeral party were given an executive lounge at Heathrow Airport as we prepared to bring Philip home to Ireland for the last time. On the plane, my distress reached such black depths that I can distinctly remember feeling that I would not care if the plane crashed. At that point, I felt my life was over anyway. But then, I was struck by feelings of guilt at such a horrible thought, since there were several children on board, children who deserved the chance to grow into loving adults.

I was so completely devastated by the whole experience that I cannot even remember now whether the casket came to Glen Corr, or proceeded directly from Dublin Airport to a Requiem Mass at the Church Of The Assumption in Howth. Not that it matters – its destination was the same either way. Everywhere, the house, the church, even the roads, seemed to be teeming with people but, once again, I closed my eyes in an attempt to shut out the horrible truth. I was led about, as if I was a blind person.

I was later told that the men of Howth, dozens upon dozens of them, had taken the casket out of the hearse and passed it along at shoulder-height right up to the church, whereas normally it would have been carried by only four men – but I can't vouch for that because I was in such an abyss of horror at the time that I saw virtually nothing.

The traditional Irish group, Clann Éadair, for whom Philip had sung lead vocals on a single, and who included my friend Snowy in their line-up, played 'The Lord Of The Dance' and a plaintive piece from *The Brendan Voyage* that soothed the spirit just a little, but the respite didn't last. I remember one female mourner coming over to me and pulling at me and saying, "God, help you! God, help you!" – and such like lamentations. Although no doubt she meant well, she was having such an awful effect on me, that two friends escorted me away from her and helped me into the car for the journey to Saint Fintan's Cemetery in Sutton, a mere stone's throw from Glen Corr. The cortege passed the Royal Hotel in Howth where, not many Sundays ago, Philip had played what must have been his last public gig ever, joining Clann Éadair for a fun session.

At the cemetery, the bitterly cold day and my inconsolable grief combined to freeze me so rigid that I could not even leave the car until a priest helped me walk among the large, jostling crowd, some of whom had been waiting from dawn. Ten feet away from the grave, I had to stop walking. I was as close to the dead body of my son as I could possibly bear. In the long run, the fact that the funeral was attended by numerous well-known people, including former (and future) Taoiseach, the late Charles Haughey, Bono, Adam Clayton and Larry Mullen from U2, their manager Paul McGuinness, Bob Geldof, his wife Paula Yates, Eamon Carr from Horslips, Philip Chevron of The Pogues and, again members of Thin Lizzy, would mean a lot to me. There were countless others from throughout the international and local music business, including musicians, managers, promoters, journalists, disc-jockeys and, most important of all, Philip's loyal fans, who had meant so much to him. But at the time, I just felt numb. Nothing could bring Philip back. That awful truth was all that mattered.

Floral tributes were sent from all over the world, from Dire Straits, Huey Lewis and The News, Gary Moore, U2, Chas and Dave, and a special one from The Boomtown Rats which read, "All our love from one bunch of cowboys to another. God bless." I remember Brian Robertson's mum coming up to me at one point and, with tears streaming down her cheeks, saying, in an obvious reference to her Brian's own difficulties, "There but for the grace of God goes my son."

But, in general, I remained thoroughly oblivious to the clamour that surrounded me. I was sleepwalking, almost comatose with grief. All I could see in my mind's eye were visions of my beautiful Philip, at various stages during his life. I thought of his face when he was four years old, on the horrible morning when I had to kiss him goodbye as I left him in Dublin, with his grandmother and returned back to Manchester. I thought of him in an ill-fitting boiler suit one day when I went to visit him at work in Tonge & Taggart in Dublin. I thought of him proudly buying me a meal in that Italian restaurant in the first flush of his local celebrity. I thought of him lying on his bed in the Kew house with Sarah and Cathleen, and all three of them laughing their heads off at something silly he said. There were moments when I genuinely believed that my head would burst open.

Unable to suppress my pain any longer, I screamed Philip's name out over the tumult of the crowd and collapsed to the ground. Big Charlie scooped me up in his arms, carried me to the car and drove straight back to Glen Corr.

11. THE MOURNING AFTER

"Wild one
Won't you please come home
You've been away too long, will you? . . .
How can we carry on
When you are gone, my wild one."
– from 'Wild One' by Philip Lynott

For the next two years, my life was overtaken by the most profound inner torment. I barely moved from the settee in Glen Corr upon which Charlie had set me down after whisking me away from the funeral. My weight plummeted to six and a half stone. I shook constantly and one arm developed a twitch. My hair turned white, and I became a virtual recluse.

Some people may argue that had I allowed myself to see Philip's body my grief would not have been so deep or so prolonged. When I later saw my mother's body after her death, I know I felt a certain peace, but I do not believe that I could have brought myself to see the dead body of my son.

My grief was undoubtedly compounded by the manner of his death. The passing of a loved one through some terminal disease, or in an accident, seems to have different effects on their bereaved than a death from drugs, which seems so avoidable. Add to that the confusion and disappointment that stemmed from my total, but ultimately hopelessly wrong, conviction that the Philip Lynott I knew would not be so weak-willed or so stupid as to allow himself to become addicted to drugs, and I am left with a feeling that it was all a terrible misunderstanding.

It must also be remembered that Philip and I had not lived together for any substantial period of time, and it may be that this actually added to the burden of my grief. I have a lingering sense of how much we missed out on. I could not claim to miss his physical presence from the house in the way that one might a partner or a lover, but, although we had lived apart for long periods, there was a remarkable closeness between us. There was a spiritual aspect to that, but the truth is that we were also best mates. I missed his regular phone calls. He never ended a call without saying: "I love you, Ma." And his sense of romanticism meant that he would always send me flowers or perfume on appropriate occasions. I just wish we had been together more, to share the joys of being mother and son, when he was growing up. I have a fierce sense of loss that continues to haunt me – but then I think it's always especially hard for a mother to bury her young son.

I couldn't bear to listen to any of Philip's music after he died. It is ironic that people often say of artists of all kinds that it is a blessing that something of their art lives on after them. But, in my case, my pain was too raw to allow me to even bear the mention of Thin Lizzy's music for a long time. I simply couldn't endure the sound of Philip's voice on the television or radio. When I passed pictures of him in the house, I would avert my eyes from his, which seemed to look out and implore me. I even requested the Thin Lizzy management office to forewarn me about any likely publicity relating to Philip or the band, so that I could specifically take precautions to avoid it. For many years, I would spend Christmases in silence, with both my television and radio switched off, rather than run the risk of hearing his voice, singing or speaking, on or around his anniversary.

Partly, I was trying to fool myself into thinking that I had imagined it all, and that Philip was actually touring Australia or somewhere far away, and that his telephone call would come at any minute. I know this probably only makes sense to me. I knew he was dead. Of course I did. But because I had not seen his body, I could fantasise. How close to the borders of insanity I came I will never know, but it must have been a close shave.

In my anger, I cursed to hell and back those who either supplied his habit or stood idly by while he went into decline. But my anger at these people later turned into sadness and pity. Some had their own problems with drugs and have since thankfully recuperated, even if they now lower their eyes in embarrassment when we meet. Such was my anger that I was instrumental in having a former Thin Lizzy roadie, Liam Kelly, charged and convicted with supplying cocaine to Philip. He was sentenced to two years in jail in England. Eventually, however, I had to educate myself to understand that addicts, whether addicted to heroin or alcohol, tend to bond together and to lie for each other. They treat non-addicts as the enemy, foes to be ruthlessly frozen out. And I came to realise that, essentially, they were more misguided than evil.

In my profound misery, Glen Corr was transformed into a silent tomb for a long time. I often lay prostrate for long periods in the house, thinking of Philip lying in his grave just a short drive away. In my unrelenting denial, I could not bring myself to visit him.

When, at last, I felt ready for that ordeal, I persuaded a friend to take me to the cemetery, where I spent some time praying for Philip's soul and tidying up his grave. I collected some smooth stones from the beach beside the house and painted them white as decorations for the grave. I also arranged for our friend Snowy McLoughlin to make a white cross with Philip's name on it.

This gave his final resting place the appearance of a cowboy's grave, out on the prairie, an appropriate memorial image, given Philip's preoccupation with bandits, vagabonds and the romantic outlaw lifestyle. But when fans began to bring their own stones, the authorities told me that you could only have a proper, regulation cross or nothing at all. While I thought that was a bit odd and arrogant, I rang Caroline to persuade her that a proper stone cross should be placed at the grave. When she came to Dublin, we chose a piece of marble, but she was adamant that the headstone should not contain any of the usual sentiments which we had seen when walking around the graveyard, such as "Sadly missed by your ever-loving wife."

Although I appreciated that she wanted to be honest, her insistence cut deeply into me. Maybe I misinterpreted her attitude and she simply felt that any kind of conventional sentimentality would be misplaced, but it seemed somehow harsh to me. I turned to Jim Fitzpatrick, the artist who had worked on several of Thin Lizzy's album covers as far back as *Vagabonds Of The Western World* in 1973, as well as *Nightlife* and *Jailbreak*, and who had been a well-loved friend of Philip's. I asked Jim, who is a dear friend to this day as well as being a neighbour, would he design a Celtic motif for the marble headstone. Rather than simply containing Philip's name, I asked him to find an appropriate Irish-language verse which could be used and which would avoid contravening Caroline's wishes. That's why the gravestone today bears the inscription in Irish, "Go dtuga Dia suaimhneas dá anam, Róisín Dubh" – which roughly translates as "Sleep in peace, our Black Rose." Caroline heartily endorsed these sentiments, and I think Philip would have approved too. He'd have especially loved the idea of having an epitaph inscribed in Irish – Jim Fitzpatrick recalls him expressing a nationalist outlook that was eloquent and anything but narrow, during some of their many conversations together.

A death of this tragic kind affects every aspect of your life, even the most trivial. For a long time, I avoided my local supermarket where Philip and I used to shop, because so many people knew us both and would offer their heartfelt sympathy whenever they met me. As a result, every visit was likely to end with me in tears, shaking uncontrollably and upsetting everybody else.

Even when I learned to venture out again, I was still over-sensitive to anybody looking at me or offering me sympathy. I imagined that such people were pitying me, and looking at me as some kind of weird recluse, driven mad because my son died a drug addict. Which, in a way, maybe I was.

Once, in a shop in the nearby suburb of Baldoyle, I was startled to hear Philip's speaking voice, as clear as could be. For a moment, I felt he was right behind me. Dropping my purchases in horror, I put my hands over my ears. Some ladies, including one who recognised me, ran over, under the impression that I was having some kind of a fit, but I then realised that the voice I had heard was the shop's sound system pumping out a song by Philip called 'King's Call' from 1980, in which Philip does a spoken passage. As a further irony, in that song Philip tells how he consoled himself on hearing of Elvis Presley's death by going *"to the liquor store and buying a bottle of wine and a bottle of gin."*

When I recovered my composure, these good samaritans took me to a café for a recuperative cup of coffee. When one of the women explained to the waitress what had just happened, she recalled that she had once met Philip on the Dublin-Holyhead ferry, and that he had asked her for a date! The laughter which that coincidence kindled helped me over the shock of imagining I was hearing the voice of my son from beyond the grave. And in a way, that incident helped the ice to begin to thaw.

On another occasion, while visiting a friend near Gretna Green in Scotland, I had to run away from a market stall where a record player was blaring out 'Whiskey In The Jar'. My friend explained to the lad running the stall that I was Philip Lynott's mother. Immediately, he chased after me and made a present of the record to me, saying that I could listen to it when I felt able to, which I did a long time later. Now that I can listen to Philip's music again, 'Whiskey In The Jar' is a real favourite of mine. It brings back so many pleasant memories.

However, I must not pretend that I was always a big fan of all of Philip's music. As I've said, when I first saw him playing live, I could not even hear the words with the overall noise, never mind understand them. It took a while for it to grow on me since I was drawn more to artists like Frank Sinatra, Earl Bostic, The Beatles and Stan Kenton, and had long kept my jazz record collection intact. Gradually, my ears have attuned to the rock sound over the years and I take some pride in being one of the few grannies that love rock music.

Although it may at times have seemed otherwise, in the long run the constant stream of fans to Glen Corr was a tremendous source of comfort to me, as it made me realise the huge number of people who were genuinely touched by Philip's music, which lived on in the hearts of so many of them. Right up to the time the Irish courts ordered me to vacate Glen Corr, I was always delighted by visits from such passionate people, all the more so as time went by. In fact, I cannot remember deliberately turning away any genuine fan that arrived on my doorstep.

It was a different matter dealing with the media, many of whom, as I have said, are prepared to stoop to any level of deceit in order to trick their way into my confidence. I know that they all have a job to do in a very competitive business, but I find it sad that such people can only earn a living by being parasites on the grief of others. I can recall one Irish journalist in particular who came to meet me on the pretext of wanting to talk to me about Philip's life after the demise of Thin Lizzy. When he arrived armed with a bottle of wine, it should have aroused my suspicions. All he wanted to talk about were the sordid lies about the alleged state of Philip's body when he was admitted to hospital.

Another journalist wormed his way into my hospitality through a female acquaintance, who phoned me completely out of the blue after I had not heard from her for over a decade. Look at it in one way and these people are very sad cases, I suppose. Fortunately, there are many others in the media who are courteous and civil and honest, and I will always try to accommodate them whenever I can.

In fact the fans have been my lifeline through so many dark episodes back then. The cases full of mail I received from fans all over the world helped me to keep whatever problems I had with the media in perspective. But I have to admit that I could have done with secretarial help – some of the mail remained unopened for up to five years because I found it too painful to confront the loss of one who was loved by so many.

Those were dark days, but Caroline, Sarah and Cathleen often came over and their company helped me too. Caroline sometimes stayed at Adam Clayton's house in Rathfarnham. The girls were not having an easy time dealing with the aftermath of their father's death either. Sarah once got into a frightful state in London and could not stop crying. Caroline, who was at her wit's end, asked me to come over to help comfort her. Part of Sarah's problem, I discovered when we met, was her fear of having another father because Caroline was then dating a man and she could not bear to see his arms around Caroline. When I explained this to Caroline and her boyfriend, they understood Sarah's hurt. But inevitably, it would be necessary for Sarah to accept Caroline's needs too.

I don't want this to turn into a litany, but I was also blessed at Glen Corr by the close proximity of some truly marvellous friends. My partner Dennis was wonderful, of course. But there were others too and while it isn't very literary, I'd like to acknowledge them here. Helen Ruttle often came to the house and talked to me for ages about all kinds of stuff that used to take my mind off my own grieving. The friendship of people like Graham Cohen, who has been such a rock for me, Dympna McKenna, Maeve Curtis' mother Trish McMahon and the entire McMahon family, and indeed my own immediate family, helped me enormously to come through what were very difficult times in every way. In some cases, it was enough to get a phone-call from a friendly voice or to meet for a cup of coffee with someone who I felt understood my predicament and could lend a sympathetic ear. But in truth, my awakening from this grief-torn world only began properly when I became interested again in what people like Helen were doing in their own lives and with the realisation that, ultimately, others had experiences as wounding, if not even more so, than mine. Life, I slowly but surely realised, goes on, no matter what, and we all have our cup of woes.

One cold day, walking along the crisp grass in the cemetery after visiting Philip's grave, I encountered a woman engrossed in cleaning a gravestone. I quietly read the details on the stone, which related the deaths of three young people in the fire that ravaged the Stardust Disco in Dublin's Artane on St Valentine's Night, 1981, claiming a total of forty-eight lives. Looking at her ice-blue hands, and feeling a wave of simple human sympathy, it suddenly dawned on me that this woman had lost not one but *three* of her children. I dropped to the ground beside her, took her cloth, gave her a hug and started polishing the headstone. When I took her back to my house for a bowl of soup, she also confided the great difficulties she and her husband had in trying to cope with their loss. It was a story of savage, cruel misfortune that was utterly heartbreaking in its scale and finality.

No, I was not the first or only mother to have lost a beloved son. I slowly discovered that this cemetery, which I had subconsciously assumed was for old people who had lived out their lives, was actually packed with the graves of dozens of young people, not just Philip Lynott. I gradually began to understand too that I had not been singled out for some malignant fate – and I realised that it was unworthy simply to feel sorry for myself when there is tragedy all around us.

Somehow, the story got about that I had begun visiting Philip's grave every day and this was blown up into something heroic, but the truth is that I have to drive past the cemetery every day and it's no big deal to stop off. Sometimes, I find the car almost automatically turning into the parking area. I go now because I like to. There is nothing self-indulgent or morbid in it – or so I like to think! What it does do, however, is bring you closer to other people who are grieving and in pain – and in that way, it is a humbling experience.

During one visit, I happened upon one of the cemetery workers in considerable distress. This was a man whom one would expect to be hardened to tragedies, yet he was weeping uncontrollably, having witnessed the most harrowing funeral of a 12 year-old girl killed by a cowardly hit-and-run driver. He took me around to her grave, which was covered in teddy-bears and flowers and heartbreaking messages. It was a devastating sight. Another day I met a man praying at the graveside of his son, who had hanged himself only a fortnight before. And on another sombre occasion, I arrived at the graveyard unwittingly at the same time as the funeral of a young woman murdered in the Dublin Mountains.

Such encounters with the grim reality of how death impacts on people's lives helped me to put my own situation into perspective and gave me the will to live again. Sometimes, when I'm laying flowers on Philip's grave, I imagine him saying, "Ah, Ma don't be smothering me with flowers, sure I'm a Rocker." It makes me aware of other graves that might have greater need of a few flowers. I admit now that I had become very selfish and self-centred in my misery, thinking "Oh me! Why me!" and so on – as if I should have been exempt from the difficulties of life that can afflict just about anyone. My encounters with the grief of others cured me of such self-indulgence and helped me face back into the world. It also freed me from a lot of ancillary baggage and, I think, enabled me to forgive all of Philip's associates, against whom I used to rail so violently. I had harboured a vicious anger in my heart against the suppliers of his drugs and the friends who did nothing to alleviate his plight. I had mostly kept that anger hidden, but my rage now melted away, or most of it anyway.

While reading about the lives of Elvis Presley, Bob Marley and Jim Morrison, I saw many parallels between the pressures of the lives they lived and the way they died and Philip's own untimely passing. In particular, I saw how Philip's hero Jimi Hendrix had died in circumstances similar to Philip's own tragic end. All of these stars had serious and ultimately fatal drug problems of one kind or another, and learning something of their lives helped me to understand a little more about some of the crazy pressures with which high-profile people like Philip must cope. It also served to bring home to me the fact that there are those who believe they are indestructible and that they can handle virtually everything. I have a feeling that, until he was close to the end, Philip was one of those.

Different drugs have different effects on people too. Looking back I now feel that certain substances made Philip aggressive, whereas he was a gentle guy at heart. Like me, he was never a great sleeper and drugs may have helped him in that regard, who knows? Hard drugs initially may have seemed to him like an adventure or respite from the glare of the spotlight he referred to in 'Dancing In the Moonlight'. Towards the end, it is widely known that his fortunes had taken a dispiriting turn in terms of his career, and he may even have been encountering money problems. Thin Lizzy had split, and he had no record deal to compensate for his substantial investment in his new project, Grand Slam. All of this might have speeded his downward spiral or, at least, added further burdens to his existing problems.

Whatever the background details may have been, it is worth repeating, over and over again, that Philip's death was an appalling waste and a source of great pain to many people who loved him in spite of his faults – but his demise was part of life and the rest of us must carry on. Nobody, no matter how talented or how loving or how young, is safe from the ravages of death, which can overtake you at any time. This is even truer today with the prevalence of drugs, and the crime and violence that tend to go with it. Kids at parties, at school and at other gatherings are called cowards if they say 'No' to drugs, so if my adult rocker son, a great hero to so many, could not avoid the pitfalls, what chance has a young teenager?

The drugs are available in ever-increasing quantities and no government or agency anywhere in the world seems even remotely capable of preventing their continued spread. I don't know what the answer is, but it still hurts me when I see Philip referred to in the press as a 'junkie'. There is something squalid about the word and, in his case, it conjures up inaccurate images of someone down and out and living friendless on the streets.

I look at it differently. Surely, Philip would not, and could not, have hurt his beloved daughters, his mother, his other relations and friends unless he had become a very sick person? Drug addicts, I believe, are sick people and, just as society has come to understand that alcoholism is an illness, we must do likewise regarding those afflicted with other addictions, bearing in mind that heroin, and perhaps cocaine, are even more lethal than alcohol, when bought on the black market, from drug dealers, with all the attendant risks of contamination and over-dosing.

At first, in trying to avoid coming to terms with the manner of Philip's death, I had hidden myself away, but now I can cope with it and perhaps use my experience to help prevent other mothers and sons from going through the hell I suffered. And, more to the point, the hell that Philip himself must have endured.

Inevitably, there were issues that needed to be resolved in Philip's affairs, following his death. Among these, the most contentious related to the house in Glen Corr, which had such powerful associations with

Philip for me, and where I lived in the aftermath of his death. However, Caroline felt that this house should be sold – an attitude with which I just couldn't agree. A dispute developed and, as a result, Caroline began to discourage meetings between me and Sarah and Cathleen. This hurt me deeply, especially because it was I who had been there for her during the births of both children. That was part of what I did, constantly making myself available as a support and occasional surrogate mother when the going got tough or people needed me. I truly love these girls. I always did but I know them less well now than I did when they were young.

In the end, the differences between Caroline and me were bitter and could only be settled by going to court. I regret all of this now, but one of the reasons I was prepared to go this far in an effort to prevent Caroline taking possession of Glen Corr and then selling it, was that I knew Philip had bought the house as a residence for Sarah and Cathleen so that they could settle in Ireland. The way I saw it, it was always meant to be their house. Both were born in Ireland, at Philip's insistence. It was their childhood home. I distinctly recall Sarah turning to me one day and saying, "I love this house." The way I saw it, in a few years, the girls could have been given the opportunity to make their own decisions. I couldn't see the need to sell the house sooner.

Some people wrongly assume that, as his mother, I must somehow benefit from the sales of Philip's records – but there's absolutely no reason why I should. His music seems to be played on the radio in Ireland and elsewhere now more than ever before, which is wonderful. But all of the royalties accruing go to his legal next of kin, and rightly so. I do not, and never did, want any of that money for myself. I know that Caroline is a good mother who loves her children, but I wanted to do whatever I could to ensure that Philip's daughters would be taken care of to the greatest extent possible, and that's the only reason I asked the court that I be allowed to remain in Glen Corr until they were able to make their own minds up. I was definitely not claiming the house for myself, and I do not want people, no matter how well-intentioned, to feel I lost it in the courts. Since I have always believed in obeying the law, there was no option for me other than to vacate Glen Corr, painful though that experience was.

Others thought this was a scandalous outcome, and told me so, not only because of the possibility that Sarah and Cathleen might be deprived of the chance to own the house their father had bought for them to grow up in, but also because the house had, over the years since Philip's death, become the primary focal point for his fans. Without being in the least ghoulish, it had become an unofficial Philip Lynott museum. Indeed, one of the rooms was often described by visitors as a veritable shrine to Philip, so full was it of artefacts and mementos relating to various aspects of his life and career. Even if, personally, I find that description a little fanciful, it is not totally off the mark. But, once the court made its decision, it was time to move on. All of that is water under the bridge now. And while I admit that I did feel that Caroline drew the children away from me, and that I felt deeply hurt by that, I think I have a better understanding now of what was involved for her. She needed her girls. And so I cannot blame her for pursuing the maternal instinct in the way she did. I know only too well from my own experience with the children that I lost and with the joy I felt when my daughter Philomena came back into my life, just how badly a mother can suffer if it seems that her children might in some way be distanced from her.

Looking back, it is easy to see that his career had left Philip with almost no time in which to enjoy his marriage or fatherhood and the normal ups and downs of ordinary life. In the same way, he never had a proper chance to enjoy Glen Corr, or not to the full anyway. I retain a very fond memory of him walking around the rear garden and saying, "Imagine, Ma, I own all this. Isn't it lovely?" Philip loved the house, and perhaps, if his life had not taken the tragic turn it did, he would have settled down there with his family for the rest of his natural life. And this story, if told at all, would have had a genuinely happy ending.

12. DEATH IS NOT THE END

"If you see my mother
Please give her all my love
For she has a heart of gold there
As good as God above
If you see my mother
Tell her I'm keeping fine
Tell her that I love her
And I'll try to write sometime."
– From 'Philomena' by Philip Lynott

It has indeed been claimed about many artists in different fields that something of them lives on in their art beyond death. In that sense, it is gratifying to know that, through their recordings, Philip and Thin Lizzy are still bringing happiness and pleasure to people. Equally, it is not every mother whose son can leave behind a piece of music with such loving sentiments as are contained in the song 'Philomena'. Philip wrote this song especially for me and recorded it on his birthday, in 1974, for inclusion on the *Nightlife* album. In the middle of a hard rock album, it's a lovely moment of supreme romanticism.

Philip loved writing songs about real people, particularly people who were important in his life. The *Nightlife* album, for instance, also features a song called 'Frankie Carroll'; the name is an amalgam of Frank Murray, Thin Lizzy's tour manager, and Ted Carroll, their manager before the two Chrises took command. As people who know his music will be aware, he also wrote lovely songs for both of his daughters, Sarah and Cathleen. Such tributes were Philip's way of telling his friends and of course his children, how much they meant to him. For me, the song 'Philomena' is a monument not just to Philip's poetic talent and his creativity but also to his ability to love – and I treasure it greatly.

Another of Philip's friends, Smiley Bolger, has been more active than anyone in keeping Philip's memory alive, particularly through the *Ode To A Black Man* records and tapes he issued, and through his annual Vibe for Philo concert which has taken place on the anniversary of his death every year since 1987. Smiley has been unfairly maligned over the years. Some malicious individuals put round the story that Smiley was personally making capital out of these projects, but I know that he started out on the road with the Vibe For Philo for all the right reasons. And it has been a huge factor in keeping the memory of Philip and his music alive for 25 years now.

The Vibe is a special occasion. I have gone every year for so long that it seems impossible to imagine January 4th without a special gig. Over the years, so many young bands, from Ireland and abroad, some of whose members may not even have been born when the band was at its peak, have gathered in Dublin on the anniversary of Philip's death. And they have performed Thin Lizzy music with the kind of energy and dedication that lifts my heart. Well-known singers and bands like Elvis Costello, Sinéad O'Connor, Joe Elliott from Def Leppard, Glen Hansard, Leanne Harte, Philip Chevron of The Pogues, Renegade, Eric Bell and Brian Robertson and his band, have all given of their time to the various remembrance projects. Jim Fitzpatrick has read from Philip's poems.

The Vibe has produced its moments too. There had been a bit of a set-to with the late broadcaster Gerry Ryan back around 2000. The first I knew of it was when I got a call from a journalist asking me what I thought of Gerry attacking my son on the radio. I hadn't heard the broadcast, but when I did listen back to it, I was outraged with the comments he'd made to the effect that Philip was an ignorant so-and-so and was strung out on heroin when he interviewed him in RTÉ years before. A newspaper carried my angry response under the headline "You're Gerry Rude". I know: headline writing was not their greatest strength...

During the Vibe the following year, I was on-stage making my thank-you speech when I become conscious of the fans booing and somebody coming over to me. It was Gerry. He asked if he could interrupt me to say a few words, so I gave him the mike. He said that his mother and his wife had told him to apologise to me, in public, for the nasty things he'd said about Philip on the radio. I admired his guts. It took more than a bit of courage to get up in front of a crowd of fans of Philip and say this.

I was reminded of all this when in 2010 Gerry sadly passed away, and the circumstances of his death sparked lots of unpleasant speculation about Gerry's own dealings with drugs. But I had forgiven him for what he said, even if the fans didn't let him off so easily. On the night they booed and they held it against him for a very long time.

The truth is that there is no one alive who has not made mistakes. Philip made huge mistakes and died as a result of them. Gerry did too. And his family have been left grieving as a result. Unless you have been through an ordeal of that magnitude, let me assure you that you have no idea what it feels like. People who have lost a loved one in that way need time and space to grieve.

Meanwhile, the dedication to Philip's memory and his art has been growing. Thanks to Smiley Bolger's efforts in showing the way, there are now annual commemorative concerts in countries as far apart as Sweden and Japan, as well as the UK, Germany and other parts of Europe. In many ways, Smiley is like me, in that he believes in speaking the truth to people he trusts. Although this has led to us having many a dispute over the years, I love him dearly. Without his considerable efforts, Philip's memory would certainly not be as prominently cherished around the world as it is today.

The way I feel now, the more of this, the better. I've come a long way from the time when I wanted to hide from images of Philip. Consequently, it was another source of great pride to me when *Hot Press* asked for my approval for the introduction of The Philip Lynott New Band Award as part of the annual *Hot Press* Music Critic Awards. *Hot Press* had decided to honour Philip in this way because he had a reputation for helping young bands who may not have had the money for demos or the knowledge of how to go about making a good studio recording. In this way, he had been an enormous help to many bands, including of course Clann Éadair, on whose single, 'Tribute To Sandy Denny', he sang in 1984. He also produced four singles for the Dublin-based band Auto Da Fé in the early 1980s.

That said, attending the awards ceremony was something of a trial because it was one of the first occasions I had been among young rock people since my son's death, and seeing long-legged men with long hair, but with no sign of Philip among them, made me feel lost and emotional. When I was making my modest speech from the stage, I started to stammer and lose my way. As I looked down from the stage through misting eyes, I caught a glimpse of a young chap in the audience looking back at me with tears rolling down his cheeks. That helped me to carry on and, eventually, I got through what I had to say.

As the desire to commemorate Philip took a more tangible form, I felt the need also to put a shape on my own thoughts. The idea of founding the Róisín Dubh Trust, which would give a focus to our efforts to remember Philip, was a big boost for my morale. The Trust not only spread the responsibility of dealing with the growing number of activities related to Philip, but because of the calibre of people like Ailish McCourtney-Baldwin, who agreed to give their time to serve, without any kind of financial remuneration, on the committee.

Those are essential practical concerns, but there have been other events which are way beyond my understanding, but which offer a degree of hope to all of us who believe that we have some spiritual aspect to our nature. Some time after Philip's death, Caroline took Sarah and Cathleen to a small cottage in Cornwall for a much-needed break. Just after she had settled into her room, Cathleen ran out to Caroline saying, "Daddy's in the cupboard in my room and he says he's going to mind us no matter where we go." She repeated this excitedly several times as if she were totally convinced of what she had seen. The point is not necessarily that it happened, but that the little girl believed that it did.

Curiously, there have been other, similar incidents that at least confirm the powerful grip that the presence of someone like Philip holds on people's hearts, their minds and their imaginations. While I was going through a very bad time, Jim Fitzpatrick called to Glen Corr and told me he had a strange story to recount. He was a bit hesitant because he feared it might be upsetting for me. I insisted that he go ahead and he then proceeded to tell me that Philip had appeared to him in New York, not once but on two separate occasions. Subsequent to that, I heard of a young male fan in Liverpool who had written to the *Liverpool Echo* to say that a vision of Philip had appeared before him.

In a similar vein, Darren Wharton, who had joined Thin Lizzy on keyboards for the *Chinatown* and *Renegade* albums, told me in the presence of a close friend of mine that Philip had appeared to his wife and himself simultaneously, shortly after they had moved into a new house. When he was telling me this, his wife was five months pregnant. My first response was to blurt out, "I wish he'd appear to me!" – though in truth, I did not, and do not, really wish that to happen. Nevertheless, I did wonder aloud to the company whether her baby might be born on Philip's birthday. I was back in Dublin when Darren phoned me on 20th August 1990, to say that his wife had given birth that very day. It was, of course, Philip's birthday! He named his son Daniel Parris, the second name his personal tribute to Philip. I can never explain fully how much a genuine gesture like that means to me.

Something unpredictable happens when someone who is revered dies, at a young age. Their legend can grow and people in different ways feel a part of the memory as it resonates down all the days and through the months and years. I was in Sweden in 1993 for a birthday tribute concert, when a young girl told me that Philip had appeared to her and instructed her to tell me that he was at peace and happy. Do I think she was really a conduit for Philip to pass a message to me? I can't imagine that he would need to take such a roundabout route if he were indeed out there and needed to tell me something. And yet, I suppose the real point is that it made both of us feel just a little bit better: her being able to tell me and feel that she held a special place; and me knowing that his life and work had reached so many in such a deep and lasting way.

Personally, I have never encountered such inexplicable events in my own life, and I have never shown any interest in spiritualism or any related subject, so I can offer no explanation – yet those involved have little to gain in risking being branded gullible or eccentric by revealing these occurrences to a cynical world. Whereas there was certainly a time when I might have belittled such experiences, I prefer now to keep an open mind on the revelations. For what have we to gain by telling people that we don't believe them?

Of course Philip has featured in my dreams on innumerable occasions. There was one in particular, which recurred, in which I enter a room where lies a newborn baby, covered up in a cot. The phone rings and I hear Philip's voice on the line saying, "I'm still alive, come on around and see me." I run frantically around the house looking for him, and when I look into the cot it's him alright, exactly as he was as a baby. The disappointment I feel on waking up after such dreams is impossible to express. I still feel crushed and alone.

There have been other mysteries and rather strange coincidences. An elderly couple called at Glen Corr one day. As a child, the husband, whose mother was a previous owner of the house, had planted all the roses that had grown so decorously in the back garden. Over a cup of tea, I discovered that they were living in Salisbury, where Philip had died. They also told me that their son had gone to view a house for sale in Bath, not realising that Philip's ex-wife owned it. About a year later, there was a knock at the door. It was their two beautiful daughters, one of whom had taken a teaching post in Malahide, a small harbour village not much further north along the coast from Howth, come to visit. I suppose these kinds of incidents happen all the time, but they take on an added sense of mystery when someone has died.

As I already said, initially, when people told me how lucky I was to have Philip's musical legacy as a permanent memento of him, I just thought, "None of that matters. None of it can replace the person I loved so much. I'd much rather have him alive." But that legacy has become a source of great comfort to me. Similar comments have been made about the comfort the grandchildren must be to me, but, much as I love them dearly, they cannot replace Philip in my life. I can only compare the pain of a mother losing a child in death to what I imagine to be the pain of being tortured. In crude terms, Philip's death was akin to someone delivering a vicious blow to my head and the ensuing numbness has taken years to diminish.

Of course, it helps that so many love his music. But I would give it all up, willingly and instantly, just to have him back in my life.

13. FRIENDS, RELATIONS AND ACQUAINTANCES

There was, I think, less of the big-headedness around Thin Lizzy that you expect from rock bands and famous people generally. As their success grew, it was like one enormous bandwagon, as Philip invited more and more of his friends to climb on board. As many of the various members and crew who paraded through the ranks of Thin Lizzy were Irish anyway, they made a tight family – at least it seemed that way most of the time when I was around.

Inevitably, I was particularly fond of Brian Downey, a fundamentally decent, trustworthy and considerate man. An only child born to his parents late in their lives, Brian drummed with Philip's first serious band, The Black Eagles. In fact, I've known Brian since he was twelve years of age and often visited his mum and dad in Crumlin. He lives in Dublin now and we are still very close. I doubt if a serious cross word has ever passed between us.

But there were other great characters and friends whom Philip thought the world of – and who thought the world of Philip. I always liked Midge Ure, who replaced Gary Moore in the band for a while before Snowy White joined, and I always enjoyed meeting and talking to both Scott Gorham and Brian Robertson, the twin guitar heroes of the albums from *Fighting* onwards. They played on *Live and Dangerous*, which many people consider the definitive Thin Lizzy album, and I always thought that they struck a great balance visually as well as musically.

Darren Wharton, who played with Thin Lizzy during the latter part of their career, is another former member with whom I kept up contact, and I have also met his family. John Sykes, who joined Lizzy from The Tygers of Pan Tang in the early 1980s, always sends me flowers and books on my birthday and at Christmas, because he knew how much I appreciated Philip doing likewise on such occasions. It's funny: these things really do count for a lot.

I know that this might seem like a roll call, but I do want the people who have been good to me – and who were good to Philip – to know that what they gave along the way was and is appreciated.

Another great pal was Frank Murray, who worked with Philip from the early days and who, with his wife Ferga, spent their honeymoon with us in Ibiza. Philip was always very loyal to those who were his friends or who had been supportive of the band in the past. People like Studs, who became a roadie with Lizzy after his father took him to see the band in Belfast, and who still keeps in touch, and like Gus Curtis, who was always close to Philip. And like Big Charlie McLennan, who was with him in his final hours. Sadly, Charlie has himself since passed away in tragic circumstances. He was staying in Shane MacGowan's apartment when Shane found him dead there. In many ways, backroom workers like Big Charlie are the unsung heroes of rock 'n' roll and I want to pay tribute to them here.

In 1993, I was delighted to renew my acquaintance with Thin Lizzy's early guitarist Eric Bell when I visited Sweden for a celebration of Thin Lizzy's music. It was Eric's departure from the band in 1973 that seemed to be their first major setback. He was replaced temporarily by Gary Moore, before a more permanent arrangement was made with Brian Robertson and Scott Gorham. It's great to know that Eric is still trucking away, and playing as well as ever, including a star turn at the 25th Anniversary Vibe For Philo, which was held in Vicar Street, Dublin in January 2011.

The only person in the Lizzy camp to whom I never became close was Gary Moore. It still came as a great shock when the news was announced in February 2011 that he had died while on holiday in Estepona, in Spain. He was part of Philip's life and a member of the extended Thin Lizzy family and I always knew that and respected him for it. Still, we never really hit it off in the same way as I did with the others. Matters were not helped by an incident that occurred early on, when Gary brought a bizarre girlfriend to the Clifton Grange Hotel. During the course of the day, the girl got very drunk and – quite unashamedly, I thought – started making passes at Philip. She was relatively young and perhaps a little naïve. She became quite incensed when I told her that she was the kind of woman who causes bands to split up. I think Gary innocently suspected that Philip was trying something on with her, rather than vice versa, and the incident caused bad vibes between us.

I wanted to report the incident to the band management but Philip, ever the diplomat, preferred not to upset Gary, whose guitar-playing he really admired. When Gary later abandoned Lizzy during a crucial tour of America in 1979, he certainly earned no credit in my eyes. I don't know the full circumstances, of course, but the way I saw it, he was jeopardising everybody's livelihood after all the work and preparation that had gone into putting a world tour together. I'm sure that Gary had his side of the story too – he would hardly have taken such a drastic step unless there were some deep divisions within the band.

I am aware too that some people, who shall remain nameless, had long been endeavouring to engineer a personal rift between Philip and Gary. As I understand it, he was constantly being needled about the fact that he was playing "second fiddle" to Philip Lynott. It's common knowledge that there was an ego clash between them, and I doubt that Philip was entirely innocent in that department. That said, he was the leader of Thin Lizzy and its main man – and to climb on board at all implied an acceptance of that.

Of course, Gary was a very talented character in his own right, as even a single listen to his beautiful solo on 'Still In Love With You' on the album *Nightlife* can testify. He was perfectly entitled to quit the band if he no longer felt fulfilled by the music they were making, although – a bit like the Irish footballer Roy Keane when he left the team and flew home from Saipan during the World Cup – I felt that his timing could have been more considerate. All that said, I was glad to see that he was such a success as a solo artist and that he and Philip, despite their numerous personal differences, could work together on Gary's solo album *Back On The Streets* in 1978. Brian Downey played drums on that album too, further proof that no matter what transpires to cause the occasional rift, musicians who have been together for a long time form a bond which runs very deep. Philip sang on Gary's haunting hit single 'Parisienne Walkways' in 1979, and they both sang on the anti-war song 'Out In The Fields' that was a Top Five hit for Gary in 1985. Philip attended Gary's wedding in Lincolnshire in 1985, and I believe he even did a couple of songs for the guests – so you could say that they really were compadres to the end of Philip's life. Unfortunately Gary has gone prematurely too, dying at the age of just 59. With all those years spent on the road and shifting from one hotel room to another, rock music is a cruel master. I think now regularly of the family that Gary, like Philip, left behind.

Contrary to popular belief, and his visit to Clifton Grange for his honeymoon notwithstanding, it is only in relatively recent times that I have really got to know Brush Shiels on a personal level. More than almost anybody else in Dublin, his name is linked with Philip's, because of their connection stretching back to the early days of Skid Row. Brush is outspoken and opinionated, but I respect that. Being open and honest about your feelings is far better than being hypocritical or worse still two-faced. With Brush, what you see is what you get. It has resulted in the occasional falling-out, but it has never been difficult to sort out our disagreements afterwards. In recent years he and his wife Margaret have kept in touch with me and I appreciate that. In 1986, Brush released a song he had written called 'Old Pal', and I think that song expressed his true feelings about Philip in a way that no mere conversation could. He is funny and wise in his way. But more than anything else he was a friend and a fellow warrior who started out alongside Philip and never forgot the good times they had together.

"'Schoolboy eyes
would stare in innocent fun
never told no lies
he loved Sarah."
– from 'Sarah" by Philip Lynott

Philip Lynott composed two songs with the title 'Sarah'. While the 1979 'Sarah', on the *Black Rose* album, obviously expresses his delight at the birth of his first daughter, it is generally accepted that an earlier song called 'Sarah', quoted from above and recorded on the 1972 album *Shades Of A Blue Orphanage*, is about my mother, after whom he named his first daughter.

She was a lovely, strong, generous woman and she got a great thrill out of having a pop song named after her. But that song is important in that it serves as a permanent and fitting reminder of the prominent place she occupied in Philip's thoughts and in his life. He never, ever forgot the sacrifices she had made in order to help us both at a particularly difficult time in our lives. Nor did I.

I was always grateful to her for her willingness to take Philip under her wing back in Dublin when she did. His presence was certain to be a source of unpleasant gossip, not to mention a burden on her energies, patience and what little finances she had. But she did it and became immensely proud of him as he grew up and became a bright and impressive young man. When she was reaching the end of her life, I went out of my way to ensure that she did not have to enter a home and live out her remaining days without friends or family. It was the least I could do to return just a small part of the enormous favour she had done for both Philip and I. Life takes a circuitous route but the hope is that we all get a chance to say a proper thanks in the end to those who have helped us along the way.

I can vividly remember her being in Glen Corr with me. One day as I was carrying her to the bathroom in my arms, she looked at me and said, "You're a really wonderful person." It was she who had been so wonderful to me, but I will treasure her words and her unselfishness till the day I die.

In that sense, while this book is about Philip Lynott and Philomena Lynott, in the end – like Philip's life – it is a tribute to the ordinary decent Dublin woman who truly knew what it was to give everything.

I can say that with absolute confidence, knowing that it's the way Philip would want it.

14. A NEW BEGINNING

The first edition of *My Boy* came out in 1995. It was an amazing time for me. I felt ready to tell the story of the love that Philip and I had shared, and also the grief that I had to endure when he died. But I still had no idea that I was going to be plunged into the limelight in the manner that followed. The book itself went to No.1 in the Irish charts for three weeks, and I did a string of interviews with media people from all over the world, talking about the book and about Philip and his music. While it was stressful at times, I enjoyed being able to articulate my feelings in a very public way for the first time since Philip's death. I am so proud of Philip and his music, and I loved being able to express that, in part, at least, as a way of saying that I would never be judgemental about the mistakes he made. He had his flaws, but he was a great artist and a great man. Nothing could ever diminish my conviction about that.

In the run-down to the publication of that first edition, I was still – to an extent at least – struggling to come to terms with Philip's death, and the circumstances surrounding it. But getting the book finished and talking openly about Philip actually helped me enormously, making it far easier to move through the grieving process than it had been up till then. In a way, it got me out of myself and into a new life, built around Philip's music and the love and affection that his fans have for him – which so many of them have passed on to me. That is a precious thing to experience. And as a result, in so many ways, the past fifteen years have been wonderful for me.

As part of the promotion of *My Boy,* I toured Ireland and Britain doing similar interviews. It was all very exciting – and also quite emotional for me, seeing afresh how Philip was loved by so many people everywhere. I was reaching out, not knowing what connection I might make, if any.

The response, as it turned out, was overwhelming.

Despite all of the trials and tribulations we encounter, there are times when you have to stand back, astonished, and say: life really is incredible. I try to picture the scene...

A man in his mid-forties, driving through London. He's listening absent-mindedly to the BBC and hears a voice coming from the speaker. It belongs to Philomena Lynott from Dublin though he doesn't know that yet. She has just written a book and she is talking about her life. Some of the details strike a chord with him. He pulls up at the traffic lights and listens. I can imagine the hairs beginning to stand up on the back of his neck as my voice, like a lost chord from a forgotten life, calls out to him. I suspect that somewhere deep in the heart of every mother who gives her child up for adoption there is a desire, conscious or otherwise, to remake that maternal connection. Sitting there at the lights, the thought occurs to him that the voice might be that of his mother. His natural mother. He has been searching for her. This might just be the very woman! He drives on. There is so much going on in his life that the thought might slip to the back of his mind, but he doesn't allow it to. Over the course of our lives, we let so many things slip. An idea. A connection. A moment of inspiration or magic. A phone call we intend to make but don't. But not this one. He thinks: I must follow this up. I must follow this up. I must. I have to know. He stops at a bookshop and goes in to enquire...

After a bit of detective work and several phone calls, the man rang the *Hot Press* office in Dublin and was put through to Niamh O'Reilly. She was handling the marketing of my book and so he asked Niamh had this particular Philomena Lynott, who had written *My Boy*, been in Manchester in the early 1950s? I have no doubt that it was the strangest telephone call that Niamh had ever received. How should she respond? The world is full of people who are looking to make a connection with celebrities or with those who, for whatever reason, are involved in public life. He explained that he thought the Philomena Lynott from the book might just be his mother. Niamh listened carefully to him but her mind was racing. Diplomatically, she told him that she thought he should read the book and he seemed content with that.

If he really was my son, this was potentially explosive information, both for me personally and indeed for *Hot Press* Books. Niamh urgently spoke to *Hot Press* editor Niall Stokes and to Jackie Hayden who'd written *My Boy* with me. Their initial reaction was guarded. As publishers of an often highly controversial magazine, they've dealt with all sorts in *Hot Press*, including musicians who claimed to have written half the music for Genesis' *The Lamb Lies Down On Broadway* album and never been paid a cent, and another who had claimed that Prince Charles was his father. A healthy caution comes with the territory.

There was a meeting of the management team in charge of the book division. Niall, Jackie, Niamh and the Managing Director, Mairin Sheehy, discussed the different ways in which they might proceed. Unbeknownst to me, the phone lines between the English midlands and Dublin hummed. Eventually, the decision was made that Jackie would meet the man privately at Buswell's Hotel in Dublin before getting me involved. They were being protective of me, which was the right thing to do in the circumstances. There is a fear in situations like these that a terrible sadness will unfold, with a fantasist of some kind pouring out his soul to you – and so, as you can imagine, Jackie went to that meeting in a state of some anxiety, concerned that he might have to deal with a hugely awkward encounter. It didn't turn out that way. The man introduced himself as Leslie and they began to talk. Within a few minutes Jackie was convinced that the man was indeed genuine, and that the story he was telling was true. As to whether he was my son or not, that was a different matter entirely. A misunderstanding or coincidence might still have explained everything. But the evidence in favour was mounting.

Jackie was impressed by the way he was clearly very respectful of what I might feel. Leslie explained that, if indeed he was right he was not intent on barging into my life just because he felt like it. He was aware that it would probably be better to take things gradually.

I am sometimes struck by the innate decency of people – or a lot of people at least. You can only speculate what a man might feel, all those years later, thinking that he was on the verge of finally meeting the woman who brought him into the world. It would be easy to understand if he were impatient to get on with it, and to find out definitively if this really is the woman he had been trying to track down. But he emphasised how he'd understand if I didn't feel comfortable with it, and said that he would be happy if I wanted to take my time.

How and when would they tell me what had been happening? There was an illness in the family and I was separately struck with a bout of flu myself, which presented a bit of an obstacle, and so they waited. Eventually, I felt better: the time was ripe and they told me everything. I, of course, could only think of my Leslie, the little boy I had last seen in the TB infirmary in Wales – I really couldn't believe that over 40 years had passed since then. The phone lines hummed again. We arranged to rendezvous in a hotel in Howth as soon as was convenient. The wait was as nerve-wracking for me, as it undoubtedly must have been for him. Would it actually be my son? And if so, what would he look like? Would I see a similarity to Philip? How would he greet me? And most importantly, would I like him? Or would he seem now like a character from a different world? The build-up to meeting your own flesh and blood is such a hard thing for the mother of a child who has been adopted. But it must be even harder for the child. I was on edge. I couldn't sleep. I kept trying to imagine him. I fantasized about the moment we'd look at one another for the first time. The day dawned and I got up to prepare. I was in a daze but there was also a huge sense of anticipation.

I got to the hotel first, and was waiting on the edge of my seat for him to arrive. The last thing I wanted was to be disappointed, but I was still not completely convinced that this was going to be my son. Even if he was as genuine as Jackie thought, there was a niggling paranoia that he could still be somebody who had dug into the records, got some information and was in a position to pass himself off as my lost boy. Alternatively, he might have been misinformed, or have got some facts or dates wrong. So much time had passed, after all!

But then the door opened, and right before my eyes was the very same face of the little boy I'd left back in the sanatorium in Abergele. My heart did somersaults. 'My son. Oh, my God, you look wonderful,' I thought. He came towards me and we hugged and we both cried and cried. It was him. I knew it straight away. Leslie, my Leslie. Instinctively, despite the almost overwhelming emotion of the occasion, I felt I had to take control. We had a drink but there was no point in holding back. This was for real. I decided to take him down to the house. I had a good feeling about it all. It was my lost boy. Everything was going to be alright. I felt certain of it. When we got to the house, Leslie opened the boot of his car. In it was a beautiful big bouquet with one rose for every year of his life. He said to me, "I read in your book *My Boy* that Philip always brought you these." I was so touched by that. Then he said, "I've brought you a book about Gregory Peck because I've read that you were a big fan of him too." He also gave me a book about Bette Davis, because I'd once accused her of being the cause of me taking up smoking when I was young! It was very touching and flattering. He seemed to have picked up on so many things about me.

In the house we talked and talked and talked. And talked and talked! Just like I had with my daughter Philomena when we first met. We were both struggling as hard as we could to cover the missing years. I find it dificult now to represent the thundering heart and racing emotions a mother feels in circumstances like that. You want to hear that everything was good and that the child you brought into the world grew up happy and fulfilled. But you also need to know that they missed you, that in some way you retained a place in their hearts even in your absence. I listened, and he did most of the talking – after all, he had already read my story, and I knew nothing of his. He told me he'd been brought up very strictly by his adoptive parents, but that they had both since died. After his adoptive father, a black African, had passed away, he had found a box in a press in the house in which there were documents with details about his background. That was where he had first come across my name. But until he heard my radio interview he'd had no idea that he was related to Philip Lynott of Thin Lizzy.

I was genuinely delighted that he had found me. There is a raw apprehension involved in meeting up again with someone you have known and loved only briefly, but who is part of you in the truest sense. There is always a possibility that they may be bitter and resentful, or have problems they have had to wrestle with about which you know nothing. In relation to both of my adopted children they have been entirely free of any hint of this. And so I realize that I have been lucky, so lucky, with both Philomena and Leslie. They are both fantastic people – forgiving, kind and generous – and in the long run they have proven to be great friends to the mother they once thought they might never know.

There was an initial excitement and exhilaration at having my second son back in my life and we revelled in it, both of us. Of course things have to settle back into a routine, but I travelled regularly over to Manchester, where he lived, to see him. He and his wife even set aside a room they called "Philomena's room" especially for me. It made me feel special and appreciated – which is how Philomena had also made me feel. And so everything proceeded in a way that made me very happy.

Clearly there was another part of the story that Leslie was still anxious about. He didn't discuss it with me, but inside he was imagining what it might be like if he could also find the man who was his father. And so, sometime after he had discovered me, Leslie flew across the Atlantic to South Carolina, to search for his father Jimmy Angel. I can understand why he didn't say anything to me because there was no telling how I might have reacted. In the heel of the hunt, he telephoned me from America, and I could sense that he was quite upset. He told me what he had been doing. "I've looked everywhere for him. I've gone through page after page of the telephone book," he said, "but I can't find any trace of him."

My first reaction was an emotional one. I couldn't understand why he would want to look for the man who had abandoned us both when we needed him most. But I quickly recognized that I wasn't being reasonable.

Leslie was following the same urge that had enabled him to find me, so what right did I really have to complain? After I'd reflected for a little bit, I knew that it was entirely natural for him to want to bring the whole process full circle. As long as there is a parent out there that you haven't met, then there is, potentially at least, a feeling that something remains unresolved. I don't know what I would have felt in the long run if he had found Jimmy Angel, but either way it wasn't to be. Indeed, it did make me wonder to myself what had become of the attractive young man I had known in those dimly remembered days at the start of the 1950s. The past, they say, is another country but now and then there is a longing to go back there – and to imagine the life that might have been if we had ordered our steps differently in the long ago.

I know that I've already remarked on how strange life is but perhaps it has been stranger for me than for most other people. Here I was, in 1996, with a daughter and a son who had never met one another! So it was truly amazing, a wonderfully exciting experience, to be making the arrangements for Leslie and my daughter Philomena to get together for the first time. Again, there were anxieties. There was a possibility they might not gel or feel that they had anything in common. But fortune smiled favourably on us. They got on like a house on fire. The truth is, and I can say this without any fear of contradiction, that she just worships him. For Philomena, having a brother in her life after growing-up as an only child is something she really cherishes. Leslie's wife Gillian has joked about her husband having not just one but *two* other women in his life, after she'd thought she was the only one. We all have a laugh about that, but the thing is, it's true. You'd think we were teenagers with a crush, when in fact it is all about the ideal of family, and the unique way in which ours has finally come together.

Life has settled into a more relaxed rhythm for us all now. Leslie lives above the East Lancashire Moors in England, where he has a beautiful cottage he recently renovated and moved into. It's quite isolated but it's lovely there. His wife is an estate agent and they're very happy in that idyllic spot. We keep in touch and I see him regularly. He's always been a big music fan, and so he came to Dublin to see the *War of the Worlds* show at The O2 concert hall and I was able to go too. It's hardly a coincidence that when the original album by Jeff Wayne came out in 1978, Philip was one of the artists on it, singing as well as speaking the part of Parson Nathaniel.

I keep photographs of both children by me in my house, to remind me that they're never too far away. Meeting them both again has been such a great comfort to me. There had been a danger that I would go to my grave wondering whatever had become of them but now I know and I am greatly reassured. They also provided huge consolation for me as I tried to repair my life after the death of Philip. Of course he was a remarkable man and a wonderful friend to me, in so many ways – almost like a brother, as I said – and there is no way that the terrible experience of watching him die will ever be fully healed for me. But Philomena and Leslie have been brilliant, giving my life a new sense of purpose and bringing joy and happiness to me in a way that I occasionally think I don't really deserve. But that too, of course, is wrong. Their love is in itself enough to show me that they understand the appalling choices I was faced with – as indeed were so many other young women at a time when members of the female sex were routinely treated like second-class citizens. I did my best and they know that. If I were to do it all again, would I make different decisions? If it were 2003 instead of 1953, then I doubt that the option of adoption would have even entered the frame. But that truly was then, and this is now. And I am so happy that we all found one another again.

15. THE ACE WITH THE BASS

When we formed the Róisín Dubh Trust we didn't really know what we were going to work towards. But I had a sense that not enough had been done to honour Irish musicians in general – and Philip in particular. I felt that he had written so many great songs, made wonderful records and achieved so much success and recognition internationally that it would be appropriate to have a statue erected in his honour in a prominent place in Dublin. And I was heartened to find that there were other like-minded souls who not only believed in the idea but were also willing to work with me towards making it happen. The journey that takes you from the start of an idea to the reality is often long and painful – which, I don't mind saying, in this case, it proved to be. There were times when someone less stubborn would have given up. But it made all the difference that I was not alone.

In particular my wonderful friend Graham Cohen was – as he always had been – a powerhouse from the start of the statue project to the finish, ever ready to go the extra nine yards to make things happen. In fact he has been such an important source of friendship and support in every way, going back to the 1970s, that it is impossible to imagine where I'd be without him. The Róisín Dubh team, with my good friend Audrey O'Neill to the fore, campaigned and lobbied brilliantly. We rubbed shoulders with councilors and politicians. Meetings were arranged with city officials. There was so much to be done in terms of planning and negotiation – never mind going through the process of deciding what the statue might look like and who would sculpt it.

Throughout, the support of fans from all over the world was to prove crucial to making it happen. This, after all, was where the money came from in the end, to fund a project that required well over €100,000 to bring to completion. They ran gigs, made donations and came up with all sorts of other ways of contributing. I felt humbled by their generosity, again and again.

These things are almost always fraught, especially in a situation where there are many artists who naturally feel that they are well qualified to be the one chosen to do the job – and so often what begins in a totally positive spirit can end up with feelings being hurt and people feeling polarized. There was a bit of that involved, but all of it is water under the bridge now. You can't satisfy everyone. Nor will you ever get anything done if you aren't prepared to make difficult decisions. And so we did what we felt was right, agreed the site, commissioned the sculptor and prayed that everything would work out. Well, prayed to Philip! And in the long run, more than anything else, out of all of that brain-storming and hard labour, I am left with innumerable memories of the generosity and goodwill of fans and friends, who gave so much of their time, energy and, in many cases, money to make our dream come true.

It was August 2005 when a life-size bronze statue of my boy, Philip Lynott, sculpted by the artist Paul Daly, was unveiled outside Bruxelles pub on Harry Street just off Grafton Street in the centre of Dublin city. Bruxelles is run by Dave Egan, who is another big fan of Philip and so the bar became our base for the day as we prepared for the big moment when the statue would be unveiled. It was a truly exhilarating and emotional occasion, to be there with so many of Philip's genuine fans and admirers from all corners of the globe as the ceremonial inauguration took place. For me, those fans were the real heroes of the day, alongside his fellow musicians, who gathered to pay homage. It was a lovely celebration of the man and his music.

Since then, the statue has been visited by a parade of international artists of the calibre of Adam Clayton of U2, Alice Cooper and members of his band, Jon Bon Jovi (we were actually pictured together with the first edition of *My Boy*), members of Metallica who have done a rousing cover version of 'Whiskey In The Jar', Lemmy Kilmister of Motörhead, Whitesnake, Iron Maiden, Gaslight Anthem, Glen Campbell, Anvil, the great Scottish comedian Billy Connolly and loads more. Henry Rollins, who is such an intense and articulate character, came too. He told me he worshipped Philip and has taken his music with him all over the world and had urged Madonna, of all people, to listen to it.

Of course, it's customary for Dublin people to come up with colloquial street-names for their monuments, and so the statue of Philip is now known as "The Ace with the Bass". I'm sure Philip would be proud. Visitors make the journey to Dublin to see the bronze figure and it has become one of the most iconic attractions in the city centre, with a huge number of rock stars and fans queuing up to be photographed beside it. But of course there has been wear and tear and a bit of vandalism, which I suppose is in the nature of these things. At one point the Róisín Dubh Trust had to spend about €8,000 to carry out repairs on it but that money was provided by the fans too. We've since transferred ownership of the statue to the city of Dublin so they can take care of it properly. It is a great relief to know that it is in their hands now. At last I can stop worrying about it.

The last time my daughter Philomena was over, we visited Philip's statue together for the first time. It was lovely to be able to pay our respects to Philip together.

In a strange and yet not entirely unexpected turn of events, I've also had contact with Dara Lambe, who announced in 2003 that he was Philip's son. I knew nothing about any son of Philip's, but I can hardly take the high moral ground in relation to that! I've since met him as well as his sister. Life is never simple in the Lynott household, that's for certain, but it was really nice for me to be able to give Dara's son a gift of a small replica of Philip's statue.

There was recognition of a different kind in 2002 when the Irish postal system, An Post, issued a series of stamps of Irish Rock Legends that featured Philip as well as Rory Gallagher, U2 and Van Morrison. If you had suggested when Thin Lizzy started out that the Irish

government would ultimately honour Irish rock stars like my Philip
in this way you'd have been laughed out of court. So times really have
changed and so also – in some ways at least – has the country that
Philip loved. It was a really proud moment for me as a mother when I
saw those stamps for the first time.

While in so many respects I have had a kind of Indian summer,
recovering from Philip's death, and the associated grief, to enjoy the
love and friendship of so many of his fans, these last few years have also
brought their fair share of sorrows too. My mother died while I was still
living in Philip's house in Howth. Maybe I should have summoned up
the courage to tell her about my other children before she passed away
but I didn't. People's attitudes to sex have changed so much since they
were born and she might not have been as horrified in later life as she
would almost certainly have been earlier, but I kept them a secret from
her for what I believed were the best of reasons.

Even more recently, my partner of fifty years Dennis Keeley passed
away. Dennis lived out the last two years of his life battling with lung
cancer and mostly confined to a bed in the sitting room because he
could no longer get up the stairs. Sometimes I'd sleep in the bed across
the room from him, while our faithful dog Lady would snooze close by.
Dennis was in terrible agony towards the end, but we tried to make it
as easy as possible for him, getting him anything he wanted. He loved
his food and liked fish as a treat and so if he fancied some monkfish
or crab for dinner, we went out of the way to get it for him. We never
told him he was dying, although he must have known, because there
was a mirror in the room where he must have been able to see his own
physical deterioration. It was sometimes shocking to look at him but
I loved him madly till the end. No matter how hard things were, that
love never wavered.

It was awfully sad, watching him waste away. I have to be honest:
there were nights I asked God to take him. In earlier times I used
to say to him, "Dennis, if I have a stroke, please don't leave me in a
wheelchair." He'd say he'd throw me into the water to end it all and we'd

laugh at that. We even talked once or twice about going to Switzerland together but when the reality of one of us being ill came around, that was the furthest thing from my mind or his. He was such a lovely, mild-mannered, decent and courteous man, and he maintained that until the very end. Eventually they took him to a hospice a few days before Christmas 2009. We were all there at the very end. Although he was unconscious, I kept whispering in his ear to go off and join Philip and have a good argument with him. For me! Twenty minutes into the New Year, in the first minutes of 2010, he took his final breath, just a few days away from Philip's own anniversary. The loss of Dennis was terrible and I will miss him always. It also revived in so many ways the feelings of loss and grief that I had felt when Philip died, which made it all just that bit harder. Sarah and Kathleen and Caroline came in for the funeral, which meant a lot to me. Dennis had wanted to be cremated and so his ashes are now in an urn close to Philip's grave, so people can pay their respects to both of them at the same time.

Dennis was a huge part of my life for such a long time, and as I said I miss him dreadfully. With a name like Keeley I've always assumed there was some Irish blood in him on his father's side, but whether there was or not, he fell in love with Ireland from the first moment he came here and never wanted to leave. That was a wish we were able to honour. I am proud about that. We made our lives together.

Towards the end of 2010, I celebrated my 80th birthday. Of course I still think of myself as a young girl, ready to take on the world and full, I hope, of the joys of life. Apart from the pleasure that the day brought me, receiving all the presents and messages from Philip's fans all over the world, I was also delighted to announce that I had agreed with Niall Stokes that it was time for *My Boy* to be updated to include the full details of my life, including the births of my other two children.

And so, of course, this is the book you now hold in your hand. It has been, I'm sure you'll understand, a tremendous relief for me to finally explain the full reasons for carrying the heavy burden of my secrets for so long. It wasn't easy. But I know that fans of my first son Philip, will understand that I did what I did for the best. And readers who have yet to fully get to grips with his music will, I'm sure, understand too. Life is full of hardship and tragedy for so many people. I have ploughed the furrow in front of me as best I could, doing always what I thought was right but making mistakes as young people do. And some not so young ones too.

I think, in so many ways, Philip Parris Lynott took after me. In fact I know it. But the beauty of this story is that there are two others now, carrying the flame. Life can be cruel – but sometimes it gives us back what we put in and a whole lot more besides.

Amen.

APPENDIX I: PHILO'S SISTER

INTERVIEW: JACKIE HAYDEN

There were two women named Philomena in Philip Lynott's world. As most people will be aware, his mother Philomena was one of the great loves of his life, but he also had a sister called Philomena that he never knew about, and, of course, whom he never met. But the story behind the younger Philomena's re-entry into her birth mother's life is almost the stuff of fantasy. Add in her discovery of not one but two half-brothers and you can see how life-changing the whole thing was for this careful, gentle woman.

The younger Philomena now lives in the English Midlands with her husband, whom she married forty years ago, happily surrounded by her own children and grandchildren. She has had a happy and generally conventional life, working as a schoolteacher until her retirement. Now approaching 60 years of age, she is an articulate, intelligent individual with a strong religious commitment and a caring nature.

Born in 1951 in Manchester, her name at birth was registered as Jeanette Parris, her father listed as Cecil Parris, the same father as Philip. However, as her mother Philomena has already clarified in this book, her real birth father was a white American soldier called Louis Caldwell, a man she has never met.

Her mother was under considerable pressure when her daughter was born less than two years after Philip had been brought into the world. Unmarried and with a son she was finding it difficult to provide for, the pressure was intensified when the nun who was working with social services told her that she had found a Roman Catholic family who would take the young baby girl. The decision to give Jeanette up for adoption was an agonizing one, but there seemed to be no option. Her new parents decided to change Jeanette's name to Philomena, to honour her birth mother.

Like her half-brother Leslie, Philomena grew up as an only kid. She remembers her childhood as being stable and happy, overseen by good, loving parents who took care of her exceptionally well. "I can't pinpoint any specific time when my parents sat me down and told me I had been adopted," she says now. "They must have done so at some point, because I grew up always knowing. I just accepted it. Then in my early teens, when I was nosing around in a wardrobe in the house, I came across some documents in a little brown box and was surprised to read the details of my adoption. I believe my surprise was really to do with actually seeing it written down."

She speaks very highly of her adoptive parents, whom she clearly loved deeply. "I couldn't have had a nicer father. He was wonderful. I was so lucky to have had him. He was a headmaster, and the children he taught always loved him. He seemed to know instinctively how to treat children. My husband is very similar, a fabulous teacher too. Because I had the best dad in the world, I had no need to look beyond him for a father figure of any kind," she declares emphatically. Her mother was a tailor; she had to give up her trade when the couple adopted Philomena. With teachers' wages set at a modest level in the UK back in the 1950s, the family were not particularly affluent, but they were always comfortable. "We had all we needed," Philomena recounts. "I went to the Hollies Grammar School in Manchester, a lovely school. I loved reading and sewing. We got a car and a television set like everybody else in the late 1960s, and when I was about eighteen I was able to go off to Strawberry Hill Teaching College in London, which my father had also attended."

It wasn't actually until she had reached her teens that Philomena had developed any curiosity about her birth parents. "My adoptive Mum, Mary, was very sympathetic. She understood that curiosity. When my birthday came around I'd get sad, but Mum would explain there were reasons why my birth mother had to have me adopted. She admitted she didn't know those reasons herself, but she knew that young ladies in some circumstances were not able to keep their children. She'd tell me how lucky they were to have me and she did everything she could to help me understand it. Mary was such a generous, kind-hearted woman."

However, Philomena felt such a deep love and respect for her father that she never raised the subject with him, in case he might be hurt. When I ask her if she ever felt that she had been abandoned when she was given up for adoption she disagrees with the use of the word "abandoned."

"It's a very strong word," she says. "As a woman myself, and maybe thinking this way because I'm older now, I can understand what it would have been like in the early '50s for a young girl to find herself pregnant outside marriage. I can imagine the fear of trying to bring up a baby alone, with no way of working, in order to be able to feed that baby. Maybe I'm putting too much of what I know and feel now into my thinking about this, but I never thought of myself as being abandoned at all. Never. In fact, I've had such a wonderful life, not only with my adoptive family but with my own husband and our family, that I'm so deeply grateful that my birth mother never considered taking a course of action that many pregnant women in her situation have understandably taken."

Once she had found the adoption documents as a teenager, Philomena knew her mother's name, but it never occurred to her do anything with that knowledge. In fact she was already married with two children and living in Nottingham when a change in the law enabled her to gain access to her adoption papers. At that point she became interested for the first time in knowing as much as she possibly could.

As it turned out, that involved a curious and at times arcane process, with which she was deeply unhappy. "The social service people came to our house," she recalls, with not a little bewilderment, "and sat across the room from me on a settee to see if I was suitable to be given the information I'd requested. They had all the details about my life but it was down to them to decide whether to give those details to me or not! I have no idea what criteria they used to decide whether I, by then a mother in my thirties, was fit to be told about my personal life, but it was deeply annoying. As it turned out, they had my birth mother's name and some other details, such as where I'd been living before I was adopted, but little more. It was hardly worth the effort."

Although she was still curious to delve deeper into her origins, she was very wary in case her inquiries led to any uncomfortable intrusions into another person's privacy. It is a feeling that many adopted children have, which has an element too of fear of rejection. Not having any real idea why the decision was made in the first place to give the child up for adoption, there is always a possibility that the mother – or indeed father – will want to run a mile when the knock on the door finally comes.

But then fate intervened in several bizarre ways, as if it was in the stars that mother and daughter were destined to meet. "We weren't regular readers of the *TV Times* magazine," she recalls, "but one week I bought a copy when I was out shopping. I remember I was kneeling down on the floor of our house emptying my shopping when the magazine opened and I accidentally came across a wedding picture of Philip Lynott with his wife Caroline and his father-in-law Leslie Crowther. It was part of a story about Leslie presenting a programme on television, probably *The Price Is Right*. Among the people in the photograph was a woman, who was referred to as Philomena Lynott, and I instantly knew it was her! I was looking at her and became so overwhelmed by the emotional impact of it that I burst into tears! It referred to Philip's father as a black Brazilian, and I thought "it's them! I know it's them!" I couldn't move for an hour. The penny had dropped."

But even after she had recovered her composure, the younger Philomena still felt confused – and uncomfortable about the thought of making any direct contact. "I actually sat on it for two years, not really knowing what to do," she recounts now. "On the one hand I wanted to make contact, I really did, yet on the other I was afraid in case I upset their lives."

. . . .

The death of the younger Philomena's father in 1982 gave her more freedom to explore her past. Pregnant with her fourth baby, her desire to know was becoming increasingly intense. So one day in 1985, after coming home from church, she simply picked up the phone and called directory enquiries. "I told them I wanted to trace a Philomena Lynott, so they gave me three numbers for people with that name. I told the first two I called that I was trying to trace a woman called Philomena Lynott who was in Liverpool around 1951 but they politely said I had the wrong person."

Then another simple twist of fate struck. She remembers it as an accident that would change her life forever, an apparent coincidence that still remains a mystery. She emotionally replays the sequence of momentous events. "I went to call the third and last number I had, but in dialling it I inadvertently got one of the digits wrong. But the phone was answered by a man whose name was Snowy. When I started to ask questions, it was obvious that he knew who I was talking about, but he became very cagey, in retrospect possibly suspecting I was a girlfriend of Philip's, which clearly would have caused problems since he was still with Caroline. But, thankfully as things turned out, he agreed to have a word with Philomena and to see what she had to say – and he promised to call me back the following day."

Philomena Jnr thought she'd totally blown it when she instructed Snowy – in fact, Snowy McLaughlin of the band Clann Éadair – not to call back the next day because she was attending her ante-natal clinic. Once she had put the phone down, she obsessed over the possibility that the reference might trigger suspicions for Snowy that he was dealing with a woman pregnant with Philip's child. Fortunately, Snowy contacted Philomena Snr as he had promised. Two days later he called her back to tell her that she should call the other Philomena at her home.

Her heart was in her mouth before she made the call. What a feeling! Over thirty years on, here she was, about to speak to the woman who had carried her in the womb – or so she fervently believed. She thought about picking up the phone but put it off. She rehearsed what she might say but the words somehow sounded forced. She was unconsciously delaying the moment, in fear and trepidation that something might go wrong. She played with the language again, going over it in her head. She had no idea what to expect but there was only one thing to do. If she didn't ring, she might have blown her chance forever. She finally plucked up the courage to dial right through to the end of the number. The phone rang. And rang. And then there was a voice on the other end of the line. Hearing it, she felt more at home immediately. "It was lovely!", she says, "I was still aware of not wanting to upset her or any partner or children she might have. I asked her if the name Jeanette Parris and Liverpool in 1951 meant anything to her. And she just said, 'You're speaking to your mother!' Just like that! We both broke down in a combination of joy and relief to have made that first personal contact after the passing of so much time. After a little hesitancy on both sides, that call turned out to be a really positive experience for both of us, and the start of a truly wonderful relationship that we still enjoy to this day."

There were still difficult issues to be resolved on Philomena Jnr's side. She had found her birth mother, a wonderful life-affirming thing in itself – but there were other considerations on her mind, not least how it might all seem to her adoptive mother Mary, now a widow.

"Mary had given me as loving a home as anyone could ask for. She was the one who sat up with me at night whenever I was poorly, so I didn't want to detract in any way from her key place in my life. Because I was living some distance from her by now, and she was a shy and not very confident woman, I was scared that she might see this new situation with my birth mother as being full of celebrities and that colourful lifestyle, and she might want to back out of my life. That was the last thing I wanted. And so I decided never to tell her. As a result, she never met my birth mother."

The two Philomenas met shortly after that momentous phone-call when Philomena Snr travelled over from Dublin to see her daughter's family. "It all seemed so right. We met her at the train station. She alighted from the train beside my husband Terry, and when I saw them greeting each other, I wondered why was I looking at Terry hugging me. That's how much she looked like me from the back! She looked just as lovely as she had sounded on the phone. I was concerned about taking her to our family home because it was in need of some repairs at the time.

There were worn carpets and toys everywhere, but she didn't mind one bit and made herself at home straight away! We had decades of catching up to do and we just chatted on and on. I think it all worked out so well because we were both ready at that time to welcome each other back into our respective lives."

While there are many examples of such reunions presenting real difficulties for one or both parties, this was not one of them. "She stayed with us for about three days. I remember when we went shopping for vegetables and our eyes met across the display counter and we just smiled at each other with happiness. I was proudly thinking to myself, 'that's my mother there!' It was really wonderful."

Having confirmed that Philip was her half-brother, in time she also began to show more interest in Thin Lizzy's music, and was delighted that her mother had brought some of their records with her. Interestingly, given that the brother she never met was to carve out a spectacular music career, she was never drawn to rock music. "I once had a close male friend who had a guitar and once tried to teach me, but I had little interest. He probably knew about Philip and Thin Lizzy, but not me. I was more into The Monkees, Cliff Richard, Elvis, mainstream pop I suppose you'd call it. When I moved to study in London, there was a young man who took me to some heavy rock gigs at places like The Imperial College in Kensington, but it wasn't my scene, really!"

She laughs at the memory.

It was the 1980s. Not long after the reunion of mother and daughter, the Lizzy man's personal problems escalated. She could only watch from the sidelines and was deeply upset when the news came through that he had died. "I'd been hoping that one day I'd look out the window and see Philip coming up to my door. I remember the words of Oscar Wilde in his play *The Importance of Being Ernest*, 'I always knew I had a brother'. Maybe some deep instinct was telling me, from years before that I had a brother. As a young girl I used to daydream that I had one, and I gave this imaginary boy the name Christopher. I used to talk to him about the things we would do together! So when I discovered I had a real brother

I was desperate to meet Philip, but sadly it never happened. He was so busy by then, not just with his music but all the problems in his life. He was such a talent and a lovely person by all accounts. I would have loved to have been able, just once, to put my arms around him and hug him."

But while her rock star brother Philip was never to fulfil her dream by walking up the front path to her door, her other brother Leslie did exactly that. That fateful event followed another emotion-filled phone-call from her birth mother. The first edition of *My Boy* had come out by then and Leslie had been to Dublin to meet Philomena Snr. Back in the English Midlands, Philomena Jnr greeted with great joy the news coming down the phone line from Dublin that she had a real, living, breathing brother. The two met shortly after that. They now enjoy a very close relationship.

Looking back on her life now, it's hard for even the most sceptical to deny that the hand of destiny might have been working overtime in young Philomena's life, bringing her close to her birth mother and her brother via a series of strange and unusual events. Indeed, as they all looked back, they realized that there were times when they had been uncannily close over the years. There could, for example, have been a near encounter with her mother during her schooldays. "I can certainly recall sitting on a wall opposite the Cenacle convent in Manchester. That wall actually belonged to the hotel my mother ran in Manchester! So we could very well have been physically close while being unaware each other. Furthermore, my dad used to go to Ringway Airport to socialize, just like my birth mother had done, quite probably around the same time. She also knew the priest who was effectively my dad's boss when he was a schoolteacher in the Catholic school, so there's another example of people being in close proximity to each other but without knowing they had any connection. Philip had a daughter called Cathleen, and so have I! There are so many links from all our pasts," she reflects.

Similarly, she was living in Twickenham in London when Philip was living nearby in Richmond. As she herself acknowledges, "we could have walked past each other on the street!" She has yet to meet Philip's daughters, Sarah and Cathleen, but there is time for that still. Lots of time.

She has, she says, never had any serious inclination to trace her birth father. "I didn't seem to feel the same need to trace my birth father as I had to trace my birth mother," she says. "I was never pulled enough in his direction. Now my world is blessed with my lovely husband and our extended family, the brother I always wanted, and my birth mother back in my life. It doesn't get much better than this."

Why would anyone want to argue with that?

APPENDIX II: PHILO'S BROTHER
INTERVIEW: JACKIE HAYDEN

When I first went to meet Leslie James Lynott, in a centre city hotel in Dublin, back in late 1995, I was very wary. He had called *Hot Press* announcing that he thought he might be the son of Philomena Lynott. To say that this was unusual and a little bit unnerving is to put it mildly. At no stage during the intensive interviews that I did with her for the first edition of *My Boy* had Philomena alluded to any child, apart from Philip. Equally, I was aware that people can make all kinds of claims of kinship for any number of self-serving reasons – whether money, the prospect of fame by association or the sense of self-importance that can accrue through an attachment with the kind of celebrated figure that Philip Lynott was. I was also conscious that Philomena had found some parts of the interviewing process for *My Boy* quite emotional and the last thing I wanted was to inflict pain on her by making a wrong move over such a sensitive issue.

But within minutes of meeting Leslie I knew he was on the level. It was nothing to do with his appearance: in contrast to his rangy, exuberant rock star brother, Leslie is more compact and quietly spoken. But he immediately struck me as a genuine character, who was searching for nothing more sinister than the truth about where he came from and how he had entered the world.

His story is a fascinating one.

. . . .

"I think I was told I was adopted when it was first possible to speak of things like that to me, maybe when I was around four or five," Leslie recalls. "My adoptive parents told me my mother was Irish and that my father was a black American GI. So I just accepted it as a normal part of my life from an early age. It was only a little later that I began to wonder why I was put up for adoption. But I was living as an only child in a loving family, and getting so much love and attention, that it really didn't intrude too much on me. I never harboured any sense that I had been abandoned or any negative feelings of that kind."

Leslie's adoptive father was Nigerian, while his mother was from Salford, near Manchester. They had married around 1947 and had set up a home in the Moss Side area of Manchester. He recalls the circumstances around his adoption.

"For the first three years of my life I was confined to a sanatorium in Abergele in North Wales suffering from TB. I actually have a letter, written to the couple who were later to adopt me by the local Council telling them about me being in the hospital, and asking if they might be interested in adoption. Luckily for me, they were. It was a significant commitment on their part to undergo the trek on weekends from Manchester to visit me in Abergele and in effect to take on a child who was seriously ill."

He loved his parents deeply. "They were brilliant parents, they really were," he says now. "Back then, mixed marriages were quite rare in our part of the world, and they had obviously discovered that they could not have children before deciding to go for adoption. I was very happy growing up and any thoughts of my birth parents were really only a mild curiosity at that stage. I always felt loved and cared for, and even if on occasion I wondered about my birth parents I was very conscious of not wanting to do or say anything that would upset my mother and father in any way. I was also aware that it might not be appropriate to intrude into the life of my birth parents as that could destroy their privacy too. My birth mother could have her own family – and my reappearing might affect that. Maybe it would turn out that she hadn't even told her own partner about me, so I really didn't want to be a source of pain or discomfort to anyone."

Leslie's adoptive father was a labourer and the family moved several times as fresh work opportunities arose, from Moss Side to other

Manchester suburbs like Wythenshawe and Miles Platting, requiring Leslie to change schools accordingly. "I didn't really settle down until we moved back to Moss Side and in my last two years at school I really knuckled down to my studies. I'd been moved up a grade at school and came second in the class in my last year. I started to work at the age of fifteen. Perhaps because I was earning my own money, I had some disagreements with my father, who was a strict man. He'd given me a normal Catholic upbringing – which I'd left behind when I got into my teens and decided to make my own peace with my own God. But, I suspect these arguments were probably no different from most other guys who argued with their Dad over the kind of shoes they should wear or staying out late and that kind of stuff." Indeed, his experiences in this regard seem to mirror Philip's family life, around about the same time, with his grandmother in Dublin.

Despite coming from a mixed race household, Leslie never experienced the kind of racist taunts Philip occasionally had to endure in parts of Dublin. "There were a lot of black people in our area of Manchester – and I'm very light-skinned, so that helped too. Although in summer months I go really, really dark, I've never had to put up with any racism," he says.

From an early age Leslie was a music fan. "Before my parents adopted me they had enjoyed a busy social life. They loved ballroom dancing, entering competitions and winning trophies. Of course they had to put that aside to take care of me, but they had an old-fashioned radiogram and I was able to listen to seventy-eight records by all kinds of artists from that time. I used to go with my parents to the local record store, so I developed an interest in music quite early on. At fourteen I began to frequent the local discos in church halls and started making friends, although I always regarded myself as something of a loner and was never really drawn to hanging around with the same bunch of mates all the time. I became attracted to soul music and began going to clubs like Twisted Wheel and the Blue Note clubs for special Northern Soul nights. I saw live acts like Junior Walker and began collecting records."

When the Northern Soul scene faded, Leslie began taking an interest in the burgeoning live rock music. "It was a great time for music. I saw bands like Led Zeppelin, Huey Lewis and The News, and Roxy Music. I saw Humble Pie maybe four or five times, although I never saw Thin Lizzy in concert. I was definitely aware of them, and saw them on television programmes like *The Old Grey Whistle Test*. I had a reel-to-reel tape recorder at home and I used to record radio programmes on it. By some very strange coincidence, the very first time I used that recorder Thin Lizzy were on the radio with 'Randolph's Tango'. As a result, that track with Philip's distinctive voice was always the first track on the tape any time I played it!"

As Leslie grew up he also became a dedicated football fan, following Manchester City. His brother Philip was also a serious football fan, although his chosen team was United! "I find it really intriguing to think that maybe there were local derbies between our favourite teams and I was at our end of the ground and Philip was at the same match – but at the other end with the United fans. So who knows how our paths might have crossed back then without us knowing?"

In 1981, when Leslie was about thirty, his adoptive parents both died within six months of one another. He gained access to their private papers and was intrigued to discover that his true birth name was Lynott. "Finding that document was a truly momentous occasion," he reveals. "It was quite emotional for me. Having grown up an only child and not being married then, the passing of my adoptive parents in a real sense left me alone in the world. Seeing the details of my birth parents made me realise that it might be possible for me to trace them if I wanted to, especially as I no longer needed to be careful to avoid hurting my adoptive parents. At the time I didn't really feel compelled to make any exploratory enquiries. I got on with my life, only occasionally wondering about it. But it was always there in the back of my mind."

. . . .

1995. Leslie was driving along the Euston Road in London and listening to the car radio. "I was not initially paying a whole lot of attention to what was being said, but I was aware there was an interview with a woman with an Irish voice talking about a new book. But my ears pricked up when I heard her mentioning how difficult it was in the early 1950s bringing up what I think she described as a half-caste child. Having had a similar upbringing myself and around the same time period, I started to pay closer attention to what she was saying. I could hear the pain in her voice and I could understand that pain. Unfortunately, what with the busy traffic and that, I didn't get her name, but something about the facts of her story struck a deep chord with me and I couldn't get it out of my mind."

Parking the car, he went into a nearby bookshop and enquired about this new book. No one could enlighten him. But he was like a bloodhound. He had the scent and was determined to chase it down. He phoned the BBC and they told him the programme had come from their sister station in Northern Ireland. The following day he phoned again and this time was informed that the interview had actually been recorded originally by RTE radio in Ireland. No obstacle would have seemed too great at this stage. Leslie made more phone calls and was eventually informed by RTE that the interview was with Philomena Lynott about a book titled *My Boy* and that it was published in Dublin by *Hot Press*.

Philomena Lynott. When he heard the name he was reeling. His heart pounded like a war drum in his chest. He broke into a cold sweat. Lynott was the name on the documents he had discovered after his parents' deaths. That, combined with the details he'd gleaned from the interview, convinced Leslie that he had discovered the crucial link to his past. The next day he plucked up the courage to call the *Hot Press* office in Dublin. He spoke to a young PR person by the name of Niamh O'Reilly, who was involved in the marketing of the book. "I told her about the interview I'd heard, but that the book wasn't yet available in the UK so I wasn't able to check the details. I asked her if there was any connection between Philomena Lynott and Manchester. She paused for a few moments and then told me I should read the book or talk to Jackie Hayden – as if she wanted to guide me along the right path but without giving anything away. I think I knew then that Philomena Lynott was my birth mother."

Leslie was due to take a business trip to Belfast shortly after this phone call to *Hot Press*. He decided to make a detour through Dublin, to be sure that he could find the book. He read it on the bus journey to Belfast. "The more I read the book the more I realised that it was almost certain that Philomena was my birth mother. There were too many connections: an Irish woman called Philomena Lynott, a black American GI partner, the adoption, the Manchester connection, my age, it all added up. Surely it couldn't just be coincidence?"

He called the *Hot Press* office again and arrangements were made for him to meet me. After being convinced of his bona fides I discussed the matter with *Hot Press* editor Niall Stokes. Fully aware of the sensitivities involved and knowing that she was still shattered by the death of Philip and the circumstances surrounding his passing, we had to find a way of approaching Philomena about the situation. Assuming that Leslie was her son, we could not take it for granted that this would be a welcome development for her, and so we felt that we needed to find out more before we proceeded. Meanwhile, Leslie was understandably getting impatient. "It seemed to drag on for weeks and weeks. It was explained to me that one of her family members had just taken ill, so there were valid reasons for the delay, but I was keen to move things forward," he recalls.

Leslie travelled to Dublin to attend the 10th Vibe For Philo in Dublin without making contact with Philomena, who was of course in attendance. It's impossible to imagine how he must have felt, his birth mother within yards of him – yet his basic decency and respect for her meant that he didn't make any intrusive move at this point. And he got closer to her in other ways while he waited for the okay to make contact.

"I found my way to her house near Howth and hung around outside. I probably made four separate trips in all, but I wasn't stalking her, in fact I was very careful not to upset her or intrude upon her in any way.

I even collected pebbles off the beach close to her house and kept them on my mantelpiece back at home. It wasn't like talking her in person, but it was good to have something that gave me a connection to her while I waited to see if she would be prepared to meet me in person. I also visited Philip's grave and had chats with him about my life."

. . . .

It was a strange time. For those weeks, Leslie was caught in a kind of twilight world, his emotions playing tricks on him, as he shifted from high expectation to near despair. What if Philomena decided that she didn't want to see him? He might understand – but he probably would have been devastated. Good fortune was on his side – and also a mother who was happy to turn back the clock and regain a love that had been lost in the stresses and strains of her turbulent youth. She too had retained a spark of hope within her that her past would finally come good. And so the pieces came together. I was able to confirm to Leslie that Philomena would phone him, at an agreed time, with a view to arranging to meet. Even down the phone line, as we spoke, I could sense his tremendous excitement. When it happened, when the call came from Philomena, he heard the phone ring like a clarion throughout his house, a call to arms that he will never forget. "It was such a joy and a relief to hear her voice," he remembers. "She sounded so wonderful and I was so relieved that she seemed so happy to talk to me. She even promised to meet me – which was even more exciting. The following week she phoned me again and we made the arrangements. I could hardly believe this was now all happening so fast and so easily, after so many delays."

When they actually met face-to-face in a hotel in Howth for the first time, Philomena looked exactly as she sounded on the phone. Leslie describes her as a wonderful, caring, pleasant person. "She knew I'd been to the Vibe. She said that I had the advantage of knowing what she looked like but she didn't know what I looked until she met me. It was a nice way for her to break the ice and help me feel at ease. In one sense it was extraordinary to be sitting there talking with my birth mother, but in another sense the situation was so overwhelming that we could only talk about small things to begin with. We had been apart for about forty-five years, so there was lots of catching up to do on both sides. You can't do it all at once. But to be re-united like this and to be made so welcome by her gave me a truly magnificent feeling."

Still high on the emotions of that initial meeting, mother and son retired to Philomena's house where he gave her a gift of a rose for every year of his life because he'd read in *My Boy* that she likes roses. He felt quietly elated, not only with the positive way the meeting had gone, and the ease they felt with each other, but that after one drink Philomena had invited him into her home. "To be welcomed so soon and so graciously into her home was even more than I could have expected at that first meeting. Back at her house we just talked and talked. For me, this was nearly like starting over a whole new life."

Over the course of the next few months, Leslie made several equally discreet trips to Philomena in Dublin, conscious that only a handful of people knew of their relationship – and aware too that she was not ready for everything to become public. He was pleased to get to know Philomena's partner Dennis as well as Graham Cohen. Indeed, Graham – who is so important in Philomena's life – confirmed to me how easily the relationship between Leslie and Philomena picked up, as if they'd known each other all their lives. "They were great together right from the start," he says. "There was never any stiffness or formality. And he got on really well with Dennis too."

"I remember one trip," Leslie adds, "when I chatted through the night until six o'clock in the morning with Dennis, until Philomena came down to run us both to bed. He was a lovely man and he liked nothing better than a good natter."

Through his reading of the book and his chats with Philomena, Leslie was also amazed to find that the hotel she ran in Manchester was very close to where he lived at the time. He had toyed with the notion that they might have passed each other on the street or bumped into one another in the local shops. And there were further surprises ahead when Philomena one day told him he had a sister! "She told me that she lived in the English Midlands not very far away from where I lived then. I was listening to her but my mind was somewhere else. I had a sister! Unbelievable!"

It is one of the great joys of this story how powerfully each of the three participants has taken to the other. The wheels were set in motion again and when Leslie met the younger Philomena they found they got on as famously as he and his birth mother had. It emerged that at one point, all three had lived in uncannily close physical proximity in Manchester without knowing of their connection or the lives they would later share – a family in the making, with deep loyalties that would only become apparent in the long run.

"I've since become a big fan of Thin Lizzy," Leslie explains. "I do a fair amount of research about their music. I have a Philip Lynott playlist on my PC, as well as a YouTube playlist and I've started a vinyl collection of his music too."

Now living high above the East Lancashire Moors and working as a lighting consultant, Leslie James Lynott is a happy man, who is far more aware than most of the strange bounties that a tangled world can sometimes bestow. That his life has been positively transformed by these events is an observation that his wife Gillian eagerly makes. His happiness has rubbed off on her too. "It's been really good for him," she says. "These situations don't always work out so positively, but Leslie gets on so well with his mother, his sister, his sister's family and everybody else involved that it's been the creation of a whole new life for him. And I'm delighted to be part of it too."

As Leslie prepares to depart with Philomena to attend the *War of The Worlds* concert at The O2 in Dublin, the stage adaptation of the original recording that featured Philip Lynott in a key role, you can see the man is intensely happy with his new life. "It was an extraordinary experience to finally get to meet and get close to my biological mother. It was really exciting later to find I had a sister and to meet her too! She has a terrific husband and five kids. So when you add Philomena our mother into the situation, I've gone from being totally alone in the world, after my adoptive parents had passed away, to having a mother and a sister and a ready-made family. It was a terrific turn-about, and I really appreciate the role you, your book and your colleagues in *Hot Press* played in helping us rediscover each other."

APPENDIX III:
ACKNOWLEDGEMENTS

T his book would not have been possible were it not for the generous co-operation of the following people:

Jackie Hayden, who had the difficult task of interviewing me about what were sometimes painful memories and intimate aspects of my life. This he always did with professional firmness, kindness and courtesy. Without him, I would not have been able to delve so deeply into my own thoughts and feelings. In some ways, his probing questioning helped me to face up to the reality of my life and Philip's.

Niall Stokes, for his time in carefully editing the text and selecting the photographs.

Jackie, Niall, Niamh O'Reilly and Mairin Sheehy in *Hot Press* who, despite pressures over the years, honoured my request not to divulge the hidden secrets in my life that I have finally revealed fully in this new edition.

My daughter Philomena and my son Leslie for their love and companionship, and for generously making themselves available for their first ever interviews for inclusion in this edition of *My Boy*.

Smiley Bolger and Adam Winstanley for their enthusiasm for Philip's music.

Past and present members of the Róisín Dubh Trust, including Roddie Cleere, Audrey O'Neill, Dawn McCarrick, Frank Hayes and Trevor Thompson.

The Labour Party councillor Brendan Carr for his tireless efforts in getting the green light for the Philip Lynott statue in Dublin. Also, Jack Gilligan and all the officials in Dublin City Council for supporting the project.

During the lowest periods of my grieving for Philip, I was extremely fortunate to have a number of dear friends in England who always made me welcome in their homes and took very good care of me. In this regard I owe an enormous debt to Mrs. Joan Schiavo and her family, Angela and her daughter Kim Tricket, Rita and Jack Rowles and my close friend June Ricci.

And of course there are the fans of Philip and Thin Lizzy all over the world, whose dedication has inspired me – thank you to every one of you from the bottom of my heart.

In some cases I have altered the names of individuals to protect their privacy. I have tried to check as many of the facts of my story as possible. However, I hope the reader will understand if either defective memory or the trauma of some events have lead to the occasional lapse in accuracy.

Finally, although the above individuals have all been of tremendous assistance, the thoughts and views contained in this book are mine alone. I express them not with the purpose of boosting my ego or of blaming others but simply to tell the truth as I see it. I accept that some will not agree with some of my conclusions, but I can only tell my story the way I remember it, feel it and lived it.

Philomena Lynott,
Dublin 1995/2011

Thanks to:
Bertie Ahern, Dave Allen, Simon Baurley and Liz Wood, Richard
Bennett, Smiley Bolger, Jon Bon Jovi, Daniel Breslin, Robert Calkin,
Councillor Brendan Carr, Jimmy Chops, Stuart Clark (*Hot Press*),
Roddie Cleere, Graham Cohen, John Conlon, Alice Cooper, Roger
Costa, Joe Duffy, Paddy Dunning, along with Peter, Imelda and Kay
(RIP) from the Wax Museum, John Earle (RIP), Peter Emmet, Dave
Egan (Bruxelles), BP Fallon, Dave Fanning, Jim Fitzpatrick, Sarah
Gaffney, Chris Harte, (Wild Ones), Gerry and Yvonne Harte, Jackie
Hayden, Declan Hayes, Frank Hayes, Shay Healy, Colm Henry, Leo
Higgins (Cast Ltd. Bronze Foundry), Dave and Sue Howlett, Barry
James, Dennis Keeley, Pat Kelly (Lord Mayor of Bantry), Lemmy,
Huey Lewis, Johannes Lindstrom, Beverley and Stephen Lister, Dawn
McCarrick, Heather McCavera and Sue Peters, Aimon McCormack,
Eilish and Julian McCourtney-Baldwin, Sean Meaney, Metallica,
Teruyo Miyata (Lizzy Boys), Lord Henry Mountcharles, Terry Naraine,
Audrey O'Neill, Phil Osborne, Ivan Preston, Henry Rollins, Helen
Ruttle, Pete Schofield, Brush Shiels, Slash, Status Quo, Niall Stokes,
Trevor Thompson, Alan Topping, Mr and Mrs Chris Townsend, U2,
Linda Vervaecke, Gino Vangheluwe, Vibe for Philo Team, Colm and
Mary Weadick, Ray and Bernie Wright.

Thanks also to all the artists who have performed at the following:
  Belgian tribute shows
  Birmingham Bashes
  Bolton tribute shows
  Copenhagen tribute shows
  Dedication (Peteborough) shows
  Dedication in Dumfries shows
  Derry shows
  Friends of Philo Arklow shows and exhibitions
  Japanese Philo's Call shows
  New York tribute shows

Richmond Rocks tribute shows
Rio De Janeiro shows
Roscommon tribute shows
Statue Anniversary shows
Statue Unveiling Show
Swedish King's Call shows
Toronto's celebration shows
Vasteras Thin Lizzy Bash Shows
The Vibe for Philo concerts

Plus the following bands and artists:
Big Digger
Celtic Legacy
Clann Éadair
Leanne Harte
Renegade (Ireland)
Rude Awakening
Sean O'Connor
Thin Az Lizzy
Wild Ones

I especially wish to express my heartfelt thanks and love to John & Angela Cooney and family for their unwavering kindness and loving support, particularly during Dennis's illness, and the loss of our dog " Lady ". You were a rock to me during very difficult times.

Hopefully we haven't forgotten anyone. If we have, forgive us and be sure to let us know.

PHILOMENA LYNOTT

Philomena Lynott was born in Dublin in 1930. When her rock star son Philip Lynott died in 1986 the tragic news reverberated across the globe, catapulting Philomena into the media spotlight. But Philomena grieved with remarkable grace and courage despite the intense public pressure. In 1995 she revealed the most intimate details of her life with Philip in the first edition of the book *My Boy*, written with Jackie Hayden, and which reached number one in the bookseller lists. The book was to have a deep impact on aspects of her life that she was not able to reveal in that first book, but which she has now confronted at the grand young age of 80.

JACKIE HAYDEN

JACKIE HAYDEN's career has been one of two halves – the first in the record industry and the second straddling the media and work in the education of people seeking careers in music. As Marketing Manager with CBS Ireland he signed U2 to their first record contract. In 1983 he became a director and General Manager of *Hot Press*. He was invited by the Irish government to serve on a Task Force, in relation to the development of Irish music, and was appointed Chairman of a Committee to examine the International Marketing of Irish Music. He was involved in setting up the renowned MIX (Music Industry Xplained) course. Apart from both editions of *My Boy – The Philip Lynott Story*, he has written and edited several books on music and other topics. Now a contributing editor to *Hot Press* he is regularly invited by radio stations in Ireland and elsewhere to share his insights into the world of contemporary music.

ALSO FROM HOTPRESS BOOKS

THE STORY OF O by Olaf Tyaransen
Described as Ireland's *Catcher In The Rye*, this tale of teenage sex, drugs, rock'n'roll – and of course music – is hysterically funny and poignantly moving in equal measure.

"It's like The Secret Diary Of Adrian Mole, only with cannabis-induced hazes." – *Sunday Times*.

"Very funny and searingly honest" – *Irish Times*

SEX LINES by Olaf Tyaransen
Delving into the wonderful world of sex, Olaf attempts to find a Russian bride, is asked to be an extra on a porn movie shoot, attends a fetish spanking club and much more.

"Hysterically funny" – *Sunday Independent*

PALACE OF WISDOM by Olaf Tyaransen
The "enfant terrible" of Irish journalism is back, with a remarkable book that explores the dark and dangerous currents in which artists, celebrities, musicians, writers and politicos alike – including the author himself – are wont to swim. And sometimes drown...

U2: THREE CHORDS AND THE TRUTH
The International Bestseller Edited by Niall Stokes
Critical, entertaining, comprehensive and revealing, *U2: Three Chords And The Truth* never misses a beat as it brings you, in words and pictures, a complete portrait of U2 in the process of becoming a legend.

THEY ARE OF IRELAND by Declan Lynch
They Are Of Ireland is a hilarious who's who of famous Irish characters – and chancers – from the worlds of politics, sport, religion, the Arts, entertainment and the media. Written by Declan Lynch, one of Ireland's wittiest writers, this is a book of comic writing that actually makes you laugh out loud.

ORDERING INFO

All of the above titles are available online from
www.hotpress.com/books
Or write to Hot Press Books, 13 Trinity St., Dublin 2.

TRADE ENQUIRIES Tel: + 353 (1) 2411 500 or Fax: + 353 (1) 2411 538 or email hotpressbooks@hotpress.ie.

ALSO FROM HOTPRESS BOOKS

SELECTED RECORDINGS: 2000-2010 by Olaf Tyaransen
REM man Peter Buck, porn star Ron Jeremy, *Playboy* founder Hugh Hefner, Lady Gaga, Dolly Parton, Damien Rice, Courtney Love, Sínead O'Connor, U2, ex-Pistol Steve Jones and former Ulster paramilitary leader Johnny "Mad Dog" Adair are among the fascinating and controversial figures interviewed in *Hot Press* writer-at-large Olaf Tyaransen's latest collection of work.

BEYOND BELIEF
No.2 Bestseller in Ireland by Liam Fay
Liam Fay has won a national journalism award for his brilliant and hilarious investigation into the wild side of faith in Ireland. Uproarious, revealing and thought-provoking, *Beyond Belief* is a triumph.

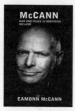

McCANN: WAR AND PEACE IN NORTHERN IRELAND
by Eamonn McCann
Published to coincide with the 30th anniversary of the Civil Rights movement, in which the author played a prominent part, *McCann: War And Peace* In Northern Ireland is essential reading for anyone interested in one of the major stories of our time.

DIARY OF A MAN by Dermod Moore
Diary Of A Man is a wonderfully open, honest, finely written – and highly sexed – account of one person's journey through the myriad attractions and pitfalls of being a free agent in contemporary society. Written from a gay perspective, it is essential reading for anyone in search of the truth about
themselves, exploring with passion and insight the needs that drive us, the choices we make and the search for fulfilment that is at the heart of our collective journey.

THE ROOMS
By Declan Lynch
The Rooms is an electrifying novel by one of the brightest stars of Irish fiction, Declan Lynch, that brings you inside the biggest secret organisation in the world. A love story that beguiles and challenges, it is at once powerful, moving and deeply revealing in its depiction of the world inside and outside of AA. In the doomy, wise-cracking Neil, it introduces a new kind of anti-hero to the pantheon of Irish fiction. One that you will never forget...